The

Strange Side of War:

A Woman's WWI Diary

"Poster showing a woman on stage, throwing off a scarlet, fur-trimmed cloak to reveal her white volunteer's uniform," (1918). Courtesy the Library of Congress.

The Strange Side of War:
A Woman's WWI Diary

Sarah Macnaughtan

Introduced & Edited by
Noël Fletcher

FLETCHER & CO. PUBLISHERS

www.fletcherpublishers.com

The Strange Side of War: A Woman's WWI Diary

By Sarah Macnaughtan
Introduced & Edited by Noël-Marie Fletcher

First published in London in October 1919 in a different form.
Copyright © of this edition, October 2014 by Fletcher & Co. Publishers LLC
All rights reserved, including the right to reproduce this book, or portions thereof, in any form without written permission except for the use of brief quotations embodied in critical articles and reviews.
ISBN-10: 1941184022
ISBN-13: 978-1-941184-02-8

Interior design & typesetting: Noël-Marie Fletcher
Cover design & illustration: Zita Steele. Cover image from a World War 1 Red Cross poster 1917, courtesy of the Library of Congress.

www.fletcherpublishers.com

Contents

Introduction	7
Chapter 1: Novelist & Adventurer: Sarah Macnaughtan	11
Key People	14
Chapter 2: 1914: The Belgian Front	25
Chapter 3: Antwerp	29
Chapter 4: Dr. Hector Munro's Ambulance Corps	53
Chapter 5: Furnes Railway Station	90
Chapter 6: Difficult Conditions	114
Chapter 7: Spring Offensive	139
Chapter 8: Last Days in Flanders	162
Chapter 9: Britain: At Home	186
Chapter 10: 1915: The Eastern Front	208
Chapter 11: St. Petersburg	210
Chapter 12: Waiting in Moscow	235
Chapter 13: Georgia & Armenia	252
Chapter 14: 1915: The War in Persia	271
Chapter 15: Travels in 3 Cities	274
Chapter 16: Last Journey Home	294
Chapter 17: Conclusion	312
Chapter 18: Afterword	323
About the Author/Editor: Noël Fletcher	328

"The Munro Ambulance Corps with Lady Dorothie Fielding (front left)," by M.E. Clark in *"A War Nurse's Diary: Sketches from a Belgian Field Hospital,"* (1918).

"The French picking up the dead in Charleroi, Belgium," *by Bain News Service* (1914). Courtesy the Library of Congress.

Introduction

BY NOËL FLETCHER

During the summer of 1914, when the Great War was still in its infancy before its terrifying acceleration, 50-year-old Scottish novelist and society matron Sarah Macnaughtan heard pleas for help in Belgium. She soon traveled across the English Channel amid a daring group of British women doctors, nurses, medical orderlies, and ambulance drivers to attend to the suffering. It was a time of political uncertainty when women had been fighting for their rights in Suffragette movements, which Sarah supported.

Aside from the hazards of working along the front lines of battlefields, Sarah and her colleagues faced other difficulties.

"When I organized the Woman's Convoy and the women were learning first aid nursing and stretcher bearing, we received nothing but opprobrium and ridicule. People wanted to know why we did it and why we should wear a uniform. I had been careful not to use khaki, to which I knew they would object, and had chosen a greeney-gray tweed. With women of all classes, rich and poor, in the convoy, I thought a uniform dress would be advisable," Mable St. Clair Stobart told *The New York Times* in 1917.

"*The Strange Side of War: A Woman's WWI Diary*" is taken from Sarah's personal records of events as she saw them unfold. Her views and patriotism are from a British stance. She had the unique opportunity to experience World War I from several cultural and political aspects during her attempts to alleviate the suffering in Belgium, France, Russia, and Persia (as Iran was known at that time). Her unique observations are about how the war impacted people—from the thrill-seekers going to battlefields for fun, to the nurses working among the wounded in darkness, and London society women venturing into foreign lands to work near dangerous enemy lines.

"War damage from German bombs in Senlis, France," by *Bain News Service* (1914). Courtesy the Library of Congress.

"British World War I poster," (1917). Courtesy the Library of Congress.

"French officers at graves of comrades," by *Bain News Service* (1914). Courtesy the Library of Congress.

Although she supported Britain and its allies during the war, Sarah was very much against the brutality of war as well as the suffering and death she witnessed. Her life of humanitarian sacrifice during World War I culminated in a premature death. She never lived to see the Armistice, but her words are with us today to present a vivid account of the many different facets of war.

The Strange Side of War: A Woman's WWI Diary" is enhanced by 130+ historic photos, maps, and propaganda posters from World War I, which bring Sarah's story to life and help us remember the bravery and sacrifice of those who died.

Flanders Fields by John McCrae

In Flanders fields the poppies blow
Between the crosses, row on row,
That mark our place; and in the sky
The larks, still bravely singing, fly
Scarce heard amid the guns below.

We are the Dead. Short days ago
We lived, felt dawn, saw sunset glow,
Loved and were loved, and now we lie
In Flanders fields.

Take up our quarrel with the foe:
To you from failing hands we throw
The torch; be yours to hold it high.
If ye break faith with us who die
We shall not sleep, though poppies grow
In Flanders fields.

A famous World War I poem written May 3, 1915 by Canadian Lt. Col. John McCrae. He penned it after the funeral in Belgium of a friend and fellow solider. The poem remains among the most popular war poems ever written. It also helped institute poppies, which grew over the graves of fallen soldiers, as a symbol to remember fallen soldiers.

Chapter 1:

Scottish Novelist & Adventurer: Sarah Macnaughtan

BY NOËL FLETCHER

"No lack of time, strength or money shall prevent me from doing anything that I want to do," was Sarah Macnaughtan's lifelong motto, first uttered in her younger years. A compassionate and daring woman ahead of her time who stood barely over 5 feet tall, Sarah let no obstacles become roadblocks in her life.

She was born at the end of Britain's Industrial Revolution in the Victorian era at a time when economic prosperity brought about influence and changes for women. Her first novel *"Selah Harrison,"* a story about a missionary in the South Seas who marries a humble Scottish girl instead of his first love from a higher social status, was deemed a moderate success at the time. It was published when Sarah was 34. A reviewer at that time described it as mixture of seriousness, subtlety and humor.

Other novels followed as she traveled the globe and gave of herself to those less fortunate despite being a fixture among the society scene. Her trips abroad took her to Canada, the United States, Argentina, India, Palestine, Egypt and Turkey.

Her London home near Park Lane was considered a literary salon. Yet she made time to volunteer to help the poor in the city's East End. During the Boer War in South Africa, she traveled there to assist the Red Cross in caring for the wounded and volunteered to fill a critical need as a cook for a hospital despite having no culinary experience. Women's rights was another important issue to her and she participated in the Women's Suffrage Movement.

Sarah Macnaughtan

"She was intensely alive, and intensely interested in all the life around her, and her interest was continually expressing itself in the most practical forms. A slight, rather delicate woman, she was never at rest and seemed to have unlimited reserves of enthusiasm and energy," according to a description of Sarah by *Littell's Living Age*, an eclectic weekly literary magazine of British and American news.

She was 50 years old when war broke out in Europe. Yet she jumped at the chance to help the needy despite the personal toll it took on her health.

Although in need of rest, Sarah used her relief trip to Britain in 1915 to become another outlet for her to share her passions. She gave 32 lectures to munitions workers around Britain to talk about her experiences in the war and rally support.

"There is no need to attempt any more elaborate study of her character; she has put herself into all of her books, and you cannot read them without growing intimately aware of her eager, joyous, resolute personality," declared *Littell's* magazine in its 1916 obituary about her life and work. "She gave herself unsparingly and died for her country as surely as any soldier who has fallen in battle."

Key People

Sarah Broom Macnaughtan
Scottish Novelist & Red Cross Volunteer

+ Born in 1864 near Glasgow, Scotland to Peter Macnaughtan, a secretary for the British Steam Navigation Co. She was one of 6 children.
+ Moved to London after her parents died and became a novelist.
+ Volunteered for the British Red Cross in 1914 and traveled to Antwerp at the outbreak of World War I to join a group of women doctors, nurses and assistants under Mrs. St. Clair Stobart's Unit.
+ Became head of the orderlies in the Ambulance Unit, working with the Belgium Red Cross.
+ Returned to Britain in May 1915 where she gave numerous lectures on the war. Later that year, she journeyed to Russia with Mrs. Hilda Wynne and an ambulance unit.

Albert I
King of Belgium

- Born in 1875, he married German princess Elisabeth in 1900.
- Entered military school at age 15. A devout Catholic, he traveled as a young man and sought out diverse experiences to learn about society. At age 22, he worked as a digger in a coal pit, a stoker in a steel foundry, and an engine driver on a train.
- Reigned from 1909 to 1934. During World War I, more than 90 % of Belgium was occupied by Germany.
- As King, refused a German request at the onset of World War I to grant the Germans passage through Belgium to attack Britain. As Germany invaded and occupied Belgium, he fought in the trenches with his troops and was known as the King-Soldier.

Elisabeth of Bavaria
Queen of Belgium

+ Born in 1876 to Karl-Theodor, Duke of Bavaria, and Maria Josepha of Portugal, whose father had been king Miguel I.
+ During World War I, lived with the king in De Panne, Belgium, along the coast of the North Sea.
+ Often visited the battlefront and earned admiration. Her other support for the war effort included sponsoring a nursing unit.

Lady Dorothie Fielding

+ Born in 1885, the second of 7 daughters of the Earl of Denbigh, a Count of the Holy Roman Empire. Her father was described as a favorite of both Pope Leo XIII and Queen Victoria, while her aunt was a nun and Sister of Charity.
+ Her family excelled in outdoor sports. She was an expert on a horse and an avid hunter.

Dr. Hector Munro

- Born in Scotland, a surgeon, psychologist, and specialist in psychotherapy.
- Worked at the Medico-Psychological Clinic in London, the first clinic in Britain providing psychoanalytic treatment.
- Formed an ambulance corps in August 1914 initially for the Belgians.
- His volunteers included a Scottish teen named Mairi Chisholm, Lady Dorothie Fielding, Mrs. Elsie Knocker and American Mrs. Helen Gleason. Chisholm and Knocker received the Military Medal and the Cross of the Order of St. John.
- Novelist May Sinclair, who also worked at the clinic, became a fundraiser for this effort.
- Operating under the Belgian Red Cross, his group started in Ghent with 4 surgeons, 5 women, 3 men to carry stretchers, and 2 ambulance drivers.

Prince Alexander of Teck

- Born in 1874 to the Duke and Duchess of Teck.
- In 1904, married Princess Alice of Albany, a granddaughter of Queen Victoria.
- In 1917, adopted the surname Cambridge when the British royal family dropped its Germanic titles.
- At the start of World War I, commanded the Life Guards in the British Army and saw action in France and Flanders.
- In 1915, became lieutenant colonel and led the British mission to the Belgian Army.

Mrs. Hilda Wynne

+ Widow of a military officer, who used her wealth to finance and worked with her secretary Ivor Bevan to start the Wynne-Bevan Ambulance Corps to assist with war wounded.
+ Drove ambulances while under fire, assisting the wounded in Belgium and France. For her efforts in Belgium, King Albert decorated her with the Order of Leopold. She also received the French Croix de Guerre.
+ After 2 years at the front, traveled to America to raise funds for an ambulance unit to serve the Russia front, which had only 600 ambulances for a 6,000-mile firing line.
+ Left for Russia with the Anglo-Russian Bevan Ambulance Care Unit, a mobile treatment unit which operated as a small hospital near the front lines.

Mabel St. Clair Stobart

- Also known as Mabel Annie Boulton. Born in 1862 to Sir Samuel Bagster Boulton and his wife Sophia in Kent.
- In 1884, married St. Clair Stobart, who died on a voyage home from East Africa in 1908. Three years later, she wed John Greenhalgh, a barrister.
- With the Bulgarian Army, founded the Women's Sick and Wounded Convoy Corps in 1912 during the Balkan War to serve wounded and sick soldiers between the field and hospital. It expanded to treat civilians and distribute medicine as well as tea and food for the wounded.
- Invited by the Belgian Red Cross to establish a hospital for Belgian and French soldiers.
- Began her WWI service in August 1914. Both she and her husband were captured by the Germans and condemned to death, but escaped and returned to Belgium in 3 weeks.

Lady Susan Elizabeth Clementine Waring

- Born in 1879, the only daughter of the William Hay, the 10th Marquis of Tweeddale. She married Major Walter Waring in 1901.
- Turned her country home Lennel House in Berwickshire to a convalescent home for Belgian, British and French officers. It housed some 15 officers at the same time. They were treated as country house guests on the estate, which had farms, woods and grand Italianate gardens.
- The medical care she provided was for the treatment of shellshock.

Millicent, Duchess of Sutherland

- Born in 1867, the eldest daughter of Scottish politician Robert St. Clair-Erskine, 4th Earl of Rosslyn. In 1884, married Lord Cromartie Sutherland-Leveson-Gower, who became the 4rd Duke of Sutherland. After her husband's death in 1913, she married Major Percy Desmond Fitzgerald, of the 11th Hussars.
- Was chosen during the 1911 coronation of King George V and Queen Mary as a canopy-bearer for the queen. A noted society hostess, she left England on Aug. 8, 1914 to join the French Red Cross and then went to the Belgian front where she organized an ambulance unit.
- Briefly trapped behind German lines, she was allowed to return to England where she wrote a book, *"Six Weeks at War,"* in 1915 based on her diary and experiences.
- Returned to duty in France, establishing a 100-bed hospital in Calais before being transferred to help British troops.

"German hussars entering Antwerp," by *Bain News Service* (circa 1914). Courtesy the Library of Congress.

"Belgian regiment going to the front lines," by *Bain News Service* (circa 1914). Courtesy the Library of Congress.

Chapter 2

1914: The Belgian Front

BY NOËL FLETCHER

Exactly one week after the start of the Great War, which became known as World War I, Germany invaded Belgium, a neutral country, on Aug. 4, 1914. Two days after Luxembourg met the same fate.

King Albert I of Belgium had refused a German request to let the German army establish itself in Belgium to better attack France. Therefore, Belgium became an enemy of Germany. A day prior to the invasion of Belgium, Germany declared war on France, telling Britain that Germany would not attack France by sea if Britain adopted a neutral stance.

Belgium requested help from France, Britain and Russia, and notified Germany it would defend its sovereignty. On the day Germany entered Belgium, Britain declared war on Germany in accordance with a pledge made to Belgium four decades earlier.

The global conflict intensified due to previous treaties and alliances, and rapidly expanded during August 1914:

- Aug. 5: Austria-Hungary declares war on Russia.
- Aug. 6: Montenegro declares war on Austria-Hungary.
- Aug. 9: Serbia declares war on Germany.

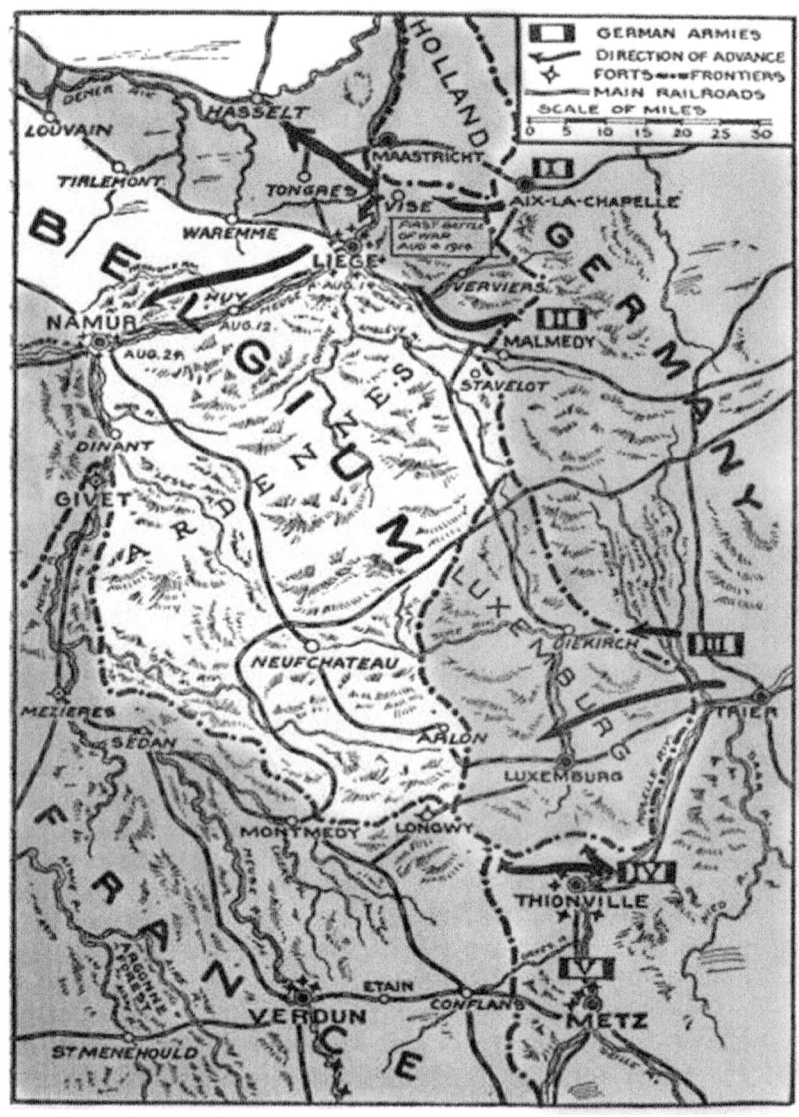

"Start of the German invasion of Belgium," in *The Story of the Great War: History of the European War,* Vol. 11, by Francis Joseph Reynolds, Allen Leon Churchill, Francis Trevelyan Miller (1916).

- Aug. 10: France declares war on Austria-Hungary.
- Aug. 12: Britain declares war on Austria-Hungary.
- Aug. 12: Montenegro declares war on Germany.
- Aug. 23: Japan declares war on Germany.
- Aug. 27: Austria-Hungary declares war on Japan.
- Aug. 28: Austria-Hungary declares war on Belgium.

"Antwerp refugees fleeing to Holland," by Bain News Service (October 1914). Courtesy the Library of Congress.

"Dr. Florence Stoney," of the New Hospital for Women in London in *Women of the War* by Barbara McLaren (1918).

Chapter 3
Antwerp

Sept. 20, 1914:

I left London for Antwerp. At the station I found I had forgotten my passport, and Mary had to run back for it. Great perturbation, but kept this dark from the rest of the staff, for they are all rather serious and I am head of the orderlies. We got under way the next morning at 4 a.m. All instantly began to be sick. I think I was the worst and alarmed everybody within hearing distance. One more voyage I hope—home—then dry land for me. We arrived 24 hours late at Antwerp on Sept. 22. The British Consul sent carriages, etc., to meet us. Drove to the large Philharmonic Hall, which has been given us as a hospital. Immediately after breakfast we began to unpack beds, etc., and our enormous store of medical things. All feeling remarkably empty and queer, but put on heroic smiles and worked like mad. Some of the staff is housed in a convent and the rest in rooms over the Philharmonic Hall.

September 23:

Began to get things in order and allot each person her task. Our unit consists of:

- Mrs. Mabel St. Clair Stobart, its head;
- Physicians Dr. Rose Turner, Dr. Florence Stoney (chief doctor and radiographer), Dr. Joan Watts (surgeon), Morris, Hanson and Dr. Mable L. Ramsey (all women); and
- Orderlies—me, Miss Randell (interpreter), Miss Perry, Dick, Stanley, Miss Benjamin, Godfrey Donnisthorpe, Cunliffe, and Mr. Glade.

Everyone very zealous and inclined to do anybody's work except their own. Keen competition for everyone else's tools, brooms, dusters, etc. Great roaming about. All mean well.

September 25:

The Defenses of the Town

Forty wounded men were brought into our hospital yesterday. Fortunately we had everything ready, but it took a bit of doing. We are all dead tired, and not so keen as we were about doing other people's work.

The wounded are not very bad, and have been sent on here from another hospital. They are enchanted with their quarters, which indeed do look uncommonly nice: 130 beds are arranged in rows, and we have a bright counterpane on each and clean sheets. The floor is scrubbed. The bathrooms, store, office, kitchens, and receiving-rooms have been made out of nothing, and look splendid. I never saw a hospital spring up like magic in this way before. There is a wide veranda where the men play cards, and a garden to stump about in.

The gratitude of our patients is boundless, and they have presented Mrs. Stobart with a beautiful basket of growing flowers. I do not think Englishmen would have thought of such a thing. They say they never tasted such cooking as ours outside Paris, and they are rioting in good food, papers, nice beds, etc. Nearly all of them are able to get out a little, so it is quite cheery nursing them. There is a lot to do. We all fly about in white caps. The keenest competition is for sweeping out the ward with a long-handled hairbrush!

I went into the town today. It is very much like every other foreign town, with broad streets, tramlines, shops and squares, but today I had an interesting drive. I took a car and went out to the second line of forts. The whole place was a mass of wire entanglements, mined at every point, and the fields were studded with strong wooden spikes. There were guns everywhere. In one place a whole wood and a village had been laid level with the ground to prevent the enemy taking cover. We heard the sound of firing last night!

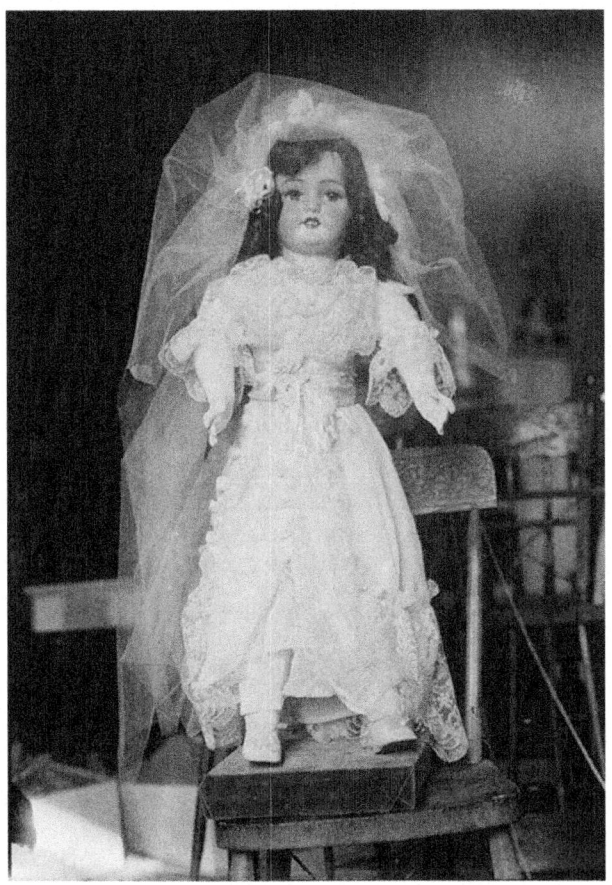

"Doll raffled for Belgian relief," by *Bain News Service* (circa 1914). Courtesy the Library of Congress.

To Mrs. Keays-Young
Rue de L'Harmonie 68, Antwerp, September 25

Dearest Babe,

It was delightful getting your letter. Our wounded are all French or Belgians, but there is a bureau of enquiry in the town where I will go to try to hear tidings of your poor friends.

We heard the guns firing last night, and 50 wounded were sent in during the afternoon. In one day 2,500 wounded reached Antwerp. I can write this sort of thing today, as I know my letter will be all right. To show you that the fighting is pretty near, two doctors went for a short drive today in the car, and they found two wounded men. One was just dying, the other they brought back in the car, but he died also. In the town itself everything seems much as usual except for crowds of refugees. Do not believe people when they say German barbarity is exaggerated. It is hideously true.

We are extremely busy, and it seems a strange side of war to cook and race around and make doctors as comfortable as possible. We have an excellent staff made up of zeal and muscle. I do not know how long it can last. We eat breakfast at 7:30, which means that most of the orderlies are up at 5:45 a.m. to prepare and do everything. The fare is very plain and terribly wholesome, but hardly anyone grumbles. I am trying to get girls to take two hours off duty in the day, but they won't do it.

Have you any friends who would send us a good big lot of nice jam? It is for the staff. If you could send some cases of it at once to Miss Stear, 39 St. James's St., London, put my name on it, and say it is for our hospital. She will bring it here herself with some other things. Some of your country friends might like to help in a definite little way like this.

Your loving, Sarah

P.S. ___ is going to England tonight and will take this.

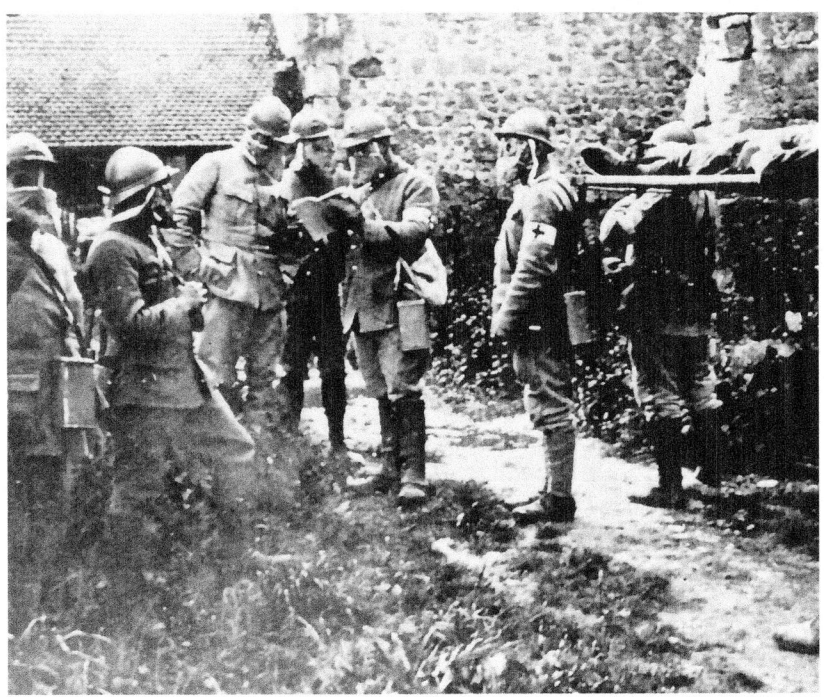

"Bringing in the wounded during a gas attack," (circa 1914 to 1918). Courtesy the Library of Congress.

September 27:
Arrival of the Wounded

Yesterday, when we were in the town, a German airship flew overhead and dropped bombs. A lot of guns fired at it, but it was too high up to hit. The incident caused some excitement in the streets.

Last night we heard that more wounded were coming in from the fighting-line near Ghent. We got 60 more beds ready, and sat up late—boiling water, sterilizing instruments, preparing operating tables and beds, etc., etc. As it got later all the lights in the huge ward were put out, and we went about with little flashlights among the sleeping men, putting things in order and moving on tiptoe in the dark.

Later we heard that the wounded might not get in until Monday.

The work of this place goes on unceasingly. We all get on well, but I have not got the communal spirit, and the fact of being a unit of women is not the side of it that I find most interesting. The communal food is my despair. I cannot eat it. All the same, this is a fine experience, and I hope we'll come well out of it. There is boundless opportunity, and we are in luck to have a chance of doing our darnedest.

September 28:

Last night two orderlies and I slept over at the hospital as more wounded were expected. At 11 p.m. word came that "les blesses" [the wounded] were at the gate. Men were on duty with stretchers, and we went out to the tramway cars in which the wounded are brought from the station—12 patients in each.

The transit is the least painful as possible. The stretchers are placed in iron brackets and are simply unhooked when the men arrive. Each stretcher was brought in and laid on a bed in the ward. The nurses and doctors undressed the men.

We orderlies took their names, their "matricule" or regimental number, and the number of their bed. Then we gathered up their clothes and put corresponding numbers on labels attached to them—first turning out the pockets, which are filled with all kinds of things from tins of sardines to loaded revolvers. They are all very pockety [full of pockets] and have to be turned out before the clothes are sent to be baked [sanitized].

We arranged everything, and then got Oxo [a beef bouillon cube drink] for the men, many of whom had nothing to eat for two days. They are a nice-looking group of men and boys, with rather handsome faces and clear eyes. Their absolute exhaustion is the most pathetic thing about them. They fall asleep even while their wounds are being dressed. When all was made straight and comfortable for them, the nurses turned the lights low again, and stepped softly about the ward with their little flashlights.

A hundred beds all filled with men in pain give one plenty to think about, and it is during sleep that their attitudes of suffering strike one the most. Some of them bury their heads in their pillows like shot partridges seeking to bury theirs among autumn leaves. Others lie very stiff and straight. All look very thin and haggard.

I was struck by the contrast between the pillared Concert Hall where they lie (with its platform of white paint and decorations) and the tragedy of suffering which now fills it.

At 2 a.m. more soldiers were brought in from the battlefield, all caked with dirt, and we began to work again. These last blinked oddly at the Concert Hall, nurses and doctors, but I think they do not question anything much. They only want to go to sleep.

A Visit from Some Deserters

I suppose that women would always be tenderhearted towards deserters. Three of them arrived at the hospital today with some absurd story about having been told to report themselves. We got them supper and a hot bath, and put them to bed. One can't regret it.

I never saw men sleep as they did. All through the noise of the wounded being brought in, all through the turned-up lights and bustle they never even stirred, but a sergeant discovered them, and at 3 a.m. they were marched away again. We got them breakfast and hot tea. At least they had a few hours between clean sheets. These men seem to carry so much, and the roads are heavy. At 5 o'clock I went to bed and slept until 8. Mrs. Stobart never rests. I think she must be made of some substance that the rest of us have not discovered. At 5 a.m. I discovered her curled up on a bench in her office—the doors wide open and the dawn breaking.

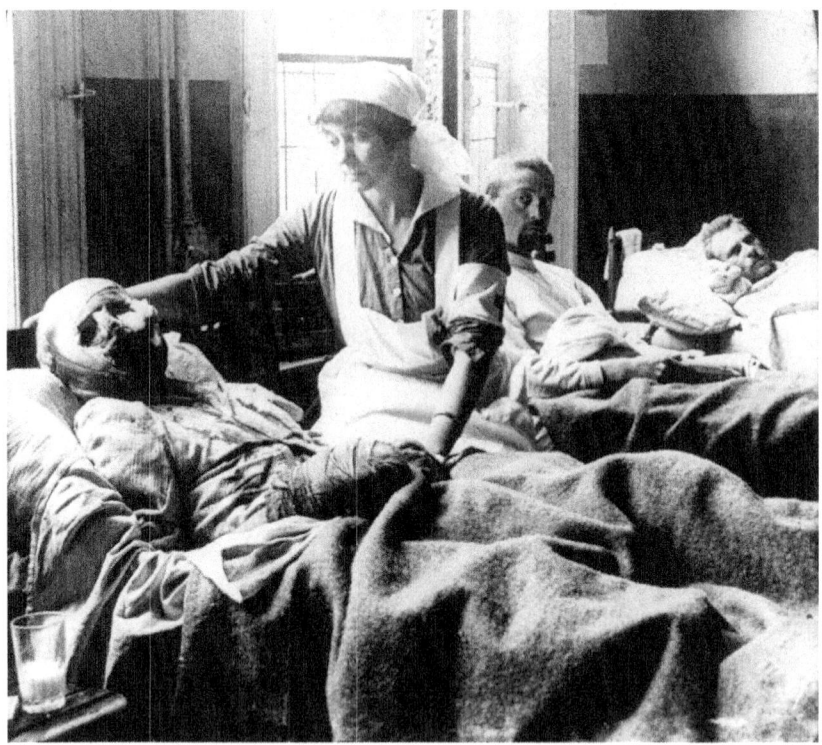

"The horror of war, ghastly glimpse of Belgian wounded in an Antwerp hospital," by *Bain News Service* (1915). Courtesy the Library of Congress.

October 2:

Here is a short account of one whole day. Firing went on all night. Sometimes it came so near that the vibration of it was rather startling. In the early morning, we heard that the forts had been heavily fired on. One of them remained silent for a long time.

Then the garrison lit cartloads of straw to deceive the Germans, who fell into the trap, thinking the fort was disabled and on fire. They rushed in to take it. They were met with a furious cannonade. But one of the other forts has fallen.

At 7 a.m. the men's bread had not arrived for their 6 o'clock breakfast, so I went into town to get it. The difficulty was to convey home 28 large loaves. So I went to the barracks, begged for a car from the Belgian officer, and came back triumphant. The military cars simply rip through the streets, blowing their horns all the time. Antwerp was thronged with these cars, and each one contained soldiers. Sometimes one saw wounded in them lying on sacks stuffed with straw.

I came down to breakfast half an hour late (8 o'clock). We had our usual fare—porridge, bread and margarine, and tea with tinned milk—amazingly nasty, but quite wholesome and filling at the price. We have reduced our housekeeping to nine pence per head per day.

After breakfast I cleaned the two houses, as I do every morning, made nine beds, swept floors and dusted stairs, etc. When my rooms were done and jugs filled, our nice little cook gave me a cup of soup in the kitchen, as she generally does. I went over to the hospital to help prepare the men's dinner. My task today was to open bottles and pour out beer for 120 men. Then, when the meat was served, I had to procure it from the kitchen and serve it out with gravy. Our own dinner is at 12:30.

Afterwards I went across to the hospital again and arranged a few things with Mrs. Stobart. I began to correct the men's diagnosis sheets, but was called to help with the arriving wounded, and to label and sort their clothes.

Just then the British Minister to the court of the Belgians, Sir Francis Villiers, and the Surgeon-General, Sir Cecil Herslet, came in to see the hospital. We proceeded to show them round, when the sound of firing began quite close to us and we rushed out into the garden.

"World War I Rumpler Taube 4C airplane," Courtesy Wikimedia Commons.

A Taube Overhead

From out the blue, clear autumn sky came a great gray dove flying serenely overhead. This was a German airplane of the class called the Taube (dove). These airplanes are quite beautiful in design and fly with amazing rapidity. This one wafted over our hospital with all the grace of a living creature "calm in the consciousness of wings." Then, of course, we let fly at it. From all round us, shells were sent up into the vast blue sky and still the gray dove went on in its gentle-looking flight. Whoever was in it must have been a brave man! All round him shells were flying—one touch and he must have dropped. The smoke from the burst shells looked like little white clouds in the sky as the dove sailed away into the blue again and was seen no more.

We returned to our work in hospital. The men's supper is at 6 o'clock. We began cutting up their bread-and-butter and cheese, and filling their bowls of beer. When that was over and visitors were going, an order came for 30 patients to proceed to Ostend and make room for the worst cases. We were sorry to say goodbye to them, especially to a nice fellow we call Alfred because he can speak English, and to Sunny Jim, who positively refused to leave.

Poor boys! With each batch of the wounded, disabled creatures carried in, one feels inclined to repeat in wonder, "Can one man be responsible for all this? Is it for one man's lunatic vanity that men are putting lumps of lead into each other's hearts and lungs, and boys are lying with their heads blown off, or with their insides beside them on the ground?" Yet there is a splendid freedom about being in the midst of death—a certain glory in it, which one can't explain.

A piece of shell fell through the roof of the hospital today—evidently part of one that had been fired at the Taube. It fell close beside the bed of one of our wounded, and he went as white as a ghost. It must be pretty bad to be powerless and have shells falling around. The doctors tell me that nothing moves them so much as the terror of the men. Their nerves are simply shattered, and everything frightens them. Rather late a man was brought in from the forts, terribly wounded. He was the only survivor of 12 comrades who stood together, and a shell fell among them, killing all but this man.

At 7 o'clock we moved all the furniture from Mrs. Stobart's office to the dispensary, where she will have more room. The day's work was then over and night work began for some. The Germans have destroyed the reservoir, and the water supply has been cut off. So we have to go fetch all the water in buckets from a well. After supper, we go with our pails and carry it home. The shortage for washing, cleaning, etc., is rather inconvenient, and adds to the danger in a large hospital and to the risk of typhoid.

"Mrs. St. Clair Stobart," in *Women of the War* (1918).

October 4:
Orders to Evacuate the Hospital

Yesterday our work was hardly over when Mrs. Stobart sent a call to all of us "heads" to come to her bureau. She had alarming news for us. The British Consul had just been to say that all the English must leave Antwerp; two forts had fallen, and the Germans were expected hourly to begin shelling the town. We were told all wounded who could travel were to go to Ostend. The worst cases were to be transferred to the Military Hospital.

I do not think it would be easy to describe the confusion that followed. All the men's clothes had to be found and they had to be put into them. Woe betides if a little cap or old candle was missing! All of them wanted help at once; all wanted food before starting. In the midst of the general mêlée I shall always remember one girl, silently, quickly, and ceaselessly slicing bread with a loaf pressed to her waist, and handing it across the counter to the men.

With one or two exceptions the staff all wanted to remain in Antwerp. I decided to abandon the unit and stay on here as an individual or go to Ostend with the men. Mrs. Stobart, being responsible, had to take the unit home. It was a case of leaving immediately. We packed what provisions we could, but the beds, x-ray machines, and all our material equipment would have to be left to the Germans. I think everyone felt as though they were running away, but it was a military order. The Consul, the British Minister, and the King and Queen were leaving. We went to eat lunch together, and as we were doing so Mrs. Stobart brought news the Consul had come to say reinforcements had arrived. The situation changed for the better, and so for the present we might remain. Anyone who wanted to leave might do so, but only four did.

We have since heard what happened. The British Minister cabled home to say Antwerp was the key to the whole situation and must not fall because once here, the Germans would be strongly entrenched, supplied with provisions, ammunition, and everything they want. A Cabinet Council was held at 3 a.m. in London, and reinforcements were ordered up. Winston Churchill is here with Marines. They say Colonel Kitchener is at the forts.

The firing sounds very near. Dr. Hector Munro, Miss St. Clair and Lady Dorothie Fielding came over today from Ghent, where all is quiet. They wanted me to return with them to rest, which was absurd, of course.

Some terrible cases were brought in to us today. My God, the horror of it! One has heard of men whom their mothers would not recognize. Some of the wounded today were among these. All the morning, we did what we could for them. One man was riddled with bullets and died very soon.

It is awful work. The great bell rings, and we say: "More wounded." The men get stretchers. We go down the long, cold covered way to the gate and number the men for their different beds. The stretchers are stiff with blood, and the clothes have to be cut off the men. They cry out terribly. Their horror is so painful to witness. They are so young, and they have seen right into hell. The doctors remove the initial dressings—sometimes there is only a lump of cotton wool to fill up a hole—and the men lie there with their tragic eyes fixed upon one. All day a nurse has sat by a man who has been shot through the lungs. Each breath is painful; it does not bear writing about. The pity of it all just breaks one's heart. But I suppose we do not see nearly the worst of the wounded.

The lights are all off at 8 o'clock now. We do our work in the dark, while the orderlies hold little flashlights to enable the doctors to dress the wounds. There are not half enough nurses or doctors out here. In one hospital there are 400 beds and only two trained nurses.

Some of our own British troops came through the town in London buses today. It was quite a moment, and we felt that all was well. We went to the gate and shook hands with them as they passed. They made jokes and did us all good. We cheered and waved handkerchiefs.

October 5–6:

I think the last two days have been the most ghastly I ever remember. Every day seems to bring news of defeat. It is awful, and the Germans are quite close now. As I write the house shakes with the firing. Our troops are falling back, and the forts have fallen. Last night we took provisions and water to the cellars, and made plans to get the wounded taken there.

They say the town will be shelled tomorrow. All these last two days, bleeding men have been brought in. Today three of them died. I suppose none of them was more than 23 years old. We have to keep up all the time and show a good face. Meals are quite cheery. Today, Tuesday, was our last chance of leaving, and only two went.

"Red Cross recruitment poster," by C.W. Anderson (circa 1914 to 1918). Courtesy the Library of Congress.

The guns boom by day as well as by night. As each one is heard one thinks of more bleeding, shattered men. It is calm, nice autumn weather; the trees are yellow in the garden and the sky is blue. Yet all the time one listens to the cries of men in pain. Tonight I meant to go out for a little, but a nurse stopped me and asked me to sit by a dying man. Poor fellow; he was 21, looked like some brigand chief, and smiled as he was dying. The horror of these two days will last always, and there are many more such days to come. Everyone is behaving well. That is all I care about.

October 7:
The Situation Gets Worse

It is a glorious morning: they will see well to kill each other today.

The guns go all day and all night. They are so close that the earth shakes with them. Last night in the infernal darkness we were turning wounded men away from the door. There was no room for them even on the floor. The Belgians scream terribly. Our own men suffer quite quietly. One of them died today.

Day and night, a stream of vehicles passes the gate. It never ceases. Nearly all are cars, driven at a furious pace, and they blast the horns all the time. These are met by a stream of carts and old-fashioned vehicles bringing in country people, who are flying to the coast. In Antwerp today it was *"sauve qui peut"* [every man for himself].

Nearly all the men are going: Mr. __, who has helped us, and Mr. __. Both of them are going to bicycle into Holland. A surgeon (Belgian) has fled from his hospital, leaving 700 beds, and there seem to be a great many deserters from the trenches.

The news is still the same—"very bad." Sometimes I walk to the gate and ask returning soldiers how the battle goes, but the answer never varies. At lunchtime today firing ceased, and I heard it was because the German guns were coming up. We got orders to send away all the wounded who could possibly go, and we prepared beds in the cellars for those who cannot be moved. The military authorities beg us to remain since so many hospitals have been evacuated.

The wounded continue to come in. One sees one car in the endless stream moving slowly (most of them fly by with their officers sitting upright, or with airplanes on long carriages), and one knows by the pace that more wounded are coming. Inside one sees the horrible six shelves behind the canvas curtain, and here and there a bound-up limb or head. One of our men had his leg taken off today and is doing well. Nothing goes on much behind the scenes. The yells of the men are plainly heard. Today, as I sat beside the lung man who was taking so long to die, someone brought a sack to me and said: "This is for the leg." All the orderlies are on duty in the hospital now. We can spare no one for rougher work. We can all bandage and wash patients. There are wounded everywhere, even on straw beds on the platform of the hall.

Darkness seems to fall early, and it is the darkness that is so baffling. At 5 p.m. we have to feed everyone while a little light remains. Then it gets dark and the groping about begins, with everyone falling over things. There is a clatter of basins on the floor or an over-turned chair. Any sudden noise is rather difficult at present because of the booming of the guns. At 7 last night they were much louder than before, with a sort of strange double sound. We were told that these were our "Long Toms," so we hope our Naval Brigade has come up.

We know very little of what is going on except when we run out and ask some returning English soldiers for news. Yesterday it was always the same reply, "Very bad." One of the Marines told me that Winston Churchill was "up and down the road among the shells." I was also told he had given orders that Antwerp was not to be taken until the last man in it was dead.

The Marines are getting horribly knocked about. Yesterday Mrs. O'Gormon went out in her own car and picked the wounded out of the trenches. She said no one knew why they were in the trenches or where they were to fire—they just lay there and were shot and then left.

I think I have seen too much pain lately. At Walworth, one saw women everyday in utter pain. Now one lives in an atmosphere of bandages and blood. I asked some orderlies today what it was that supported them most at a crisis of this sort. The answers varied and were interesting. I am surprised to find that religion is not my best support. When I go into the little chapel to pray, it is all too tender, the divine Mother and the Child and the holy atmosphere. I begin to feel rather sorry for myself, I don't know why. Then I go, move beds and feel better; but I have found that just to behave like a well-bred woman is what keeps me up best. I had thought that the flag or religion would have been stronger incentives to me.

Our own British soldiers seem to find self-respect their best asset. It is amazing to see the difference between them and the Belgians, who are terribly poor hands at bearing pain. They beg for morphine all the time. An officer today had to have a loose tooth out. He insisted on having cocaine, and then begged the doctor to be careful!

The firing now is furious—sometimes there are five or six explosions almost simultaneously. I suppose we shall read in the *Times* that "all is quiet," and in *Le Matin* that *"pour le reste tout est calme."* The staff is doing well. They are generally too busy to be frightened, but one has to speak once or twice to them before they hear.

On Wednesday night, October 7, we heard that one more ship was going to England, and a last chance was given to us all to leave. Only two did so; the rest stayed on. Mrs. Stobart went out to see what was to be done. The Consul said we were under his protection, and if the Germans entered the town he would see we were treated properly. We had a deliberately cheerful supper. Afterwards a man called Smits came in and told us the Germans had been driven back 9 miles. I did not believe this, but we went to bed and even took off our clothes.

At midnight, the first shell came over us with a shriek. I went down and awoke the orderlies, nurses and doctors. We dressed and went to help move the wounded at the hospital. The shells began to scream overhead. It was a bright moonlight night, and we walked without haste—a small body of women—across the road to the hospital. Here we found the wounded all yelling like mad things, thinking they were going to be left behind. The lung man has died.

"A library (left) on a bombed street in Louvain, Belgium where the Germans bombed and looted the town and executed civilians for 5 days starting Aug. 24, 1914," by *Bain News Service* (1914). Courtesy the Library of Congress.

Nearly all the moving to the cellars had already been done—only three stretchers remained to be moved. One wounded English sergeant helped us. Otherwise women did everything. We laid the men on mattresses, which we fetched from the hospital overhead. Then Mrs. Stobart's mild, quiet voice said, "Everything is to go on as usual. The night nurses and orderlies will take their places. Breakfast will be at the usual hour." She and the other ladies whose night it was to sleep at the convent then returned to sleep in the basement with a Sister.

"Ruins in Visé after the Aug. 4, 1914 destruction of the Belgian town by German forces," by *Bain News Service* (1914). Courtesy the Library of Congress.

The Bombardment

We came in for some of the most severe shelling at first, either because we flew the Red Cross flag or because we were in the line of fire with a powder magazine that the Germans wished to destroy. We sat in the cellars with one nightlight burning in each and 70 wounded men to care for. Two of them were dying. There was only one line of bricks between us and the shells. One shell fell into the garden, making a hole 6 feet deep, while the next crashed through a house on the opposite side of the road and set it on fire. The danger was twofold. We knew our hospital, which was a cardboard sort of thing, would ignite like matchwood; and if it fell, we would not be able to get out of the cellars. For this reason some people on our staff were much against us using a cellar at all. I myself felt it was the safest place. As long as we stayed with the wounded, they minded nothing. We sat there all night.

The English sergeant said that at daybreak the firing would probably cease, as the German guns stopped when daylight came in order to conceal the guns. We just waited for daybreak. When it came, the firing grew worse. The sergeant said, "It is always worse just before they stop," but the firing did not stop. Two hundred guns were turned on Antwerp, and the shells came over at the rate of 4 per minute. They have a horrid screaming sound as they come. We heard each one coming and wondered if it would hit us, and then we heard the crashing somewhere else and knew another shell was coming.

The worst cases among the wounded lay on the floor and were in need of constant attention. The others, in their greatcoats, stood about the cellar leaning on crutches and sticks. We wrapped blankets around the rheumatism cases and sat through the long night. Sometimes when we heard a crash nearby, we asked: "Is that the convent?" However, nothing else was said. Everyone spoke cheerfully, and there was some laughter in a further cellar. One little red-haired nurse enjoyed the whole thing. I saw her carry three wounded men in succession on her back down to the cellar. I found myself wishing, that for me, a shot would come and finish the horrible night. Still we all chatted and smiled and made little jokes. Once during that long night in the cellar I heard one wounded man say to another as he rolled himself round on his mattress, "Que les Anglais sont comme il faut."

At 6 o'clock, the convent group came over and began to prepare breakfast. The least wounded men began to steal away. We were left with between 30 and 40 of them. The difficulty was to know how to get away and how to remove the wounded, two of whom were nearly dead. Miss Benjamin went to stand at the gate while the shells still flew and picked up an ambulance. In this way, we moved six men, including the two dying ones. Mrs. Stobart was walking about for 3 hours trying to find anything on wheels to remove the wounded and us. At last we got an ambulance, where we packed in 20 men—that was all it would hold. We told them to go as far as the bridge and send it back for us. It never came. Nothing seemed to come. The Vice-Consul had told us we were under his protection, and he would, as a neutral, march out to meet the Germans and give us protection. But when we asked, we heard he had bolted without telling us. The next to give us protection was the Field Hospital, which said they had a ship in the river and would not move without us. But they also left without saying anything.

We got dinner for the men, and then the strain began to be much worse. We had seven wounded plus ourselves and nothing in which to get out of Antwerp. I told Mrs. Stobart we must leave the wounded at the convent in charge of the Sisters. This we did, telling them where to take them in the morning. The young nurses fetched them across on stretchers.

A Harrowing Escape

About 5 o'clock the shelling became more violent, and three shells came with only an instant between each. We heard Mrs. Stobart say, "Come at once." We went out and found three English buses with English drivers at the door. They were carrying ammunition and were the last vehicles to leave Antwerp. We got into them and lay on the top of the ammunition, and the girls began to light cigarettes! The noise of the buses prevented for a time us hearing the infernal sound of shells and our cannons' answering roar.

As we drove to the bridge many houses, and sometimes a whole street, were burning. No one seemed to care. No one was there to try and save anything. We drove through the empty streets. We saw the burning houses and great holes where shells had fallen. Then we got to the bridge and out of the line of fire. We set out to walk towards Holland, but a Belgian officer got us some Red Cross ambulances. Into these we went and were taken to a convent at St. Gilles, where we slept on the floor until 3 a.m. At 3 o'clock a message was brought: "Get up at once—things are worse." Everyone seemed to be leaving. We got into the Red Cross ambulances and went to the station.

"Three British soldiers in trench under fire during World War I," (circa 1916). Courtesy the Library of Congress.

October 9:

We have been all day in the train in very hard 3rd-class carriages with the Royal Marines Light Infantry. The journey of 50 miles took from 5 o'clock in the morning, when we got away, until 12 o'clock at night, when we reached Ostend. The train hardly crawled. It was the longest I've ever seen. All Ostend was in darkness when we arrived—a German airship having been seen overhead. We always seem to be tumbling around in the dark. We went from one hotel to another trying to get accommodation. At last the St. James allowed us to lie on the floor of the restaurant. The only food they had for us was 10 eggs for 25 hungry people and some brown bread, but they had champagne at the house, and I ordered it for everybody. We made little speeches and tried to end on a good note.

October 10:
The Unit Returns to England

Mrs. Stobart took the unit back to England today. The wounded were found in a little house that the Red Cross had made over to them. Dr. Ramsey, Sister Bailey, and the two nurses had much to say about their perilous journey. One man had died on the road, but the others all looked well. Their joy at seeing us was pathetic, and there was a great deal of handshaking over our meeting.

Miss Donnisthorpe and I got decent rooms at the Littoral Hotel, where our luggage was brought over. We had baths, which we much needed. Dr. Hanson had gotten out of the train at Bruges to bandage a wounded man, and she was left behind—and is still lost. I suppose she has gone home. She is the doctor I like best, and she is one of the few whose nerves are not shattered. It was a sorry little party that Mrs. Stobart took back to England.

Chapter 4
Dr. Hector Munro's Ambulance Corps

"Interior view of a French ambulance," by *Bain News Service* (circa 1914 to 1915). Courtesy the Library of Congress.

Oct. 12, 1914:

Everyone has returned to England except Sister Bailey and me. She is waiting to hand over the wounded to the proper department. I am waiting to see if I can get on anywhere. It does seem so hard that when the men need us the most we should all run home and leave them.

The noises and racket in Ostend are deafening. There is panic everywhere. The boats go to England packed every time. I called on Sir Francis Villiers yesterday, and heard his wife is leaving Tuesday. But they say the British Minister dare not leave or the whole place would go wild with fear. Some ships lie close to us on the gray misty water, and the troops are passing along all day.

"English ladies doing Red Cross work in France, Mairi Chisholm (left) and Elsie Knocker, the Baroness de T'Serclaes," *The Illustrated War News*, (July 26, 1916).

Later:

We heard tonight the Germans are coming into Ostend tomorrow, so once more we fly like dust before a broom. It is horrible having to clear out for them. I am trying to discover what courage really consists of. It isn't only a lack of imagination. In some people it is transcendent; in others it is only a sort of stupidity. If proper precautions were taken, the need for courage would be much reduced—the "tight place" is so often the result of sheer muddle. This evening Dr. Hector Munro came in from Ghent with his oddly dressed ladies; at first one was inclined to call them masqueraders in their knickerbockers [capri pants], puttees [leather leggings], and caps, but I believe they have done excellent work. It is a strange side of war to see young, pretty English girls in khaki and thick boots, coming in from the trenches, where they have been picking up wounded men within 100 yards of the enemy's lines, and carrying them away on stretchers. Wonderful little Valkyries in knickerbockers, I lift my hat to you! Dr. Munro asked me to come onto his convoy. I gladly did so as he sent home a lady whose nerves were gone. I was put in her place.

October 13:
Meeting a New Team

We had an early breakfast, during which everyone spoke in a high voice and urged others to hurry. Then we collected luggage and went to see the General. Afterwards we all got into our ambulances en route for Dunkirk. The road was filled with flying inhabitants, and down at the dock both the wounded and well struggled to board a steamer [steamship].

People were begging us for a seat in our ambulance. Well-dressed women were setting out to walk 20 miles to Dunkirk. The rain was falling heavily.

It became a dripping day as we and a lot of English soldiers found ourselves in the square in Dunkirk, where the few hotels are located. We had an expensive lunch at a greasy restaurant before trying to find rooms.

I began to figure out who was among us in our party. There is Lady Dorothie Fielding—probably 22, but capable of taking command of a ship, and speaking French like a native; Mrs. Decker, an Australian, plucky and efficient; Mairi Chisholm, a blue-eyed Scottish girl, with a thick coat strapped around her waist and a haversack [bag] slung from her shoulder; a tall American, whose name I do not yet know, whose husband is a journalist; three young surgeons, and Dr. Munro.

It is all so quaint. The girls rule the company—they carry maps, find roads, see about provisions, and carry the wounded.

We could not get rooms at Dunkirk and so went to St. Malo les Bain, a small seaside place that had been shut up for the winter. The owner of a hotel there opened up some rooms for us, and got us some ham and eggs. The evening ended very cheerily.

To me, our party seems amazingly young and unprotected.

October 14:
War & Simplicity

Today I took a car into Dunkirk and bought some things, as I have lost nearly all I possessed at Antwerp. In the afternoon, I went to the dock to get some letters mailed and walked around there for a long time. War is such a disorganizer. Nothing starts. No one is able to move because of wounded arms and legs; it seems to make the world helpless and painful. In minor matters, one lives nearly always with damp feet, and rather dirty and hungry. Drains are all choked, and one does not get much sleep. These are trifles of course.

Tonight as we sat at dinner, a message was brought that a woman outside had been run over and was going to have a baby immediately in a tramway shelter. So out we went and got one of our ambulances. A young doctor with his fiancée went off with her. There was a lot arguing about where the woman lived, until one young man said: "Well, get in somehow, or the baby will have arrived." There is a simplicity about these tragic times, and nothing matters but to save people.

October 15:
Women at the Front

Today we went down to the docks to get a passage for Dr. Munro, who is going home for money. A German Taube flew overhead and men were firing rifles at it. An Englishman hit it, and down it came like a shot bird. So that was the end of a brave man, whoever he was, and it was a long drop, too, through the still autumn air. Guns have begun to fire again, so I suppose we shall have to move on once more. One does not unpack. It is dangerous to part with one's linen to be washed. Yesterday I heard a man—a man in a responsible position—say to a girl: "Tell me, please, how far we are from the firing line." It was one of the most remarkable speeches I ever heard. I go to these girls for all my news.

"British Tommies rescuing a comrade under shell fire," (1916) Courtesy Wikimedia Commons.

Lady Dorothie Fielding is our real commander, and everyone knows it. One hears on all sides: "Lady Dorothie, can you get us tires for the ambulances? Where is the gasoline?" "Do you know if the General will let us through?" "Have you been able to get us any stores?" "Should we have '*laissez-passer's*' or not?" She goes to all the heads of departments, is the only good speaker of French, and has the only reliable information about anything. All the men acknowledge her position. They say to me, "It's very odd being run by a woman, but she is the only person who can do anything." In the firing line she is quite cool and so are the other women. They seem to be interested, not dismayed, by shots and shrapnel.

October 16:
The Ironies of War

Today I have been reading of the "splendid retreat" of the Marines from Antwerp and their "unprecedented reception" at Deal. Everyone appears to have been in a state of wild enthusiasm about them, and it seems almost like Mafeking [in South Africa] over again.

What struck me most about these men was the way in which they blew their own trumpets in full retreat -- while flying from the enemy. We traveled all day in the train with them and had long conversations with them all. They were all saying: "We will bring you the Kaiser's head, Miss." I replied, "Well, you had better turn around and go the other way." Some people like this "English" spirit. I find the conceit of it most trying.

Belgium is in the hands of the enemy, and we flee before him singing our own praises loudly as we do so. The Marines lost their kit, spent one night in Antwerp, and went back to England, where they had an amazing reception amid scenes of unprecedented enthusiasm! The [British] Government will give them a fresh kit, and the public will cheer itself hoarse!

I could not help thinking, when I read the papers today, of our tired little body of nurses, doctors, and orderlies going back quietly and unproclaimed to England to rest at Folkestone for three days—and then to return here again. They had been for 18 hours under heavy shellfire without so much as a rifle to protect them and with the immediate chance of a burning building falling about them.

The nurses sat in the cellars tending wounded men, whom they refused to leave. Then they hopped onto the outside of an ammunition bus "to see the fun" before coming home to buy their little caps and aprons out of their own slender purses and start work again. I shall believe in Britishers to the day of my death, and I hope I shall die before I cease to believe in them, but I do get some disillusions.

At Antwerp not a man remained with us, and the worst of it was they made elaborate excuses for leaving. Even our sergeant, who helped during the night, took a comrade off in the morning and disappeared. Both were wounded, but not badly, and two young English Tommies, very slightly wounded, left us as soon as the firing began. We saw them afterwards at the bridge, and they looked pretty mean.

Tonight at dinner, some officers came in when the food was pretty well finished. Only some drumsticks of chicken and bits of ham were left. I am always slow at beginning to eat, and I had a large wing of chicken still on my plate. I offered this to an officer, who accepted it and ate it, although he asked me to have a little bit of it. I do hope I shall meet some cases of chivalry soon.

Firing ceased about 5 o'clock this afternoon, but we are short of news. The English papers rather annoy one with their continual victories, of which we see nothing. Everyone talks of the German big guns as if they were some happy chance. But the Germans were drilling and preparing while we were making speeches at Hyde Park Corner. Everything had been thought out by them.

People talk of the difficulty they must have had in preparing concrete floors for their guns. Not a bit of it. There were innocent dwelling houses, built long ago, with floors in just the right position and of just the right stuff, and when they were wanted the top stories were blown off and the concrete gun-floors were ready. There were local exhibitions, too, to which firms sent exhibition guns, which they "forgot" to remove! While we were going on strike, they were making an army, and as we have sown so must we reap.

One almost wonders whether it might not be possible to eliminate the personal element in war, so constant is the talk about victorious guns. If guns decide everything, then let them be trained on other guns. Let the gun that drives farthest and goes surest win.

If every siege is decided by the German 16-inch howitzers, then let us put up brick and mortar or steel against them, but not men. The day for the bleeding human body seems to be over now that men are mown down by shells fired from eight miles away. War used to be splendid because it made men strong and brave, but now a little German in spectacles can stand behind a Krupp gun and wipe out a regiment.

"An operating ambulance in France," by *Bain News Service* (circa 1914 to 1915) Courtesy the Library of Congress.

Life or Property?

I suppose women will always try to protect life because they know what it costs to produce it, and men will always try to protect property because that is what they themselves produce. At Antwerp, our wounded men were begging us to go up to the hospital to fetch their wallets from under their pillows! At present, women are only repairers, darning socks, cleaning, washing up after men, bringing up reinforcements in the way of fresh life, and patching up wounded men. But some day they must and will have to say, "The life I produce has as much right to protection as the property you produce, and I claim my right to protect it." There seems to me a lack of connection between one man's desire to extend the area he occupies and young men in their teens lying with their lungs shot through or backs blown off.

October 19:

Our time is now spent in waiting and preparing for work, which will probably come, soon, as there has been fighting near us again. One hears the boom of guns a long way off, and always there is the sound of death in it. One has been too near it not to know now what it means.

Yesterday I went to church in an empty little building, but a few of our hospital men turned up and made a small congregation. In the afternoon, a couple of people came to tea in my bedroom, as we could not make our usual expedition to De Poorter's bun shop. The pastry habit is growing on us all.

We went to the arsenal today to see about some repairs to our ambulances. I saw a German bus that had been captured, and the eagles on it had been painted out with stripes of red paint and the French colors put in their place. The bus was one mass of bullet holes. I have seen wagons at Paardeberg, but I never saw anything so knocked about as that gray bus. The engines and sides were shattered, and the chauffeur, of course, had been killed. We went on by car to the "Champs des Aviateurs." We saw one naval airplane man, who told us that he had been hit in his machine when it was 4,000 feet up in the air. A bullet tore his jacket and his machine dropped, but he was uninjured and got away on a bicycle.

The more I see of war the more I am amazed at the courage and nerve that are shown. Death or the chance of death is everywhere. We meet it not as fatalists do or those who believe they can earn eternal glory with a sacrifice, but lightly and with a song. An English girl at Antwerp was horribly ashamed of some Belgians who skulked behind a wall when the firing was hottest. She herself remained in the open.

It has been a great comfort to me that I have had a room to myself so far on this campaign. I find the communal spirit is not in me. The noisy meals, the heavy bowls of soup, the piles of labeled dinner napkins, give me an unexpected feeling of oppressive seclusion and solitude. Only when I get away by myself do I feel that my soul is restored.

Mr. Gleeson, an American, joined his wife here a couple of days ago; it was odd to have a book talk again.

October 21:
What Is Heroism?

A still gray day with a level sea and a few fishing boats going out with the tide. On the long gray shore shrimpers are wading with their nets. The only color in the soft gray dawn is the little wink of white that the breaking waves make on the sand. This small empty seaside place, with its row of bathing machines [small structures for changing clothes] drawn up on the beach, has a look about it as of a theatre seen by daylight. All the seats are empty, and the players have gone away, and the theatre begins to whisper as empty buildings do. I think I know quite well some of the people who come to St. Malo les Bain, just by listening to what the empty little place is saying.

Firing has begun again. We hear our ships are shelling Ostend from the sea. The news that reaches us is meager, but I prefer that to the false reports circulated at home.

This afternoon we came out in cars and ambulances to establish ourselves at Furnes in an empty Ecclesiastical College. Nothing was ready. Everything was in confusion. The wounded from the fighting nearby had not begun to come in, but the infernal sound of the guns was quite close to us and gave the sensation of a horn blow on the ear. Night was falling as we came back to Dunkirk to sleep since no beds were ready at Furnes. We passed many vehicles of every description going out to Furnes. Some of them were filled with bread, and one saw stacks of loaves filling to the roof some once beautifully appointed vehicle. Now all was dust and dirt.

All my previous ideas of men marching to war have had a touch of heroism, crudely expressed by quickstep and smart uniforms. Today, I see tired dusty men, very hungry looking and unshaved, slogging along, silent and tired, and ready to lie down wherever chance offers. They keep as near their convoy as they can, and are eager to stop and cook something. What is heroism? It baffles me.

October 22: Furnes
A Wild Car Ride

The bulk of our party did not return from Furnes yesterday, so we thought the wounded must be coming in. We left Dunkirk early and came here. As I packed my things and rolled my rugs at 5 a.m., I thought of Mary, and "Charles to fetch down the luggage," as well as the fuss at home over my delicate health!

A French officer called Gilbert took us to Furnes in his Brooklands racing car, so that was a bit of an experience too since we sat curled up on some luggage and were told to hang on to something. The roads were empty and level; the little seats of the car were merely an appendage to its long big engines.

When we got our breath back, we asked Gilbert what his speed had been. He told us 75 mph. There was a crowd of vehicles in the yard of the Ecclesiastical College at Furnes, engines throbbing and clutches being jerked. We were told that all last night the fighting had gone on and the wounded had been coming in. There are three wards already fairly full, nothing quite ready, with the inevitable and reiterated "where" heard on every side.

"Where are the stretchers?" "Where are my forceps?" "Where are we to eat?" "Where are the dead to be put?" "Where are the Germans?" No one stops to answer. People ask everybody 10 times over to do the same thing and use anything that is around.

A Daring Rescue Attempt

There are two war correspondents here—Phillip Gibbs [one of 5 official British reporters covering WWI who was knighted for his war coverage] and Ellis Ashmead-Bartlett [famed British Fleet Street journalist]—and they told me about the fighting at Dixmude last night. I must try to get Mr. Gibbs's newspaper account of it, but nothing will ever be so simple and so dramatic as his own description.

"Belgian Red Cross fundraising poster from London," by Charles A. Buchel (circa 1915). Courtesy the Library of Congress.

He and Mr. Bartlett, Mr. Gleeson and Dr. Munro, with young Mr. Brockville, the War Minister's son, went to the town, which was being heavily shelled. Dixmude was full of wounded, and the church and the houses were falling. The roar of things was awful. The bursting shells overhead sent shrapnel pattering on the buildings, the pavements, and the cars.

Young Brockville went into a house, where he heard wounded were lying, and found a pile of dead Frenchmen stacked against a wall. A bursting shell scattered them. He went into a cellar and found some living men, got the stretchers, loaded the cars and bade them drive on. In the darkness, and with the deafening noises, no one heard his orders properly. The two ambulances moved on and left him behind among the burning houses and flying shells. It was only after going a few miles that the rest of the party found he wasn't with them. Mr. Gleeson and Mr. Bartlett went back for him. Nothing need be said except that they went back to hell for him, and the other two waited in the road with the wounded men. After an hour of waiting, these two also went back.

I asked Mr. Gibbs if he shared the contempt that some people expressed for bullets. He and Mr. Gleeson both said, "Anyone who talks of contempt for bullets is talking nonsense. Bullets mean death at every corner of the street, and death overhead and flying limbs and unspeakable sights." All these men went back. All of them behaved quietly and like gentlemen, but one man asked a friend of his over and over again if he was a Belgian refugee, and another said that a town steeple falling looked so strange that they could only stand around and light cigarettes. In the end, they gave up Mr. Brockville for lost and came home with the ambulances. But he turned up in the middle of the night to everyone's huge delight.

October 23:
Daybreak on the Front Lines

A crisp autumn morning, a courtyard filled with vehicles and brancardiers [orderlies who transport patients] and men in uniform, and women in knickerbockers and puttees, all lighting cigarettes and talking about repairs, gears, and a box of bandages. The mornings always start happily enough. The guns are nearer today or more distant, the battle sways backwards and forwards, and there is no such thing as a real "base" for a hospital. We must just stay as long as we can and fly when we must. About 10 a.m. the ambulances that have been out all night begin to come in, the wounded on their pitiful shelves.

"A Taube," by C.R.W. Nevinson (1916). The painting by the famed British war artist shows a French boy injured by a shell from a Taube. Courtesy Wikimedia Commons.

"Take care. There are two awful cases. Step this way. The man on the top shelf is dead. Lift them down. Steady. Lift the others out first. Now carry them across the yard to the overcrowded ward, and lay them on the floor if there are no beds, but lay them down and go for others. Take the worst to the theater. Get the shattered limbs amputated and then bring them back, for there is a man just dead whose place can be filled; and these two must be shipped off to Calais; and this one can sit up."

The Weird Tired Hour

I found one young German with both hands smashed. He was not ill enough to have a bed, of course, but sat with his head fallen forward trying to sleep on a chair. I fed him with porridge and milk out of a little bowl. When he had finished half of it he said, "I won't have any more. I am afraid there will be none for the others." I got a few cushions for him and laid him in a corner of the room. Nothing disturbs the deep sleep of these men. They seem not so much exhausted as dead with fatigue. A French boy of 16 years of age is a favorite of mine. He is such a beautiful child, and there is no hope for him; shot through the abdomen. He can retain nothing and is sick all day. Every day he is weaker.

I don't find that the men want to send letters or write messages. Their pain is too awful even for that, and I believe they can think of nothing else. All day the stretchers are brought in and the work goes on. It is about 5 o'clock that the weird tired hour begins—when the dim lamps are lighted, people fall over things, nearly everything is mislaid, the wounded cry out, and one steps over forms on the floor. From then until one goes to bed, it is difficult to be just what one ought to be, the tragedy of it is too pitiful. There is a boy with his eyes shot out, and there is a row of men all with head wounds from the cruel shrapnel overhead. Bloodstained mattresses and pillows are carried out into the courtyard. Two ladies help move the corpses. There is always a pile of bandages and rags being burnt, and a youth stirs the horrible pile with a stick. A queer smell permeates everything. The guns never cease. The wounded are coming in at the rate of 100 per day.

The Queen Elisabeth of the Belgians called to see the hospital today. Poor little Queen, coming to see the remnants of an army and the remnants of a kingdom! She was kind to each wounded man, and we were glad of her visit, if for no other reason than that some sort of cleaning and tidying was done in her honor. Tonight Mr. Nevinson arrived, and we went round the wards together after supper. The beds were all full—so was the floor. I was glad so many of the wounded were dying. The doctors said, "These men are not wounded, they are mashed." I am rather surprised to find how little the quiet young girls seem to mind the sight of wounds and suffering. They are bright and witty about amputations, and do not shudder at anything. I am feeling rather out-of-date among them.

"The Queen of Belgium," by *Bain News Service* (circa 1914 to 1918). Courtesy the Library of Congress.

The Tragedy of Pain
Oct. 23, 1914
Letter to Sarah's Sisters,
Dr. Hector Munro's Ambulance, Furnes, Belgium

My Dear People,
I think I may get this posted by a war correspondent who is going home, but I never know whether my letters reach you or not, for yours, if you write them, never reach me. I can't begin to tell you all that is happening, and

it is really beyond what one is able to describe. The tragedy of pain is the thing that is most evident, and there is the roar and the racket of it and the everlasting sound of guns. The war seems to me now to mean nothing but torn limbs and stretchers. All the doctors say that never have they seen men so wounded.

The day that we got here was the day that Dixmude [city in West Flanders] was bombarded, and our 10 ambulances went out to fetch in wounded. These were shoved in anywhere, dying and dead, and our men went among the shells with buildings falling about them and took out all they could. Except where the fire is hottest one woman goes with each car. So far I have been doing ward work, but one of the doctors is taking me on an ambulance this afternoon. Most of the women who go are very good chauffeurs themselves, so they are chosen before a person who can't drive. They are splendid creatures, and funk nothing, and they are there to do a little dressing if it is needed.

The firing is awfully heavy today. They say it is the big French guns that have got up. Two of our ambulances have had miraculous escapes after being hit. Things happen too quickly to know how to describe them. Today when I went out to breakfast an old village woman aged about 70 was brought in wounded in two places. I am not fond of horrors.

We have been given an empty house for the staff, the owners having quitted it in a panic and left everything, children's toys on the carpet, and beds unmade. The hospital is a college for priests, all of whom have fled. Into this building the wounded are carried day and night, and the surgeons are working in shifts and can't get the work done. Alas, we are losing so many patients. Nothing can be done for them, and I always feel so glad when they are gone. I don't think anyone can realize what it is to be just behind the line of battle. I fear there would not be much recruiting if people at home could see our wards. One can only be thankful for a hospital like this in the thick *of things, for we are saving lives, and not only so, but saving the lives of men who perhaps have lain three days in a trench or a turnip field undiscovered and forgotten.*

As soon as a wounded man has been attended to and is able to be put on a stretcher again he is sent to Calais. We have to keep emptying the wards for other patients to come in, and besides, if the fighting comes this way, we shall have to fall back a little further.

We have a river between us and the Germans, so we shall always know when they are coming and get a start and be all right.

Your loving,

S. Macnaughtan

October 25:

A glorious day. Up in the blue even Taubes—those birds of prey—look beautiful, like eagles wheeling in their flight. It is all far too lovely to leave; yet men are killing each other painfully with every day that dawns.

I had a tiresome day in spite of the weather because the hospital was evacuated suddenly owing to the nearness of the Germans, and I missed going with the ambulance, so I hung around all day.

October 26:
My Birthday

This morning several women were brought in horribly wounded. One girl of 16 had both legs smashed. I was taking one old woman to the civil hospital and I had to pass 18 dead men; they were laid out beside some women who were washing clothes. I noticed how tired even in death their poor dirty feet looked.

The Edge of the Frontline

We started early in the ambulance today and went to pick up the wounded. It was a wild gusty morning, one of those days when the sky takes up nearly all the picture and the world looks small. The mud was deep on the road, and a cyclist corps plunged heavily along through it. The car steered badly. We drove to the edge of the fighting line.

First one comes to a row of ammunition vans, with men cooking breakfast behind them. Then come the long gray guns, tilted at various angles, and beyond are the shells bursting and leaving little clouds of black or white in the sky. We signaled to a gun not to fire down the road in much the same way as a bobby [policeman] signals to a hansom [horse-drawn carriage]. When we got beyond the guns, they fired over us with a long streaky sort of sound. We came back to the road and picked up the wounded wherever we could find them.

The churches are nearly all filled with straw, the chairs piled anywhere, and the sacrament removed from the altar. In cottages and little inns it is the same thing—a litter of straw, and men lying on it in the chilly weather. Here and there through some little window one sees surgeons in their white coats dressing wounds. Half the world seems to be wounded and inefficient. We filled our ambulance and stood about in curious groups of English men and women who looked as if they were on some shooting party. When our load was complete we drove home.

Dr. Munro told me that last night he met a German prisoner quite naked being marched in, proudly holding his head up. Lots of the men fight naked in the trenches. In the hospital we meet delightful German youths. Among others who were brought in today was Mr. "Dick" Reading, the editor of a sports newspaper. He was serving in the Belgian army and behind a gun carriage when it was fired upon and started. Reading clung on behind with both his legs broken, and he stuck to it until the gun carriage was pulled up! He came in on a stretcher as bright as a button, smoking a cigar and laughing.

Brief Luxuries

Late this afternoon we had to leave Furnes and fly to Poperinghe in West Flanders. The drive was intensely interesting, through crowds of troops of every nationality. The town seemed large and well lit. It was crowded with people to see all our ambulances arrive. We went to a café, where there was a fire but nothing to eat. So some of the party went out and bought chops. I cooked them in a stuffy little room that smelt of burnt fat.

After supper, we went to a convent where the Queen of the Belgians had made arrangements for us to sleep. It was delightful. Each of us had a snowy white bed with white curtains in a long corridor, and there was a basin of water, cold but clean, and a towel for each of us. We thoroughly enjoyed our luxuries.

October 28:

The tide of battle seems to have swung away from us again, and we were recalled to Furnes today. The hospital looked very bare and empty as all the patients had been evacuated. There was nothing to do until fresh ones should come in. Three shells came over today and landed in a field near us. Some people say they were sent by our own naval guns firing wide. The souvenir grafters went out and got pieces of them.

November 2:

An Unpopular Boat

I have been spending a couple of nights in Dunkirk, where I went to meet Georgie Fyfe [sister of Times journalist Henry Hamilton Fyfe]. The S.S. *Invicta* [British troop ship] got in late because the *HMS Hermes* [a protected cruiser for the Royal Navy] had been torpedoed and they had gone to her assistance. No doubt the torpedo was intended for the *Invicta*, which carries ammunition, and consequently is becoming an unpopular boat. Forty of the *Hermes* men were lost.

"HMS Hermes cruiser for the Royal Navy" (circa 1913). The vessel was recommissioned in August 1914 as a depot ship and aircraft ferry. German torpedoes sunk it in October 1914 in the straits of Dover.

Dunkirk is full of people, and one meets friends at every turn. I had tea at the Consulate one afternoon and was rather glad to get away from the talk of shells and wounds, which is what you hear most at Furnes.

I saw Lord Horatio Herbert Kitchener, British Field Marshal, in the town one day. He had come to confer with French General Marshal Joseph Joffre, Field Marshal Sir John French, French President Monsieur Raymond Poincaré, and Winston Churchill at a meeting at the Hotel du Chapeau Rouge in Dunkirk.

Rather too many valuable men in one room, I thought—especially with so many spies about! The other day three men in English officers' uniforms were discovered to be Germans, and taken out and shot.

"Millicent, Duchess of Sutherland, as a Red Cross worker in Belgium," *The Sketch* (Oct. 28, 1914).

The Duchess of Sutherland has a hospital at our old Casino at Malo les Bain and has made it very nice. I had a long chat with a Coldstream man who was there. He told me he was carried to a barn after being shot in the leg with a shattered bone. He lay there for 6 days with nothing to eat but a few biscuits before he was found. He dressed his own wound.

"But," he said, "the string of my puttee had been driven in so far by the shot I couldn't find it to get the thing off, so I had to bandage over it."

I went down to the station one day to see if anything could be done for the wounded there. They are coming in at the rate of 700 per day and are laid on straw in an immense shed. They get nothing to eat, and the atmosphere is so bad that their wounds can't be dressed. They are all patient, as usual, only the groans are heartbreaking sometimes. We are arranging to have soup given to them, and a number of ambulance men arrived who will remove them to hospital ships and trains. But the shed is a shambles, and let us leave it at that. [Sarah's time in Flanders was all spent behind the French and Belgian lines.]

A Courageous Woman

Mrs. Elsie Knocker [a divorcee who was a trained nurse] came into Dunkirk for a night's rest while I was staying there. The previous day she had been out the whole time driving an ambulance in a windstorm with rain. The ambulance was heavily weighed down with the wounded, and shells were dropping very near. The most courageous woman that ever lived, she was quite unnerved at last. The glass of the car she was driving was dim with rain and she could carry no lights, and with this swaying load of injured men behind her on the rutty road she had to stick to her wheel and go on.

Someone said to her, "There is a doctor in such-and-such a farmhouse, and he has no dressings. You must take him these."

She demurred (a most unusual thing for her), but men do not protect women in this war, and they said she had to take them. She asked one of the least wounded of the men to get down and see what was in front of her, and he disappeared altogether. The dark mass she had seen in the road was a huge hole made by a shell! After steering into dead horses and going over awful roads, Mrs. Knocker came bumping into the yard, steering so badly they ran to see what was wrong and found her fainting. She was carried into the house. At Dunkirk, she got a good dinner and a night's rest.

November 5:
Hopeless Cases

The hospital is beginning to fill up again, and the nurses are depressed because only those cases which are nearly hopeless are allowed to stay—so it is death on all sides and just a hell of suffering. One man yelled to me tonight to kill him. I wish I might have done so. The tragedy of war presses with a fearful weight after being in a hospital, and wherever you are you hear the infernal sound of the guns. On Sunday about 40 shells came into Furnes, but I was at Dunkirk. This morning about 5 shells dropped onto the station.

A Nightmare Town

Today I went out to Nieuport, in West Flanders. It is like some town you see in a horrible nightmare. Hardly a house is left standing, but that does not describe the scene. Nothing can adequately describe it except perhaps such a pen as Victor Hugo's. The cathedral at Nieuport has two outer walls left standing. The front leans forward helplessly, while the aisles are gone. The trees around it are burnt up and shot away. In the roadway are great holes that shells have made. The very cobbles of the street are scattered by them. Not a window remains in the place; all are shattered and many hang from their frames. The fronts of the houses have fallen out. You see glimpses of wretched domestic life—a baby's cradle hangs in mid-air, some tin boxes have fallen through from a storage room in the attic to the ground floor. Shops are shivered and their contents strewn on all sides; the interiors of other houses have been hollowed out by fire. There is a toyshop with dolls grinning vacantly at the ruins or bobbing brightly on elastic strings.

In a wretched cottage, some soldiers are having breakfast at a fine-carved table. In one house, surrounded by a very devastation of wreckage, some cheap ornaments stand intact on a mantelpiece. From another, a little ginger-colored cat strolls out unconcernedly! The bedsteads hanging midway between floors look twisted and thrown—nothing stands up straight. Like the wounded, the town has been rendered inefficient by war.

November 6:
The Ghosts of Furnes

Furnes always seems to me a weird tragic place. I don't know why I think this, but its influence on me is rather strange. I feel as if all the time I was living in some blood-curdling ghost story or a horrid dream. Everyday I try to overcome the feeling, but I can't succeed. This afternoon I made up my mind to return to our villa and write my diary. The day was lovely. I meant to enjoy a rest and a scribble, but so strong was the horrid influence of the place that I couldn't settle to anything. I can't describe it, but it seemed to stifle me, and I can only compare it to some second sight in which you see death. I sat as long as I could doing my writing, but I had to give in at last. I tucked my book under my arm and walked back to the hospital, where at least I was with human beings and not ghosts.

Our life here is made up of many elements and many people, all rather incongruous, but the average of human nature is good. A villa belonging to a Dr. Joos was given to our staff. It is a pretty little house, with three beds in it. We are a group of 18 people, so most of us sleep on the floor. It wouldn't be a bad little place (except for the drains) if only there wasn't this horrid atmosphere everywhere. I always particularly dislike following after people like a little lost dog, but here I find myself doing that with somebody if the ghosts get the better of me.

I fear we are ruining the villa, but I have a woman to clean it and am trying to keep it in order. It is a cold little place since we have no fires. By pumping, we can get a little very cold water. There is a faucet in the bathroom and one sink where everyone tries to wash and shave at the same time. We get our meals at a butcher's shop, where there is a large room which we more than fill. The town lights all out by 6 o'clock, so we grope about in the dark, but there is a lamp in our dining room. When we leave, we have to pass through the butcher's shop, and you may find yourself running into the interior carcass of a sheep.

We get up about 7 o'clock and fight for the sink. Then we walk around to the butcher's shop and have breakfast at 7.30 a.m. Most people think they start off for the day's work at 8, but it is generally around 10 o'clock before all the brown-hooded ambulances with their red crosses have moved out of the yard. As a rule, we do not meet again until dinnertime, and even then many of our group are absent. They come in at all times, very dirty and hungry, and the greeting is always the same, "Did you get many?" "Have you picked up many wounded?"

"French soldiers resting after a march," by *Bain News Service* (1914). Courtesy the Library of Congress.

One night Dr. Munro got knocked over by the actual force in the air created by a shell, which however did not hit him. Yesterday Mr. Secher was shot in the leg. I am amazed that not more get hit. They are all very cheery about it.

Today we heard that a cheerful French boy with white teeth, who has been very good at making coffee at our picnic lunches, was put up against a tree and shot at daybreak. Someone had made him drunk the night before, and he had threatened an officer with a revolver.

November 7:
A Dramatic Incident

Lady Theodosia Bagot turned up here today, and I lunched with her at the Hôtel des Arcades. Just before lunch, a bomb was dropped from a Taube overhead, and we had hardly sat down to lunch when a revolver shot rang through the room.

"In Paris, Turcos soldiers wounded during the Battle of Charleroi in Belgium," by *Bain News Service* (1914). Courtesy the Library of Congress.

A French officer had discharged his pistol by mistake, and he lay on the floor in his scarlet trousers. The scene was really the Adelphi, and as the man had only slightly hurt himself. You are able to appreciate the scenic effect and notice how well staged it was. A waiter ran for me. I ran to one of our ambulances for dressings, and we knelt in the right attitude beside the hero in his scarlet clothes, while the "lady of the bureau" begged for the bullet!

In the evening, Lady Bagot and I worked at the railway sheds until 3 a.m. One immense shed had 700 wounded in it. The night scene, with its inevitable accompaniment of low-lit lamps and gloom, was one I shall never forget. The railway lines on each side of the covered platform were spread with straw. On these slept the wounded men, bedded down like cattle. There were rows of them sleeping feet to feet, with straw over them to make a covering. I didn't hear a grumble and hardly a groan. Most of them slept heavily.

Near the door was a row of Senegalese, their dark faces and gleaming eyes looking strange above the straw; and further on were some Germans, whom the French authorities would not allow our men to touch; then rows of men of every color and blood; Zouaves [French Army Light Infantry], with their picturesque dress all grimed and colorless; Turcos [tirailleurs, or French Army shooting skirmishers], French, and Belgians. Nearly all had their heads and hands bound up in filthy dressings. We went into the dressing station at the far end of the great shed and dressed wounds until about 3 o'clock. Then we passed through the long, long lines of sleeping wounded men again and went home.

The Hunger of the Wounded
Nov. 8, 1914
To Lady Clémentine Waring

My Dearest Clemmie,

I have a big job for you. Will you do it? I know you are the person for it, and you will be prompt and interested.

The wounded are suffering from hunger as much as from their wounds. In most places, such as dressing stations and railway stations, nothing is provided for them at all. Many men are left for two or three days without food.

I wish I could describe it all to you! These wounded men are picked up after a fight and taken anywhere—very often to some farmhouse or inn, where a Belgian surgeon claps something onto the wounds or ties on a splint, and then our (Dr. Munro's) ambulances come along and bring the men into the Field Hospital if they are very bad, or if not they are taken direct to a station and left there. They may, and often do, have to wait for hours until a train loads up and starts.

Even those who are brought to the Field Hospital have to leave long before they can walk or sit. They are carried to the local station and put into covered horseboxes on straw, and must wait until the train loads up and starts.

You see everything has to be done with a view to sudden evacuation. We are so near to the firing line that the Germans may sweep on our way at any time. Then every man has to be cleared out somehow (we have a heap of ambulances), and the staff is moved off to some safer place.

We did an escape of this sort to Poperinghe one day. But after being there two days, the fighting swayed the other way and we were able to come back.

Well, during all these shiftings and waitings the wounded get nothing to eat. I want some traveling kitchens, and I want you to see about the whole thing. You may have to come from Scotland because I have discussed this subject with Mr. Burbidge, of Harrods' Stores. A Harrods' man is over here. He takes back this letter. I particularly want you to see him.

Mr. Burbidge has, or can obtain, old horse vans that can be fitted up as traveling kitchens. He is doing one now for Millicent, Duchess of Sutherland. It is to cost £15, which I call very cheap. I wish you could see it since I know you could improve upon it. It is fitted, I understand, with copper for boiling soup and a chimney. There is also a place for fuel. I would like a strongbox that would hold vegetables, dried peas, etc., whose top would serve as a table. Then there must be plenty of hooks and shelves where possible, and I believe Burbidge makes some sort of protection against fire in the way of lining to the van. Harrods' man says he doesn't know if they have any more vans or not.

I want someone with push and energy to see the thing right through and get the vans off. Sailing daily from the Admiralty Pier in Dover, the Invicta brings Red Cross things free.

The vans would have to have the Red Cross painted on them, and in small letters, somewhere inconspicuous, "Miss Macnaughtan's Traveling Kitchens." This is only for identification. I thought we might begin with three, and get them sent out at once, and go on, as they are required. I must have a capable person and a helper in charge of each, so that limits my number. The Germans have beautiful little kitchens at each station, but I can't be sure what money I can raise, so must go slow.

I want also two little trollies, just to hold a tin jug and some tin cups hung round, with one oil lamp to keep the jug hot. The weather will be bitter soon, and only "special" cases have blankets. Clemmie, if only we could see this thing through without too much red tape! No permission needs to be given for the work of these kitchens since we are under the Belgian Minister of War and act for Belgium.

I thought of coming over to London for a day or two. I can still do so, only I know you will be able to do this thing better than anyone, and will think of things no one else thinks of. I can get voluntary workers, but meat and vegetables are dreadfully in short supply, so I won't be able to spend a great deal on the vans. However, any day they may be taken by the Germans, so the only thing that really matters is to get the wounded a mug of hot soup.

Last night I was dressing wounds and bandaging at Dunkirk station until 3 a.m. The men are brought there in heaps—all helpless, all suffering. Sometimes there are 1,500 in one day. Last night, 700 lay on straw in a huge railway shed, with straw to cover them—bedded down like cattle and all in pain. Still, it is better than the trenches and shrapnel overhead!

At the Field Hospital the wounds are ghastly, and we are losing so many patients! Mere boys of 16 come in sometimes mortally wounded, and there are very many cases of wounded women. You see, no one is safe. And, oh, my dear, have you ever seen a town that has been thoroughly shelled? At Furnes, we have many shells dropping in, but no real bombardment yet. After Antwerp I don't seem to care about these visitors.

We were under fire there for 18 hours. It was a bit of a strain as our hospital was in a line with the Arsenal, which they were trying to destroy, so we got more than our share of attention.

"A tirailleur, an infantry man in uniform from French Equatorial Africa, possibly Senegal, preparing to assist France in World War I," by *Bain News Service* (1914). Courtesy the Library of Congress.

The noise was horrible, and the shells came in at the rate of 4 per minute. There was something quite hellish about it. Do you remember that great bit of writing in Job, when Wisdom speaks and says: "Destruction and Death say, it is not in me"? The wantonness and sort of rage of it all appall you. Our women behaved splendidly. I'll come over to England if you think I had better, but I'm sure you are the person I want. If anything should prevent your helping, please send a wire to me. Otherwise I will know things are going forward.

Your loving,
S. Macnaughtan

P.S. The vans should be strong since they may have rough usage. Also, to take them to their destination they may have to be hitched onto an ambulance. One or two strong trays in each kitchen would be useful. The little trollies would be for train-station work. As we go on, I hope to have one kitchen for each dressing station as well.

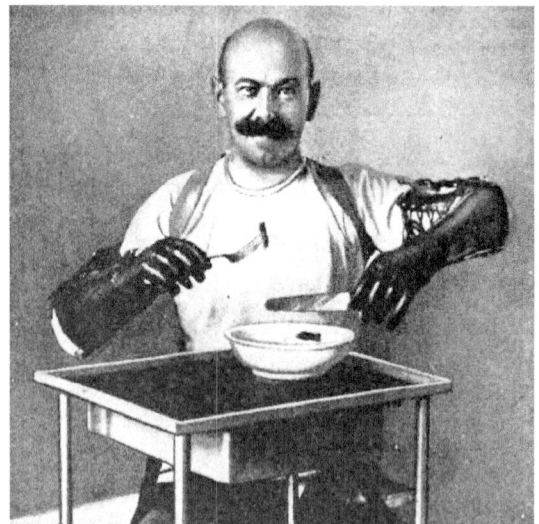

"The war cripple found that science had come most unexpectedly to his aid. One of the wonders of the war was the success with which a soldier's amputated hand, arm or leg was replaced by an artificial one, and he was taught how to earn his living in spite of his handicap." *Harper's Pictorial Library of the World War*, Vol. 7 (1920).

November 8:

An Act of Mercy

This afternoon I went down to the Hôtel des Arcades, which is the general meeting place for everyone. The drawing room was full and so was the central square called the Place Jean Bart, on which it looks. Suddenly we saw people beginning to fly! Soldiers, old men, children in their Sunday clothes—all running for cover. I asked what was up and heard that a Taube was at that moment flying over our hotel. These are the sort of pleasant things you hear out here! Then Lady Gertude Decies [a widow who became a decorated Red Cross nurse] came running in to say that two bombs had fallen and 20 people were wounded.

Once more we got bandages and hurried off in a car, but the civilian doctors were looking after everyone. By good luck, the bomb had fallen into a little garden with the least damage imaginable, but every window in the neighborhood was smashed.

At night we went to the railway sheds and dressed wounds. I made them do the Germans; but it was too late for one of them—a handsome young fellow with both his feet deep blue with frostbite, his leg broken and a great wound in his thigh. He had not been touched for eight days. Another man had a great hole right through his arm and shoulder. The dressing was rough and ready. The surgeons clapped a great wad of lint [boracic lint was a medical dressing] into the hole and we bound it up. There is no hot water, no sterilizing, no cyanide gauze even, but iodine saves many lives, and we have plenty of it. The German boy was dying when we left. His eyes above the straw began to look glazed and dim. Death, at least, is merciful.

We work so late at the railway sheds that I lie in bed until lunchtime. Lady Bagot and I go to the sheds in the evening and stay there until 1 a.m.

November 11:
Who Will Be Left?

I got a letter from Julia yesterday, telling me that Alan [her nephew Capt. Alan Young, 2nd Battalion, the Welch Regiment] is wounded and in hospital at Boulogne, and asking me to go and see him.

I came here this morning and had to run around for a long time before I started getting a *"laissez-passer"* for the road, as spies are being shot almost at sight now. By good chance, I got a car that brought me all the way; trains are uncertain, and filled with troops, and you never know when they will arrive.

I found poor old Alan, at the Base Hospital, in terrible pain, poor boy, but not dangerously wounded. He has been through an awful time and nearly all the officers of his regiment have been killed or wounded. For my part, in spite of his pain, I can thank God that he is out of the firing line for a bit. The horror of the war has got right into him, and he has seen things that few boys of 18 can have witnessed. Eight days in the trenches at Ypres under heavy fire day and night is a pretty severe test, but Alan has behaved splendidly. He told me the most awful tales of what he had seen. I believe it did him good to get things off his chest, so I listened.

The thing he found the most ghastly was the fact that when a trench has been taken or lost, the wounded, the dying and the dead are left out in the open. He says the firing never ceases, and it is impossible to reach these men, who die of starvation within sight of their comrades.

"Sometimes," Alan said, "we see them raise themselves on an arm for an instant and yell to us to come to them, but we can't."

His own wound was received when the Germans "got their range to an inch" and began shelling their trenches. A whole company next to Alan was wiped out and he started to go back to tell his Colonel the trench could not be held.

The communication trench through which he went was not quite finished, and he had to get out into the open and race across to where the unfinished trench began again. Poor child, running for his life! He was badly hit in the groin, but managed just to tumble into the next bit of the trench, where he found two men who carried him, pouring with blood, to his Colonel. He was hastily bound up and carried 4 miles on crossed rifles to the hospital at Ypres, where his wound was properly dressed. After an hour he was put on the train for Boulogne.

Alan had one story of how he was told to wait at a certain spot with 130 men. "So I waited," he said, "but the fire was awful." His regiment had, it seems, gone around another way. "I got 30 of the men away," Alan said, "the rest were killed." It means something to be an officer and a gentleman. Each day the list of casualties grows longer, and I wonder who will be left.

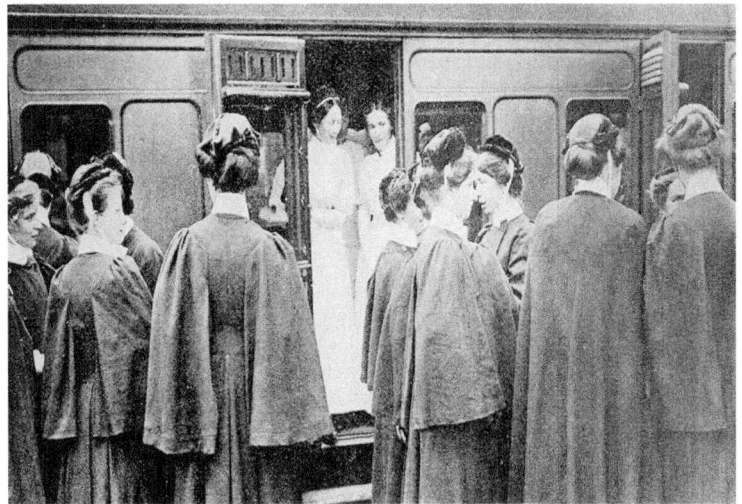

"English nurses training in London," by *Bain News Service* (from 1914 to 1915). Courtesy the Library of Congress.

November 19:
Cold & Wet

Early on Monday, November 16, I left Boulogne in Lady Bagot's car and came to Dunkirk, where I was laid up with a cold for 2 or 3 days. It was very uncomfortable, as no one ever answered my bell, etc. However, I had a bed, which is always such a comfort, and the room was heated so I got my things dry. Very often I find the only way to do this or to get clothing to dry is to take things to bed with you—it is rather chilly, but better than putting on wet things in the morning.

The usual number of unexpected people keep coming and going. In Boulogne, I met Lady Eileen Elliot, Ian Malcolm [politician and British Red Cross officer], Lord Francis Scott, and various others—all very English, clean and well fed. It was quite different from Furnes, to which I returned on Wednesday. Most of us sleep on mattresses on the floor in Furnes. But even these were all occupied, so I hopped around getting in where I could. The cold weather "set in in earnest" as newspapers say. When it does that in Furnes it seems to be particularly in earnest.

Censorship & Changes

Nov. 18, 1914
To Lady Clémentine Waring
Hotel des Arcades, Dunkirk

Dearest Clemmie,

Forgive the delay in writing again. I was too sick about it all at first. Then I was called to go to Boulogne to see my nephew, who is badly wounded.

I can't explain the present situation to you because it would only be censored, but I hope to write about it later.

I shall manage the soup kitchens soon, I hope, but next week will decide that and many things. The objection to the pattern is that those vans would overturn going around corners when hitched behind ambulances.

Some wealthy people are giving a regular motor kitchen to run about to various "dressing" stations—this will be very useful, but it doesn't do away with the need to eat something during those interminable waits at train stations.

Tomorrow I begin my own little soup kitchen at Furnes. I have a room but no van, which is very unsatisfactory since any day the room (so near the station) may be commandeered. A van would make me quite independent, but I must feel my way around.

The situation changes very often, as you will of course see. When you are quite close to the Front, you must always be changing with it.

I want helpers, and I want vans. However, rules are becoming stricter than ever. Even Adeline, Duchess of Bedford, whose good work everyone knows, has waited a week for a permit at Boulogne and has now gone home.

When all the useful women have been expelled there will follow the usual tale of soldiers' suffering and privations: when women are around, they don't let them suffer.

The only plan (if you know of any man who wants to come out) is to know how to drive a car and then to offer it as well as his services to the Red Cross Society.

I have set my heart on station soup kitchens because I see the men put into horse-boxes on straw straight off the field, and there they lie without water or light or food while the train jolts on for hours. I wish I had you here to back me up! We could do anything together.

As ever, yours gratefully,
Sally

P.S. The motor kitchens cost £600 fitted, but the maker is giving the one I speak of for £300. Everyone has given so much to the war I don't feel sure I could collect this amount. I might try America, but it takes a long time.

Chapter 5
Furnes Railway Station

"Volunteers in a Belgian soup kitchen," by the *National Photo Co.* (circa 1914). Courtesy the Library of Congress.

Nov. 21, 1914:
Feeding the Wounded

I am up to my eyes in soup! I have started my soup kitchen at the station, and it gives me a lot to do. Bad luck, though, as my cold and cough are pretty bad!

It is odd to wake in the morning in a frozen room with every pane of glass green and thick with frost. I do not dare think of Mary and morning tea! When I can summon enough moral courage to put a foot out of bed, I jump into my clothes at once. Half dressed, I go to a little tap of cold water to wash. We brush our own boots here, put on all the clothes we possess, and then descend to a breakfast of Quaker oat porridge with bread and margarine. I wouldn't have it different, really, until our men are out of the trenches. But I am hoping most fervently that I won't break down, as I am so "full with soup."

Our kitchen at the railway station is a little bit of a passage, measuring 8 feet by 8 feet. In it are two small stoves. One is a little round iron thing that burns, while the other is a sort of little "kitchener" which doesn't! With this equipment, and various huge "marmites" [pottery containers] we make coffee and soup for hundreds of men every day. The first convoy gets into the station about 9.30 a.m., with all the men frozen, the black troops nearly dead with cold. As soon as the train arrives I carry out one of my boiling "marmites" to the middle of the stone entrance and ladle out the soup, while a Belgian Sister takes around coffee and bread.

These Belgians (three of them) deserve much of the credit for the soup kitchen, if any credit is going around. They started with coffee before I came and did wonders with nothing. Now that I have bought my pots, pans, and stoves we are able to do soup and much more. The Sisters do the coffee on one side, while I work with my vegetables and stove on the other side. We can't ask people to help because there is no room in the kitchen. Besides, there are so many people who like raising a man's head and giving him soup, but who don't like cutting up vegetables.

After the first convoy of wounded has been served, other wounded men come in from time to time. Then about 4 o'clock there is another trainload. At 10 p.m. the largest convoy arrives. The men seem too stiff to move and many are carried in on soldiers' backs. The stretchers are laid on the floor. Those who can *"s'asseoir"* sit on benches. Every man produces a "quart" or tin cup. One and all they come out of the darkness and never look around them, but rouse themselves to get fed, and stretch out poor grimy hands for bread and steaming drinks. There is very little light—only one oil lamp, which hangs from the roof, and burns dimly. Under this, we place the "marmites." All that I can see is one brown or black or wounded hand stretched out into the dim ring of light under the lamp, with a little tin mug held out for soup.

"King Albert I of Belgium, inspecting the trenches," by *Bain News Service* (circa 1915). Courtesy the Library of Congress.

Wet, ragged, and covered with sticky mud, the wounded lie in the hallway of the station. Except under the lamp, it is all quite dark. There are dim forms and frosty breaths, and a door that bangs continually. Then the trainloads up, the wounded depart, and a heavy smell and an empty pot are all that remain. We clean up the kitchen and go home about 1 a.m. I do the night work alone.

November 24:

We are beginning to get into our stride. The small kitchen turns out it gallons and buckets of liquid. Mrs. ___ has been helping me with my work. It is good to see anyone so beautiful in the tiny kitchen and quaint to see anyone so absolutely ignorant of how a pot is washed or a vegetable peeled.

I have a little electric lamp, which is a great comfort to me since I have to walk home alone at midnight. When I get up in the morning, I have to remember anything I will need during the day, as the villa is a mile from the station. So I take my light out at 9.30 a.m.! I saw a Belgian regiment march back to the trenches today. They had a poor little band and some foggy instruments. A bugler flourished a trumpet. I stood by the roadside and cried until I couldn't see.

A Letter Home
Nov. 27, 1914
To Miss Mary King,
Furnes, Belgium

Dear Mary,

You will like to know that I have a soup kitchen at the station here, and I am up to my neck in soup. I make it all day and a good bit of the night too, for the wounded are coming in all the time, and they are half frozen, especially the black troops. People are being so kind about the work I am doing, and they are all saying what a comfort the soup is to the men. Sometimes I feed several hundreds in a day.

I am sure everyone will grieve to hear of the death of Field-Marshal Lord Frederick Roberts, but I think he died just as he would wish to have died—among his old troops [in France], who loved him, and in the service of the King. He was a fine soldier and a Christian gentleman, and you can't say better of a man than that.

I feel as if I had been out here for years, and it seems quite odd to think that I used to wear evening dress and have a fire in my room. I am promising myself, if all goes well, to get home around Christmas time. I wish I could think that the war would be over by then, but it doesn't look like it.

Remember me to Gwennie, and to all your people. Take care of your old self.

Yours truly,
S. Macnaughtan

"Panoramic view of almost totally destroyed town," by the U.S. Air Service (1918). Courtesy the Library of Congress.

December 1:
The Blind Sentinel

Mrs. Knocker, Miss Chisholm and Lady Dorothie went out to Pervyse, a small rural village near the Yser Front, a few days ago to make soup, etc., for the Belgians in the trenches. They live in the cellar of a house, which has been blown inside out by guns, and take out buckets of soup to men on outpost duty. Not a glimpse of fire is allowed on the outposts. Fortunately the weather has been milder lately, but soaking wet. Our three ladies walk out to the trenches at night, and I come home at 1 a.m. from the station. Meanwhile, the men of our party do some housework. They sit over the fire a good deal and clear away the tea-things; when we come home at night we find they have put hot-water bottles in our beds and turned down some lamps. I feel like Alice in Wonderland or I'm in some other upside-down world. We live in much discomfort, which is a little unnecessary; but no one seems to want to do housekeeping. I make soup all day, and there is not much else to write about. All along the Yser river, the Allies and the Germans confront each other, but things have been quieter lately. The piteous list of casualties is not so long as it has been. A wounded German was brought in today. Both his legs were broken and his feet frostbitten. For 4 days, he had been in water with nothing to eat and with his legs unset. He is doing well.

On Sunday I drove out to Pervyse with a kind friend, Mr. Tapp. At the end of the long avenue leading to the village, Pervyse church stands, like a sentinel with both eyes shot out. Nothing is left but a blind stare. Hardly any of the church remains. The churchyard is as if some devil had stalked through it, tearing up crosses and kicking down graves. Even the dead are not left undisturbed in this awful war. The village (like many other villages) is just a mass of gaping ruins—roofs blown off, streets full of holes, not a window left unshattered, and the guns still booming.

Shelling of a Church
Dec. 5, 1914
To Mrs. Charles Percival
Furnes, Belgium

Darling Tab,

I have a chance of sending this to England to be posted, so I must send you a line to wish you many happy returns of the day. I wish we could have our yearly kiss. I will think of you a lot, my dear, on the 8th, and drink to your health if I can raise the wherewithal. We are not famous for our comforts. It would amaze you to see how very nasty food can be, and how very little you can get of it.

I have an interesting job now, and it is my own, which is rather a mercy, as I never know which is most common, dirt or muddle. I can have things as clean as I like, and my soup is getting quite a name for itself. The first convoy of wounded generally come into the station about 11 a.m. It may number anything. Then the men are put into the train. There begins a weary wait for the poor fellows until more wounded arrive and the train is loaded up. Sometimes they are kept there all day. The stretcher cases are in a long corridor, and the sitting-up cases in ordinary 3rd-class carriages. The sitters are worn, limping men, with bandaged heads, and hands bound up, who are yet capable of sitting up in a train.

The transport is well done, I think (far better than in South Africa), but more women are needed to look after details. To give you one example, all stretchers are made of different sizes, so that if a man arrives on an ambulance, the stretchers belonging to it cannot go into the train. The poor wounded man has to be lifted and "transferred," which causes him (in the case of broken legs or internal injuries, especially) untold suffering. It also takes up much room and gives endless trouble for the sake of an inch and a half of space, which is the usual difference in the size of the stretchers. But that prevents them slipping into the sockets on the train.

Another thing I have noticed is, that no man, even lying down in the train, ever gets his boots taken off. The men's feet are always soaked through, as they have been standing up to their knees in water in the trenches. Of course, slippers are unheard of. I do wonder if ladies could be persuaded to make any sort of list [cloth] or felt or even flannel slippers? I saw quite a good pattern the other day, and will try to send you one in case Eastbourne should rise to the occasion. Of course, there must be hundreds of pairs, and heaps would get lost. I do believe other centers would join, and the cost of material for slippers would be quite trifling. A priest goes in each corridor train, and there is always a stove where the boots could be dried. I believe slippers can be bought for about a shilling a pair. The men's feet are enormous. Cases should be marked with a red cross, and sent per S.S. Invicta, Admiralty Pier, Dover.

The fighting has had a sort of lull here for some time, but there are always horrible things happening. The other day at Lampernesse, 500 soldiers were sleeping on straw in a church. A spy informed the Germans, who were 12 miles off, but they got the range to an inch and sent shells straight into the church, killing and wounding nearly everyone in it, while leaving men under the ruins. We had some terrible cases that day. The church was shelled at 6 a.m. By 11 a.m. all the wounded were having soup and coffee at the station. I thought their faces were more full of horror than any I had seen.

The parson belonging to our convoy is a particularly nice young fellow. I have had a bad cold lately, and every night he puts a hot-water bottle in my bed. When he can raise any food, he lays a little supper for me, so that when I come in between 12 and 1 o'clock I can have something to eat, a lump of cheese, plum jam, and perhaps a piece of bully beef, always three pieces of ginger from a paper bag he has of them. Last night when I got back I found I couldn't open the door leading into a sort of garage through which we have to enter this house. I pushed as hard as I could, and then found I was pushing against horses. A whole squad of troop horses had been shoved in there for the night, so I had to make my entry under their noses and behind their heels. Pinned to the table inside the house was a note from the parson, "I can't get you any food, but I have put a bottle of port-wine in your room. Stick to it."

I had meant to go early to church today, but I was really too tired, so I am writing to you instead. Now I must be getting up since "business must be attended to."

Well, goodbye, my dear. I am always too busy to write now, so would you mind sending this letter onto the family?

Your loving sister,
S. Macnaughtan

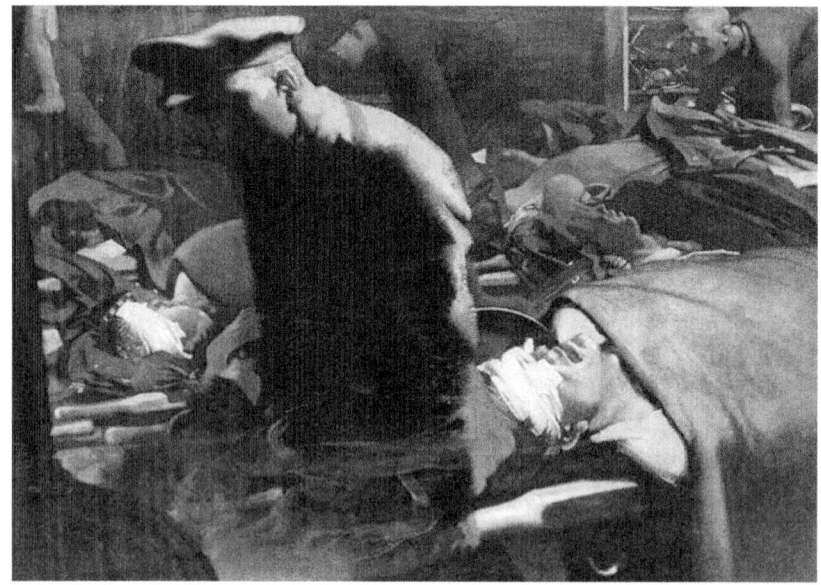

"Inside a World War I field hospital with gassed and wounded soldiers on stretchers," by Eric Kennington, who enlisted with the London Regiment and became a war artist with the Ministry of Information (1918). Courtesy Wikimedia Commons.

December 1914:

Unexpected people continue to arrive at Furnes. Madame Marie Curie and her daughter are in charge of the x-ray apparatus at the hospital. Sir Bartle Compton Frere is there as a guest. Gertrude Vaughan, assistant editor of the *Nursing Times*, came in out of the dark one evening. Today King Albert I of Belgium has been here. God bless him! He always does the right thing.

December 6:
Stretchers & Shrapnel

My horizon is bounded by soup and the men who drink it. There is a commotion outside the kitchen, and someone says, *"Convoi."* So then we begin to fill pots and take steaming "marmites" off the fire. The "sitting cases" come in first, hobbling, or carried on their comrades' backs—heads and feet bandaged or poor hands maimed. When they have been carried or stiffly and slowly marched through the entrance to the train, the *"brancard"* [stretcher] cases are brought in and laid on the floor. They are hastily examined. A doctor goes around reading the labels attached to them that describe their wounds. An English ambulance and a French one wait to take serious cases to their respective hospitals. The others are lifted onto train stretchers and carried to the train.

Two doctors came out from England on inspection duty today. They asked if I had anything to report. I made them come to the station to go into this matter of the different-sized stretchers. It causes agony to the men to be shifted. Dr. Wilson has promised to take up the question. The transport service is now much improved. The trains are heated and lighted, and priests travel with the lying-down cases.

December 8:
A Close Call

I have a little *"charette"* [small wagon] for my soup. It is painted red and provides a lot of amusement to the wounded. The trains are very long, and my small carriage is useful for cups and basins, bread, soup, coffee, etc. Clemmie Waring designed and sent it to me.

Today I was giving out my soup on the train and three shells came in in quick succession. One went just over my head and lodged in a hay stall on the other side of the platform. The wall of the store has an enormous hole in it, but the thickly packed hay prevented the shrapnel scattering. The stationmaster was hit, and his watch saved him, but it was crumpled up like a rag. Two men were wounded; one of them died. A whole crowd of refugees came in from Coxyde along the North Sea coast, which is being heavily shelled. There was not a scrap of food for them. So I made soup in great quantities and distributed it among them in a crowded room whose atmosphere was thick. Ladling out the soup is great fun.

December 12:
The Nameless Soldier

The days are very short now, and darkness falls early. All the streets are dark, so are the houses, so is the station. Two candles are a rare treat, and oil is difficult to get.

Such a nice boy died tonight. We brought him to the hospital from the station, and learned that he had lain for 8 days wounded and untended. Strangely enough he was naked and had only a blanket over him on the stretcher. I do not know why he was still alive. Everything was done for him that could be done, but as I passed through one of the wards this evening the nurses were doing their last kindly duty to him. Poor fellow! He was one of those who had "given even their names." No one knew who he was. He had a woman's portrait tattooed on his breast.

December 19:
The War Within

Not much to record this week. The days have become more stereotyped, and their variety consists in the number of wounded who come in. One day we had 280 extra men to feed—a batch of soldiers returning hungry to the trenches, and some refugees. So far we have never refused anyone a cup of soup, or coffee and bread.

I haven't been well lately and get terribly bad headaches. I go to the station at 10 a.m. every morning and work until 1 p.m. Then to the hospital for lunch. I like the staff there very much. The surgeons are not only skillful, but are men of education. We all get on well together, in spite of that curious form of temper which war always seems to bring.

No one is friendly here, except those who have just come from home, and it is quite common to hear a request made and refused, or granted with, "Please do not ask again." Newcomers are looked upon as aliens, and there is a queer sort of jealousy about all the work.

Oddly enough, few people seem to show at their best at a time when the best should be apparent. No doubt, it is a form of nerves, which is quite pardonable. Nurses and surgeons do not suffer from it. They are accustomed to work and seeing suffering, but amateur workers are a bit reckless at times. I think the expectation of excitement (which is often frustrated) has a good deal to do with it.

Those who "come out for thrills" often have a long waiting time, and energies unexpended in one direction often show themselves unexpectedly and a little unpleasantly in another.

In my own department, I always let zeal spend itself unchecked. I find that people who ferociously claim work or a job are the first to complain of over-work if left to themselves. Afterwards, if there is any good in them, they settle down into their stride. They are only like young horses, pulling too hard at first and sweating off their strength—jibbing one moment and shying the next—when it comes to *"'ammer, 'ammer, 'ammer, on the 'ard 'igh road,"* you find who is going to stick it and who is not.

There has been some heavy firing round about Nieuport and south of the Yser lately. An unusual number of wounded have been coming in, many of them *"gravement blessés"* [seriously injured].

One evening, a young French officer came into the kitchen for soup. It was on Wednesday, December 16, the day the Allies assumed the offensive. All night cases were being brought in. He was quite a boy and utterly shaken by what he had been through. He could only repeat: "It was horrible, horrible!" These are the men who tell brave tales when they get home. But we see them dirty and worn when they have left the trenches only an hour before and have the horror of battle in their eyes.

There are scores of *"pieds gelés"* [frozen feet] at present. I now have bags of socks for these. So many men come in with bare feet. In time, I hope to get carpet slippers and socks for them all.

One night no one came to help. I had a great deal of trouble getting down a long train, so Mrs. Logette has promised to come every evening. The kitchen is much nicer now, as we are in a larger passage and we have three stoves, lamps, etc. Many things are being "straightened out" besides my poor little corner. The war seems better understood. There is hardly a thing that isn't thought of and done for the sick and wounded, and I must say having a grievance was impossible.

I still stay at the Villa Joos and am beginning to enjoy a study of middle-class provincial life. The ladies do all the housework. We have breakfast (a bite) in the kitchen at 8.30 a.m. Then I go to make soup. When I come back after lunch for a rest, "the family" are dressed and sitting around a stove, and this they continue to do until a meal has to be prepared. There is one lamp, one table, and one stove. Unless Papa plays the pianola there is nothing to do but talk. No one reads, and only one woman does a little embroidery, while the small girl of the party cuts out scraps from a fashion newspaper.

The poor convoy! It is becoming very squabbly and tiresome. There is a good deal of "talking over," which is one of the weakest sides of "communal life." It is petty and ridiculous to quarrel when death is so near, and things are so big and often so tragic. Yet human nature has strict limitations.

Ramsay MacDonald [British statesman] came out from the committee to see what all the complaints were about. So there were strange interviews, in storerooms, etc. (No one has a place to call their own!) Everyone "explained" and "gave evidence" and tried to "put matters straight."

It rains every day. This may be "providence," as the floods are keeping the Germans away. The sound of constant rain on the windowpanes is a little melancholy. Let us pray that in singleness and cheerfulness of heart we may do our little bit of work.

December 23:
A Dangerous Expedition

Yesterday I drove into Dunkirk and did a lot of shopping. By accident our car went back to Furnes without me, and there was not a bed to be had in Dunkirk! After many vicissitudes I met Captain Whiting, who gave up his room in his own house to me and slept at the club. I was in clover for once, and nearly wept when I found my boots brushed and hot water at my door. It was so like home again.

I was leaving the station today when shelling began again. One shell dropped not far behind the bridge, which I had just crossed, and wrecked a house. Another fell into a boat on the canal and wounded the occupants badly. I went to tell the Belgian Sisters not to go down to the station, and I lunched at their house. Then I went home until the evening work began. People are always telling you that danger is now over—a hidden gun has been discovered and captured, and there will be no more shelling. *Quel blague* [what a joke]! The shelling goes on just the same whether hidden guns are captured or not.

I can't say at present when I shall get home, because no one ever knows what is going to happen. I don't quite know who would take my place at the soup kitchen if I were to leave.

December 25:
Battle

My Christmas Day began at midnight when I walked home through the moonlit empty streets of Furnes. At 2 a.m. the guns began to roar and roared all night. They say the Allies are making an attack.

"Prince Alexander of Teck," by *Bain News Service*. Courtesy the Library of Congress.

I got up early and went to church in the untidy schoolroom at the hospital, which is called the nurses' sitting room. Mr. Streatfield had arranged a little altar, which was quite nice. He had set some chairs in an orderly row. From the altar linen to the white artificial flowers in the vases—all was as decent as could be and there were candles and a cross. We were quite a small congregation, but another service had been held earlier. The wounded heard Mass in their ward at 6 a.m. The priests put up an altar there, and I believe the singing was excellent. Inside we prayed for peace, and outside the guns went on firing. Prince Alexander of Teck [a British military commander] came to our service—a big soldierly figure in the bare room.

After breakfast, I went to the soup kitchen at the station, as usual, then home—i.e., to the hospital to lunch. At 3:15 p.m. came a sort of evensong [evening prayers] with hymns. Then we went to the civil hospital where there was a Christmas tree for all the Belgian refugee children. I never saw anything more touching and to be with them made you blind with tears. One tiny mite, with her head in bandages, and wearing a little black shawl, was introduced to me as *"une blessée, Madame"* [the wounded]. Another little boy in the hospital is always spoken of gravely as "the civilian."

Every man, woman, and child got a treat, present, or a good dinner. The wounded had turkey, and all they could eat. The children got toys and sweets off the tree. I suppose these children are not accustomed to presents for their delight was almost too much for them. I have never seen such excitement! Poor mites, without homes or money and with their relatives often lost—yet little boys were gibbering over their toys, and little girls clung to big parcels, and squeaked dolls or blew trumpets. The bigger children had rather good voices and all sang our national anthem in English. "God save our nobbler King"—the accent was quaint, but the children sang lustily.

We had finished and were waiting for our own Christmas dinner when shells began to fly. One came whizzing past Mr. Streatfield's storeroom as I stood there with him. The next minute a little child, in floods of tears, came in grasping her mother's bag, to say *"Maman"* just had her arm blown off. The child herself was covered with dust and dirt. In the streets people were sheltering in doorways and taking little runs for safety as soon as a shell had finished bursting. The bombardment lasted about an hour. We all waited in the kitchen and listened to it. At such times, when everyone is rather strung up, someone always and continually lets things fall. A nun clattered down a pail, and Maurice the cook seemed to fling saucepan lids on the floor.

About 8:15 p.m. the bombardment ceased, and we went in to a cheery dinner—soup, turkey, and plum pudding, with crackers and speeches. I believe no one would have guessed we had been a bit "on the stretch."

At 9:30, I went to the station. It was very melancholy. No one was there but myself. The fires were out, or smoking badly. Everyone had been scared to death by the shells and talked of nothing else, usually shells would be forgotten immediately.

"Belgian orphans leaving Paris for country homes," by *Bain News Service* (circa 1914). Courtesy the Library of Congress.

I got things in order as soon as I could. The wounded in the train got their hot soup and coffee as usual, which was satisfying. Then I came home alone at midnight—keeping as near the houses as I could because of possible shells—and so to bed, very cold, and rather too inclined to think about home.

December 26:
Belgian Hospitality

I went to the station. Oddly enough, very few wounded were there, so I came away and had my first day at home. I got a little oil stove put in my room, wrote letters, tidied up, and thoroughly enjoyed myself.

A Taube came over and hovered above Furnes, dropping bombs. I was at the Villa. The Joos family and I stood and watched it—a nasty dangerous moth is how it looked way up in the sky. Presently it came over our house, so we went down to the kitchen. A few shots were fired, but the Taube was far too high up to be hit. Max, the Joos' cousin, went out and *"tirait"* [fired shots], to the admiration of the women. Of course, *"Papa"* had to have a try. The two men, with their little gun, their talk and gesticulations, lent a queer touch of comedy to the scene. The garden was so small, the men in their little hats were so suggestive of the "broken English" scene on the stage, that you could only stand and laugh.

The Joos family is quite a study and so kind. On Christmas Eve, I dined with them, and they gave me the best of all they had. There was a pheasant, which someone had given the doctor (I fancy he is a very small practitioner among the poor people); surely, never did a bird give more pleasure. I had known of its arrival days before by seeing Fernande, the little girl, decorated with feathers from its tail. Then the good Papa must be decorated also. These small jokes delighted the whole family to the point of ecstasy.

On Christmas Eve, Monsieur Max conceived the splendid joke, carefully arranged, of presenting Madame Joos—who is young and pretty—and the doctor with two parcels, which on being opened contained the child's umbrella and a toy gun. There wasn't even a comic address on the parcels; but Yrma, the servant, carefully trained for the part, brought them in having fits of delight. All the family laughed with joy until the tears ran down their cheeks. As they wiped their eyes, they admitted they were sick with laughter. After supper we had the Pianola, played by Papa. I must say that when you can get nothing else, this instrument gives a great deal of pleasure. You get a sort of ache for music, which is just as bad as being hungry.

December 27:
The Risk of Spies

Bad, bad weather again. It has rained almost continuously for 5 weeks. Yesterday it snowed. Always the wind blows, and something lashes itself against the panes. You can't leave the windows open, as the rooms get flooded. It is amazingly cold o' nights, I can't sleep for the cold.

"Wreckage of a German Albatross D. III fighter biplane," by unknown (circa 1916). Courtesy the Library of Congress.

We have some funny incidents at the station sometimes. A particularly amusing one occurred the other day, when three ladies in knickerbockers and khaki and badges appeared at our soup kitchen door and announced they were "on duty" there until 6 o'clock. I was not there, but the scene that followed has been described to me, and has often made me laugh.

It seems the ladies never got further than the door! Some people might have been firm in the, "Too sorry! Come-some-other-day-when-we-are-not-so-busy" sort of way. Not so for Miss ___. In more primitive times, she would probably have gone for the visitors with a broom, but her tongue is just as rough as the hardest besom [broom], and from their dress ("skipping over soldiers' faces with breeches on, indeed!") to their corps there was very little left of them.

It wasn't really from the dog-in-the-manger spirit that the little woman acted. The fact is that Belgians and French run the station together. They all agree on one thing, no one but an authorized and registered person is to come within its doors. Heaven knows the trouble there has been with spies, and this rule is absolutely necessary. Two Red Cross khaki-clad men have been driving everywhere in Furnes and were discovered to be Germans. Had we permitted itinerant workers, the authorities notified us that the kitchen would have to close. In the evening, when I went to the station, another knickerbockered lady sat there! I told her about our difficulties, but allowed her to do a little work rather than hurt her feelings. The following day Miss ___ engaged in deadly conflict with the lady who had sent our unwelcome visitors. Over the scene, we will draw a veil, but we never saw the knickerbockered ladies again!

Dec. 31, 1914:
Under Fire

The last day of this bad old year. I feel quite thankful for the summer I had at the Grange. It has been something to look back upon all the time I have been here—the pergolas of pink roses, the sleepy fields, the dear people who used to come and stay with me, and all the fun and pleasure of it, help a great deal now.

Yesterday was a fine day in the middle of weeks of rain. When I came down to breakfast in the Joos' little kitchen. I remarked, of course, on the beauty of the weather. "What a day for Taubes!" said Monsieur Max, looking up at the clear blue sky. Before I had left home there was a shell in a street close by. Already you hear these horrible birds of prey had been at work and had thrown two bombs, which destroyed two houses in the Rue des Trèfles. The pigeons that circle round the old buildings in Furnes always seem to see the Taubes first, as if they knew by sight their hateful brothers. They flutter disturbed from roof and turret, and then, with a flash of white wings, they fly far away. I often wish I had wings when I see them.

I went to the station and then to the hospital for slippers for some wounded men. Five airplanes were overhead—Allies' and German. There was a good deal of firing. I was struck by the fact that the night before I'd seen exactly this scene in a dream. Second sight always gives me much to think about.

"Clearing up after the Battle of Haelen in Belgium," by *Bain News Service* (1914). Courtesy the Library of Congress.

The inevitableness of things seems much accentuated by it. In my dream, I stood by the other people in the yard looking at the war in the air and watching the circling airplanes amid bursts of smoke.

At the station there was a nasty feeling that something was going to happen. The Taubes wheeled around and hovered in the blue. I went to the hospital for lunch. Afterwards I asked Ivor Bevan to come to the station to look at some wounded men, whose dressings had not been touched for too long. He said he would come in half an hour, so I said I wouldn't wait since he knew exactly where to find the men. Instead, I returned to the villa for my rest.

As I walked home, I heard that the station had been shelled. I met one of the Belgian Sisters and told her not to go on duty until after dark, but I had no idea until evening came of what had happened. Ten shells burst in or around the station. Men, women, and children were killed. They tell me that limbs were flying, and a French chauffeur, who came here, picked up a man's leg in the street. Mr. Bevan sent word that none of us was to go to the station for the present.

At Dunkirk, seven Taubes flew overhead and dropped bombs, killing 28 people. At Pervyse, shells are coming in every day. I can't help wondering when we will move out of this. If the bridges are destroyed it will be difficult to get away. The weather has turned very wet again this evening. We have only had two or three fine days in as many months. The wind howls day and night, and the place is so well known for it that *"vent de Furnes"* is a byword. No doubt the floods protect us, so you mustn't grumble about a sore throat.

Jan. 1, 1915:

The station was shelled again today. Three houses were destroyed. One person was killed and a good many more were wounded. A rumor got around that the Germans had promised 500 shells in Furnes on New Year's Day.

In the evening, I went down to the station. Evidently, I was evidently not expected. Not a thing was ready for the wounded. The man in charge had let all three fires out, and he and about 7 soldiers (mostly drunk) were making merry in the kitchen. None of them would budge. I was glad I had young Mr. Findlay, who was in uniform, with me, as he helped to get things straight. But these French seem to have very little discipline. Even when the military doctors came in, the men did nothing but argue with them. It was amazing to hear them. One night a soldier, who is always drunk, was lying on a brancard in the doctor's own room, and no one seemed to mind.

January 3:

I have had my usual rest and hot bath. I find I never want a holiday if I may have my Sundays. I spent a lazy afternoon in Miss Scott's room (she was ill), then went to Mr. Streatfield's service, dinner, and the station. A new officer was on duty there and was introduced to the kitchen. He said, "*Les Anglais,* of course. No one else ever does anything for anybody."

"Burying horses killed on the battlefield following the Battle of Haelen," by *Bain News Service* (1914). Courtesy the Library of Congress.

I believe this is very nearly the case. God knows, we are full of faults, but the superiority of the British race to any other that I know is a matter of deep conviction with me, and it is founded, I think, on wide experience.

January 6:
The Shelling Gets Worse

Two days ago, I went to Adinkerke in Western Belgium near the French border to establish a soup kitchen there since the Furnes station is too dangerous. We have been given a nice little waiting room and a stove. We heard today that the stationmaster at Furnes has been signaling to the enemy, so that is why we have been shelled so punctually. His daughter is engaged to a German. Two of our hospital people noticed that before each bombardment a blue light appeared to flash on the sky. They reported the matter, as a result the signals were discovered.

There has been a lot of shelling again today. Several houses are destroyed. A child of two years is in our hospital with one leg blown off and the other broken. One only hears people spoken of as, "the man with the abdominal trouble," or "the one shot through the lungs." Children know the different airplanes by sight, and one little girl, when I ask her for news, gives me a list of the *"obus"* [shells] that have arrived, and which have *"s'éclaté"* [blast] and which have not. One can see that she despises those which *"ne s'éclatent pas"* [don't burst]. You say *"Bon soir, pas des obus,"* as in English one says, "Goodnight, sleep well."

January 10:

Prince Alexander of Teck dined at the hospital last night, and we had a great spread. Madame Sindici did wonders. There were loaned plates and finger bowls, and food galore! We felt very grand. An old General (the head of the Army Medical Corps) gave me the most grateful thanks for serving the soldiers. It was gracefully and delightfully done. I am going home for a week's holiday.

January 14:

I went home via Calais. Mr. Bevan and Mr. Morgan took me there. It was a fine day, and I felt happy for once, that is, for once out here.

Some people enjoy this war. I think it is far the worst time, except one, I ever spent. Perhaps I have seen more suffering than most people. A doctor sees a hospital, and a nurse sees a ward of sick and wounded, but I see them by the hundred passing before me in an endless train all day. I can make none of them really better. I feed them, and they pass on.

You review your life a little as each one departs. Always I shall remember Furnes as a place of wet streets and long dark evenings, with gales blowing, and as a place where I have been always alone. I have not once all this time exchanged a thought with anyone. I have lived in a very damp attic and talked French to some kind middle-class people, and I have walked a mile for every meal I have had. So I shall always think of Furnes as a wet, dark place, and of myself with a lantern trudging about its mean streets.

Chapter 6
Difficult Conditions

"British poster to alert public during World War I," by unknown military artist (1915). Courtesy Wikimedia Commons.

January 1915:

I have not written in my diary for many weeks. I went home to England and stayed at Rayleigh House. On my way home, I met Mr. F. Ware, who told me submarines were around. As I had but just left a much-shelled town, I think he might have held his peace. I had the usual warm welcome at Rayleigh House, with Mary there to meet Emily Strutt and me.

I wasn't very tired when I first arrived, but fatigue came out on me like a rash afterwards. I got more tired every day and ended by having a sort of breakdown. This rather spoilt my holiday, but it was very nice seeing people again. It was difficult, I found, to accommodate myself to small things, and you are amazed to find people still driving serenely in closed broughams [horse-drawn carriages]. It was like going back to live on earth again after being in rather a horrible other world. I went to my own house and enjoyed the very smell of the place. My little library and an hour or two spent there made my happiest time. Different people asked me to things, but I wasn't up to going out. The weather was amazingly bad.

I was to have gone back to work on the Thursday week after I arrived home, but I got a telegram from Madame Magda Sindici [who organized civilian volunteers] saying Furnes was being shelled, and the hospital, etc., was to be evacuated. Dr. Perrin, who was to have taken me back, had to start immediately without me. It was difficult to get news. Hearing nothing I went over on Saturday, January 23, as I had left Mrs. Clitheroe in charge of my soup kitchen. I thought I had better do the burning deck act and get back to it.

Mr. Bevan and Mr. Morgan met me at Calais, and told me to wait at Dunkirk, as everyone was leaving Furnes. One of our poor nurses was killed, and the Joos' little house was much damaged. I stopped at Mrs. Clitheroe's place, very glad to be ill in peace after my seedy condition in London and a bad crossing. Rested quietly all Sunday there by myself. It is an empty, bare little place, with neither carpets nor curtains, but there is something home-like about it, the result, I think, of having an open fire in one room.

On Monday, the 25th, I went back to work at Adinkerke station, where our soup kitchen has been moved. I got a warm welcome from the Belgian Sisters. It is very difficult doing the station work from Dunkirk, as it is 10 miles from Adinkerke; but the place itself is nice, and I just have to trust to lifts. I fill my pockets with cigarettes and go to the *"sortie de la ville,"* and just wait for something to pass—and some odd, bumpy rides I get. Still, the soldiers who drive me are delightful, and the cigarettes are always taken as good pay.

One day I went and spent the night at Hoogstadt, where the hospital now is, and that I much enjoyed. Dr. Perrin gave up his little room to me. The nurses and staff were all so full of welcome and pleasant speeches.

"Women in England training with a dog as part of the Women's Sick and Wounded Convoy Corps during World War I," by *Bain News Service* (circa 1915). Courtesy the Library of Congress.

On Monday, February 8, I went out to La Panne to start living in the hotel there; but I was really dreadfully ill and suffered so much that I had to return to the flat at Dunkirk again to be nursed. My day at La Panne was therefore very sad, as I nearly perished with cold and felt so ill. Not a soul came near me. I wished I could be a Belgian refugee and might have had a little attention from somebody.

On Tuesday, February 9, a Belgian officer came into Adinkerke station, claimed our kitchen as a bureau, and kicked us out onto the platform. I am trying to get General Millis to interfere, but, indeed, the rudeness of this man's act makes you furious.

February 14:
Illness at Dunkirk

I have been laid up for some days in the room at Dunkirk. It is amazing to realize that this place should be your present idea of comfort. It has no carpets, no curtains, not a blind that will pull up or down, and rather dirty floors, yet it is so much more comfortable than anything I have had yet that I am too thankful to be here. There is a gas ring in the kitchen, on which it is possible to cook our food, and there are shops where things can be purchased.

Mr. Strickland and I are both laid up here, and Miss Logan nurses us devotedly. Our joy is having a sitting room with a fire in it. Was there ever anything half so good as that fire, or half so homely, half so warm or so much your own? I lie on three chairs in front of it, and headache and cold and throat are almost forgotten. The wind howls, the sea roars, and airplanes fly overhead, but at least we have our fire and are at home.

February 17:

Another cold, wet day. I am alone in the flat with a *"femme de ménage"* [housekeeper] to look after me. A doctor comes to see me sometimes. Miss Logan and Mr. Strickland left this morning. There was a tempest of rain, and I couldn't think of being moved. They were sweet and kind, and felt bad about leaving me; but I am just loving being left alone with some books and my fire. I have been lying in bed correcting proofs. Oh, the joy of being at your own work again! Just to see print is a pleasure. I believe I have forgotten all I ever knew before the war began. A magazine article comes to me like a language I have almost forgotten.

February 18:
Arrogant Newcomers

This is the day that German "piracy" is supposed to begin. We heard a great explosion early this morning, but it was only a mine found on the shore being blown up. The sailors' airplane corps is opposite us. We see Air Commander Charles Rumney Samson and others flying off in the morning and whirling back at night. Then we hear there has been a raid somewhere. When a Taube comes over here, the sailors fire at it with a gun just opposite us—and then tell us they only do it to give us flower vases, i.e., empty shell cases!

Mr. Holland came here today and told me some humorous sides of his experiences with ambulances. One man from the Church Army marched in, and said: "I am a Christian and you are not. I come here for petrol, and I ask it, not for the Red Cross, but in the name of Christ." Another man came dashing in, and said: "I want to go to Poperinghe. I was once there before and the mud was beastly. Send someone with me."

My own latest experience was with an American woman of awful vulgarity. I asked her if she was busy, like everyone else in this place. She said: "No. I was suffering from a nervous breakdown, so I came out here. What is your war is my peace, and I now sleep like a baby."

I want adjectives! How are you to describe the people who come for one brief visit to the station or hospital with an intense conviction that they and they only feel the suffering or even notice the wants of the men. Some are good workers. Others I call, "This-poor-fellow-has-had-none." Nurses may have been up all night, doctors may be worked off their feet, 700 men may have passed through the station, all wounded and all fed, but when our visitors arrive they discover that "This poor fellow has had none," and firmly, and with a high sense of duty and of their own efficiency, they make the thing known.

No one else has heard a man shouting for water; no one else knows that a man wants soup. The man may have appendicitis, or colitis, or pancreatitis, or he may have been shot through the lungs or the abdomen. It doesn't matter. The casual visitor knows he has been neglected, and she says so, and quite indiscriminately she fills everyone up with soup. Only she is tenderhearted. Only she could never really be hardened by being a nurse. She seizes a little cup, stoops over a man gracefully, and raises his head. Then she wants things passed to her. Someone must help her. Someone must listen to what she has to say. She feeds one man in half an hour and goes away horrified at the way things are done. Fortunately these people never stay for long.

"Recruiting poster for the Coldstream Guards," by Ernest Ibbetson (1914). Courtesy the Library of Congress.

Then there is another. She can't understand why our ships should be blown up or why trenches should be taken. In her own mind, she proves herself of good sound intelligence and a member of the Empire who won't be bamboozled, when she says firmly and with heat: "Why don't we do something?" She would like to scold a few Generals and Admirals, and she says she believes the Germans are much cleverer than ourselves. This last taunt she hopes will make people "do something." It stings, she thinks.

I could write a good deal about this "solitary winter," but I have not had time either to write or to read. I think something inside me has stood still or died during this war.

February 21:
Community Disorder

The Munro Corps has swooped down in its usual hurry to distribute letters and say someone is waiting down below so they can't stop. They eat a hasty sardine, drink a cup of coffee, and are off!

Today I have made this flat tidy at last, and have had it cleaned and scrubbed. I have thrown away old papers and empty boxes, and can sit down and sniff contentedly. No convoy-ite sees the difference!

I think I have learned every phase of muddle and makeshift this winter, but chiefly have I learned the value of the Biblical recommendation to put candles on candlesticks. In the "*Convoi Munro*" I find them in bottles, on the lids of mustard tins, in metal cups, or in the necks of bedroom carafes. Never is the wax removed. Where it drips there it remains. Where matches fall, there they lie. Stumps of cigarettes grace even the insides of flowerpots, knives are wiped on bread, and overcoats of enormous weight (khaki in color, with a red cross on the arm) are hung on inefficient loose nails and fall down. Towels are always scarce; but then, they serve as dinner napkins, handkerchiefs, and even as pillowcases, so no wonder we are a little short of them. There is no necessity for muddle. There never is any necessity for it.

The communal life is a mistake.

On Sundays I always want to rest and something always makes me write. The attack comes on quite early. It is irresistible. At last, I am a little happy after these dreary months. It is only because I can think a little and because the days are not quite so dark. I think the nights have been longer here than I have ever knew them. No doubt it is the bad weather and the small amount of light indoors that makes the days seem so short.

I am going back tomorrow to the station, with its trainloads of wounded men. I want to go and give them soup, comforts, and cigarettes. Just 10 days' of illness and idleness have "balmed my soul."

February 22:

Waited all day for a car to come and fetch me away. It was dull work as I could never leave the room. All my things were packed up, and there was no coal.

February 23:
Brutality

Waited again all day. I got very tired of standing by the window looking out on a strip of beach at the bottom of the street, and on the people passing to and fro. Then I went down to the dock to try and get a car there, but the new police regulations made it impossible to cross the bridge. I went to the airmen opposite. No luck.

There is a peculiar brutality that seems to possess everyone out here during the war. I find it nearly everywhere, and it involves a good deal of unnecessary suffering. Always I am reminded of birds on a small ledge pushing each other into the sea. The big bird that pushes another one over goes to sleep comfortably.

I remember one evening at Dunkirk when we couldn't get rooms or food because the hotel landlady had lost all her servants. The staff at the ___ gave me a meal, but there was a strange lack of courtesy about it. I said that anything would do for my supper, and I went to help get it myself. I spied a roll of cold veal on a shelf, and said helpfully that it would do splendidly. But the answer was: "Yes, but I believe that is for our next meal." However, in the end I got a scrap, consisting mostly of green stuffing.

"But when thou art bidden, go and sit down in the lowest room." Ah, my dear Lord, in this world one may certainly take the lowest place, and keep it. It is only the great men who say, "Friend, come up higher."

"You can't have it," is on everyone's lips, and a general sense of bustle goes with the brutality. "You can't come here," "We won't have her," are quite common phrases. God help us, how nasty we all are!

I find one can score pretty heavily nowadays by being a "psychologist." All the most disagreeable people I know are psychologists, notably ___, who breaks his promises and throws all his friends to the wolves, but who can still explain everything in his sapient way by saying he is a psychologist.

"The Duchess of Sutherland," *The Sketch*, (Nov. 14, 1915).

One thing I hope—that no one will ever call me "highly strung." I wish good old-fashioned, bad temper was still the word for highly-strung and nervy people.

I am longing for beautiful things, music, flowers, fine thoughts....

February 25:
This Is War

At last I have succeeded in getting away from Dunkirk! The Duchess of Sutherland brought me here in her car. Last night I dined with Mrs. Clitheroe. She was less bustled than usual, and I enjoyed a chat with her as we walked home through the cold white mist that enshrouded La Panne, on the coast of the North Sea.

This long war has settled down to a long wait. Little goes on except desultory shelling, with its occasional quite useless victims. At the station we have mostly *"malades"* and *"éclopés"*; in the trenches the soldiers stand in the bitter cold and occasionally are moved out by shells falling by chance among them. The men who are capable of big things wait and do nothing.

If it weren't for the wounded, how would you stand the life here? A man looks up patiently, dumbly, out of brown eyes, and you are able to go on again.

February 27:

I have been staying for three nights at the Kursaal Hotel, but my room was needed and I had to leave. So I packed my things and came down to the Villa les Chrysanthèmes, where I shared Mrs. Clitheroe's room for a night. In the morning all our party packed up and left to go to Furnes, so I took on these rooms. I may be kicked out any minute for *"le militaire,"* but meanwhile I am very comfortable.

The heroic element (a real thing among us) takes odd forms sometimes. "No sheets, of course," is what you hear on every side. To eat a meal standing and with dirty hands is to "play the game." Maxine Elliott said, "The nervous exhaustion attendant upon discomfort hinders work," and she "does herself" very well, as also do all the men of the regular forces. But volunteer corps—especially women—is heroically bent on being uncomfortable. In a way, they like it. They eat strange meals in large quantities and feel that this is war.

Lord Francis Dudley Leigh took me into Dunkirk in his car today, and I managed to get lots of vegetables for the soup kitchen, and several other things I wanted. A lift is everything at this time, when you can "command" nothing. If you might for once feel that by paying a fare, however high, you could ensure having something—a railway journey, a car, or even a bed!

My work isn't so heavy at the kitchen now, and the hours are not so long, so I hope to do some work of a literary nature.

Silent Death
Sunday, Feb. 28, 1915
To Sarah's Sisters
Villa les Chrysanthèmes la Panne, Belgium

My Dear Family,

It is so long since I wrote a decently long letter that I think I must write to you all, to thank you for yours, and give you what news there is of myself.

Of war news there is none. The long war is now a long wait. The huge expense still goes on, while we lock horns with our foes (and just sway backwards and forwards a little. This, as you know, we have done for weeks past. Every day at the station there is a little stream of men with heads or limbs bandaged. Our work goes on as before, although it is not on quite the same lines now. I used to make every drop of the soup myself and give it out all down the train. Now we have a receiving room for the wounded, where they stay all day, and we feed them four times. Then they are sent away. The whole thing is more military than it used to be. The result, I think, of officers not having much to do, and with a passion for writing out rules and regulations with a nice broad pen. Two orderlies help in the kitchen; the soup is "inspected," and what used to be "la cuisine de la dame écossaise" [the cooking of a Scottish lady] is not so much a charitable institution as it was.

You see a good deal of that sort of thing during this war. Women have been seeing what is wanted and have done the work themselves at really enormous difficulty, and in the face of opposition. And when it is a going concern, it is taken over, and, in many cases, the women are kicked out. This was the case at Dunkirk station, which was known everywhere as "the shambles." I myself tried to get the wounded attended to, and I went there with a naval doctor, who told me he couldn't uncover a single wound because of the awful atmosphere (it was quite common to see 15,000 men lying on straw). One woman took this matter in hand, purged the place, got mattresses, clean straw, stoves, etc., and when all was in order the voice of authority turned her out.

This long waiting is being much more difficult for people than actual fighting. In every corps, the old heroic outlook is a little bit fogged by petty things. You see the result of it in some wrangling and jealousy, but this will soon be forgotten when fighting with all its realities begin again.

I think Britain on the subject of "piracy" is about as fine as anything in her history. Her determination to ignore ultimatums and threats is really quite funny. English people still put out in boats as they have always done and are quite undismayed. Our own people here continue to travel by sea, as if submarines were rather a joke. When going over to England on some small and useless little job they say apologetically: "Of course, I wouldn't go if I hadn't got to." The fact is, if there is any danger about they have to be in it.

Some of our own corps have gone back to Furnes—I believe because it is being shelled. The rest of us are at La Panne, a cold seaside place among the dunes. In summer time, I think it is fashionable, but now it contains nothing but soldiers. They are quartered everywhere. You never know how long you will be able to keep a room. The station is at Adinkerke, where I have my kitchen. It is about 2 miles from La Panne and also crammed with soldiers. There seems to be no attempt at sanitation anywhere.

I wish I had more interesting news to tell you, but I am at my station all day. If there is anything to hear (which I doubt), I do not hear it. There is a barge on the canal at Adinkerke that is our only excitement. It is the property of Maxine Elliott [American stage actress], Lady Kathleen Drogheda, and Miss Close, and to go to tea with them is everyone's ambition. The barge is crammed with things for Belgian refugees, and Maxine told me that the cargo represents "nearer £10,000 than £5,000." It is piled with flour in sacks, clothing, medical comforts, etc. The work is good.

I am sending home some long pins like nails. They are called "Silent Death" and dropped from German airplanes. Boys pick them up and give them to us in exchange for cigarettes.

I want to tell Tabby how immensely pleased everyone is with her slippers. The men who have stood long in the trenches are in agonies of frostbite and rheumatism. Now that I can give them these slippers when they arrive at the station, they are able to take off their wet boots caked with mud.

If J. would send me another little packet of groceries I would love it. Just what can come by mail. That Benger's Food of hers nearly saved my life when I was ill at Dunkirk. What I should like better than anything is a few good magazines and books. I get Punch and the Spectator, but I want the English Review and the National, and perhaps a Hibbert. I enclose 10 shillings for these. What is being read? Stephen Coleridge seems to have brought out an interesting collection, but I can't remember its name. I wonder if any notice will be taken of "They who Question." The reviews speak well of the Canadian book.

Love to you all, and tell Alan how much I think of him. Bless you, my dears. Write often.

Yours as ever,
Sarah

March 1:
Thieving and Giving

Woe betides the person who owns anything out here: he is instantly deprived of it. "Pinching" [thieving] is proverbial, and people have taken to carrying as many of their possessions as possible on their person, with the result that they are the strangest shapes and sizes. Still, you hope the goods are valuable until you discover that they generally consist of the following items: a watch that doesn't work, a fountain pen that is never filled, an electric flashlight that won't light, a much-used hanky, an empty iodine bottle, and a scarf.

March 5:

I went as usual today to the muddy station and distributed soup, which I no longer make now that the station has become militarized. My hours are from noon to 5 o'clock. This includes the men's dinner hour and the washing of the kitchen. They eat and smoke when I am there, and loll on the little bench. They are Belgians, and I am English. And you are always being warned that the English can't be too careful! We are entertaining 40,000 Belgians in England, but it must be done "carefully."

It is a great bore out here that everything is stolen. You can hardly lay a thing down for an instant that it isn't taken. Today my Thermos flask in a leather case, in which I carry my lunch, was stolen from the kitchen. Things like metal cups are stolen by the score, and everyone begs! Even well-to-do people are always asking for something. They simply whine for tobacco. The fact is, I think, the English are giving things away with their usual generosity and want of discrimination, and—it is a horrid word—they are already pauperizing a nice lot of people. I can't help thinking that the thing is being run on wrong lines. We should have given or lent what was necessary to the Belgian Government, and let them provide for soldiers and refugees through the proper channels. No lasting good ever came of gifts—every child begs for cigarettes, and they begin smoking at five years old.

I often think of our poor at home, and wish I had a few sacks full of things for them! I have not myself come across any instances of poverty nearly as bad as I have seen in England. I understand from Dr. Joos and other Belgians who know about these things that there is still a good deal of money tucked away in this country. I hope there is, and we all want to help the Belgians over a bad time, but it would be better and more dignified for them to get it through their own Government.

I had tea with Lady Bagot the other day, and afterwards I had a chat with Prince Francis at the English Mission. Another afternoon I went down to the Kursaal Hotel for tea. The stuffy sitting room there is always filled with knickerbockered, leather-coated ladies and with officers in dark blue uniform, who talk loudly and pat the barmaid's cheeks. She seems to expect it; it is almost etiquette. A cup of bad tea, some German trophies examined and discussed, and then I came away with a "British" longing for skirts for my ladies, and for something graceful and (odious word) dainty about them. Yesterday evening Lady Bagot dined with me. This villa is the only comfortable place I have been in since the war began, and it makes an amazing difference to my health.

It is odd to have to admit that I have hardly ever been unhappy for a long time before this war. The year my brother died, the year I went through a tragedy, the year of deadly dullness in the country—but now it isn't so much a personal matter. War and the sound of guns as well as the sense of destruction and death abroad, the solitude of it, and the disappointing people! Oh, and the poor wounded—the poor, smelly, dirty wounded, whom you see all day, and for whom you just stick this out.

I have only twice been for a drive out here, and I have not seen a single place of interest, nor, indeed, a single interesting person connected with the war. That, I suppose, is the result of being a *"cuisinière"* [cook]! It is rather strange to me, because for a very long time I always seem to have had the best of things. Today I hear of this General or that Secretary, or this great person or that important functionary, but the only people whom I see are three little Sisters and two Belgian cooks.

To give up work seems to me a little like divorcing a husband. There is a feeling of failure about it, and the sense that you are giving up what you have undertaken to do. So, however dull or tiresome the husband or work may be, you mustn't give them up.

March 6:
The Power of the Bible

Today I have been thinking, as I have often thought, that the real power of the Bible is that it is a universal human document. The world is based upon sentiment—the personality of man and his feelings brought to bear upon facts. It is also the world's dynamic force. Now, the books of the Bible—especially, perhaps, the magical, beautiful Psalms—are the most tender and sentimental (the word has been misused, of course) ever written. They express the thoughts and feelings of generations of men who always did express their thoughts and feelings, and thought no shame of it. And so we northern people, with our passionate inarticulateness, love to find ourselves expressed in the old pages.

I find in the Gospels one of the few complaints of Christ. "Have I been so long time with you and yet hast thou not known me, Philip?" All you have ever felt is said for you in a phrase, all that you find most isolating in the world is put into one sentence. There is a weak feeling of wonder in it; "so long," and yet you think that of me! "so long," and yet such absolute inability to read my character! "so long," and yet still quite unaware of my message! The humor of it (to us) lies in the little side of it! The dear people who "thought you would like this or dislike that"—the kind givers of presents even, the little people who shop for you! The friends who invite you to their strange, soulless, thin entertainments, with their garish lights; the people who choose a book for you, who advise you, even with annoyance, to go to some play which they are "sure we shall like." "So long"—they are old friends, and yet they thought we should like that play or that book! "So long"—and yet they think you capable of certain acts or feelings that don't remotely seem to belong to you!

"So long"—and yet they can't even touch one chord that responds!

We are always quite alone. The communal life is the loneliest of all because "yet thou hast not known me." The world comes next in loneliness, but it is big, and with a big soul of its own. The family life is almost naïve in its misunderstanding—no one listens, they just wait for pauses....

The worship of the "sane mind" has been a little overdone, I think. The men who are prone to say of everyone that they "exaggerate a little," or "are morbid," are like weights in a scale—just, but oh, how heavy! This war is fine, fine, FINE! I know it, and yet I don't get near the fineness except in the pages of Punch! I see streams of men whose language (Flemish) I don't speak, holding up protecting hands to keep people from jostling a poor wounded limb. I watch them sleeping heavily, or eating oranges and smoking cigarettes down to the last hot stump. But I don't hear of the heroic stands which I know are made, or catch the volition of it all. Perhaps only in a voluntary army is such a thing possible. Our own boys make your heart beat, but these poor, dumb, sodden little men, coming in caked with mud—to be patched up and sent into a hole in the ground again, are simply tragic.

March 7:
"*The Woman's Touch*"

"The woman's touch." When a woman has been down on her knees scrubbing for a week and washing for another week, a man, returning and finding his house in order, and vaguely conscious of a newer and fresher smell about it, talks quite tenderly of "a woman's touch." There are some people who never care to enter a door unless it has "*passage interdite*" upon it....

The guns are booming heavily this morning. Nothing seems to correspond. Are men really falling and dying in agony quite close to us? I believe we ought to see less or more—be nearer the front or further from it. Or is it that nothing really changes us?

The Strange Side of War: A Woman's WWI Diary 131

"Remains of dead World War I soldier hanging on barbed wire in No Man's Land," (circa 1914 to 1918). Courtesy the Library of Congress.

Only war pictures and war letters remain as a fixed, blazing standard. The soldiers in the trenches are quite as keen about sugar in their coffee as we are about tea. No wonder men have decided that one day we must put off flesh. It is far too obtrusive....

To comfort myself I try to remember that the Duke of Wellington took his old nurse with him on all his campaigns because she was the only person who washed his stocks properly.

Surely the expense of the thing will one day put a stop to war. We are spending 2 million sterling per day, the French certainly as much, the Germans probably more, and Austria and Russia much more—in order to keep men most uncomfortably in unroofed graves and to send high explosives into the air, most of which don't hit anything. Surely, if fighting was (as it is) impossible in this flooded country in winter, we might have called a truce and gone home for three months, and trained and drilled like Christians on

Salisbury Plain! Health—i.e., bad health—obtrudes itself tiresomely. I am ill again, and, fortunately, few people notice it, so I am able to keep going on. A festered hand makes me awkward. As I wind a bandage around it and tie it with my teeth, I once more wish I was a Belgian refugee, as I am sure I would be interesting and people would do more things for me!

A sick Belgian artist, M. Rotsartz is doing a drawing of me. I go to Lady Bagot's hospital, where he is laid up, and sit with him in the intervals of soup. That little wooden hospital is the best place I have known so far. Lady Bagot is never bustled or fussy, or even "busy." Her staff is made of up excellent men with the "mark of the Lamb" on them.

I gave away a lot of things today to a regiment going into the trenches. The soldiers were delighted with them.

March 11:
The Promise of Spring

There was a lot of firing near La Panne today, and a British warship was repeatedly shelled by the Germans from Nieuport. I went into Dunkirk with Mr. Clegg, and got the usual hasty shopping done. No one can ever wait a minute. If you have time to buy a newspaper you are lucky. The difficulty of communicating with anyone is great—no telephone—no letters—no car. I am stranded.

I generally go in the train to Adinkerke with the French Marines, nice little fellows, with labels attached to them stating their "case"—not knowing where they are going or anything else—just human lives battered about and carted off. I don't even know where they get the little bit of money, which they always seem able to spend on strong-smelling oranges and cigarettes. The place is littered with orange peels—today I saw a long piece lying in the form of an "S" amid the mud. Like a story of a century old, I thought of ourselves as children throwing orange peels around our heads and onto the floor to read the initial of our future husband. I seemed to hear mother say, "'S' for Sammy—Sammy C__," a boy with thick legs whom we secretly despised! I have found a whole new household of *"éclopés"* [the lame] at Adinkerke, who want cigarettes, socks, and shoes all the time. They are a pitiful lot, with earaches, toothaches, and all the minor complaints, which I myself find so trying. They lie on straw until they are able to go back to the trenches again. The pollard willows between here and Adinkerke are all being cut down to build trenches. They were big with buds and the promise of spring.

March 14:

I went to the station yesterday, as usual. Suddenly I couldn't stand it any more. Everyone was cleaning. I was getting swept up with straw and mopped up with dirty cloths. The kitchen work was done. I ate my lunch in a filthy little outer building and then I fled. I had to get into the open air. I hopped onto an ambulance and drove to Dunkirk. I had much to do there getting vegetables, cigarettes, etc. We got back late to the station, where I heard the Queen of Belgium had paid a visit. Rather bad luck on almost the only day I have been away.

I am waiting anxiously to hear if the report of the new British advance yesterday is true. When fighting really begins we are going to be in for a big thing; you dread it for the sake of the boys we are going to lose. I want things to start now just to get them over, but I rather envy the people who died before this unspeakable war began.

March 17, 1915
To Mrs. Keays-Young,
Care of Field Post Office, Dunkirk

My Dearest Baby,

I have (of course) been getting letters and parcels very badly lately. I am sending this home by hand, which is not allowed except on Red Cross business, but this is to ask how Lionel is, so I think I may send it. My poor Bet! What anxiety for her!

This spring weather is making me long to be at home, and when people tell me the crocuses are up in the park! Well, you know London and the park belong to me! Are the catkins out? We can get flowers at Dunkirk, but not here.

Not a word of war news, because that wouldn't be fair. A shilling wire about Lionel would satisfy me—just "Better, and Bet well," or something of that sort.

Always, my dear,
Your loving,
S. Macnaughtan

P.S. Your two letters and Bet's have just come. To be in touch with you again is very pleasant. I can't tell you what it was like to sit down to a pretty, clean breakfast today with my letters beside me. Someone brought them here early. I heard today that I am going to be decorated by the King of the Belgians, but don't spread this news as anything might happen in war.

"A boy and his dog amid debris overlooking the Cathedral at Rheims, France damaged during the German bombardment," (1914). Bombing destroyed 60% of Rheims and some 5,000 people died there during World War I. Courtesy the Library of Congress.

March 20:
Madmen

I met an Englishman belonging to an armored car in Dunkirk a couple of days ago. He told me that the last four days' fighting at La Bassée in northern France has cost the British 13,000 casualties. Three lines of holes in the ground and fighting only just beginning again! Bet's fiancé has been shot through the head, but is still alive. My God, the horror of it all! And England is still cheerful, I hear, and is going to hold race meetings as usual.

At the station today I saw a mad man, who fought and struggled. I thought madmen raved. This one fought silently, like a man you see in a dream. Another soldier shook all over like an old man. Many were blind.

"A soldier stands among poor people and their dogs sleeping in a church in northern France," (circa 1915). Courtesy the Library of Congress.

"On the whole," someone said to me in England, "I suppose you are having a good time."

There is a snowstorm today. It is bitterly cold. It is very odd how many small "complaints" seem to attack you. I can't remember the day out here when I felt well all over.

Last night some Belgians came in to dinner. It was like old times trying to get things nice. I had some flowers and a tablecloth. I believe in making a contrast with the discomfort I see out here. We forced open a piano, and had some perfect music.

March 21:

The weather is brighter today. The sound of firing is more distant. It is possible to think of other things besides the war.

Mrs. ___ came to the station this morning. I think she has the untidiest mind I have ever met with.

With all our faults, I often wish that there were more Macnaughtans in the world. Their simple and plain intelligence gives you something to work upon. Mrs. ___ came and told me today that last night "they laughed until they cried" over her attempt at making a pudding. I should have cried, only, about a woman of 50 who wasn't able to make a pudding. She and ___ are twin nebula who think themselves constellations.

Longing for Home

March 22, 1915
To Mary King,
Care of Field Post Office, Dunkirk

Dear Mary,

My plans, like those of everybody else, are undecided because of the war. If it is going to stop in May I would like to stay until the end. But if it is likely to go on for a long time, I will come home. I don't think hot soup (which is my business) can be wanted much longer, as the warm weather will be coming.

I have been asked to take over full charge of a hospital here. It is a great compliment, but I have almost decided to refuse. I have other duties, and I have some important writing to do. I am busy with a book on the war. I begin work as early as ever, and then go to my kitchen.

When I do come home I want to be in my own house. I am longing to be back. Many of my friends go backwards and forwards to England all the time, but when I return, I would like to stay.

I am in wonderfully comfortable rooms at present. The landlady is most kind and attentive. She gives me a morning cup of tea. The care and comfort are making me much better. I get some soup before I go off to my station, and last night I was really a fine lady.

When I came in tired, the landlady, who is a Belgian, took off my boots for me! When I come home I think I'll lie in bed all day. Poor old Mary will get quite thin again nursing me. The things you will have to do for me, and all the pretty things I shall see and have are a great pleasure to think about!

Yours truly,
S. Macnaughtan

Chapter 7
Spring Offensive

"British recruiting poster," by unknown (1915). Courtesy the Library of Congress.

Spring 1915:
The Storm of Life

I have been to London for a few days to see about the publication of my little war book, *"A Woman's Diary of the War."* I got frightful neuralgia there, and find that as soon as I begin to rest I get ill. I went to a daffodil show and found myself in the very hall where the military bazaar was held last year. I saw the place where the Welch had their stall. What fun we had! How many of the regiment is left? Only one officer not killed or wounded. Lord Roberts, who opened the bazaar, is gone too. All the soldiers whom I knew best have been taken, and only a few tough women seem to weather the storm of life.

I had to see publishers in London and do a lot of business. Just when I was beginning to love it all again my holiday was over. There had been heavy fighting out here, and I felt I must come back. My dear people didn't want me to return and were very severe on the subject. Mary scolded me most of the time. It was all affection on their part although it made "duty" rather a criminal affair!

There was endless difficulty about my passport when I returned. People besieged the French Consulate. I had to go there at 8.30 a.m. and wait until the doors opened. I was then told I must first go to the Foreign Office to get an order from Colonel Walker. I went down to Whitehall from Bedford Square and was told I must get a letter from Mr. Coventry. I went to Pall Mall, and Mr. Coventry said it was quite impossible to do anything for me without instructions from Mr. Sawyer. Mr. Sawyer said the only thing he could do (if I could establish my identity) was to send me to a matron who would make every enquiry about me. Perhaps in three days I might get an Anglo-French certificate, through which Mr. Coventry might be induced to give me a letter to give to Colonel Walker, who might then sign the passport, which I could then take to Bedford Square to for a visa.

I got Sir John Furley [active in the Red Cross] to identify me. Then I began a dogged process of going from place to place and from official to official until at last I got the thing through. I felt just like a Russian being "broken." There is a regular system, I believe, in Russia of wearing people out by this sort of official tyranny. I do not know anything more tiring or more discouraging! I had all my papers in order—my passport, my *"laissez passer,"* a letter from Mr. Bevan, explaining who I was and asking for "every facility" for me, and my photograph, properly stamped. I am now so loaded with papers I feel as if I were carrying a library around with me. Oh, give me intelligent women to do things for me! The best-run things I have seen since the war began have been our women's unit at Antwerp and Lady Bagot's hospital at Adinkerke.

I came back refreshed. I think everyone (every woman) out here has noticed how indifferent and really "nasty" people are to each other at the front. It is one of the singular things about the war, because you always hear it said that it deepens people's characters, purifying them, and so on. As far as my experience goes, it has shown me the reverse. I have seldom known so much quarreling. There is a sort of strange unhappiness that has nothing to do with the actual war or loss of friends. I can't be mistaken about it because I see it on all sides.

At the hospital, both the men and women alike are quarreling all the time. Resignations are frequent. So-and-so has got so-and-so kicked out. Someone has written to the committee in London to report on someone else. A nice doctor is dismissed. Every nurse has given notice at different times. Most people are hurt and sore about something. Love seems quite at a discount, and you can't help wondering if hate can be infectious! It is all very disappointing for surely your heart beat high when you made up your mind to do what you could for suffering Belgium and for the sake of the English name.

Those two poor girls at ____! I know they meant well and had high ideas of what they were going to do. Now they "use langwidge" to each other (although I know a very strong affection binds them) and very, very strong that language is.

Poor souls, the people here aren't a bit happy. I wonder if the work is sufficiently "sanctified." You never know. Lady Bagot's is the happiest and most serene place here. Her men are Church Army people, and they have evening prayers in the ward. It does make a difference.

Scandals also exist out here, but they are merely silly, I think, and very unnecessary, though acting a little more conventional wouldn't hurt anyone. Sometimes I think it would be better if we were all at home since Belgians are particular. I hate breeches [short pants] and gaiters [leggings] for girls, and a silly way of going on. I do wish people could sometimes leave sex at home, but they never seem to. I wonder if Crusaders came back with scandals attached to their names!

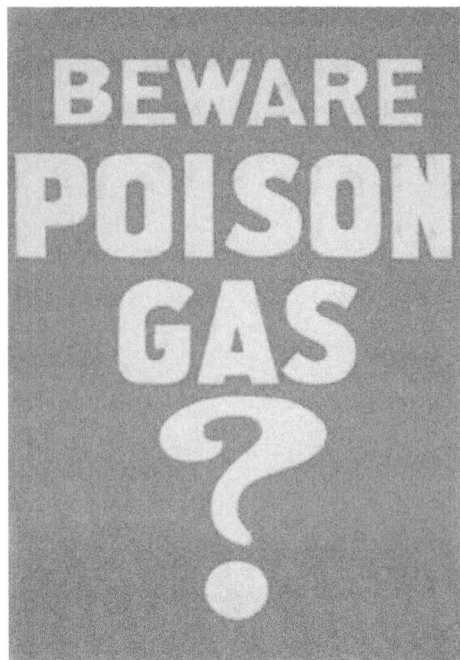

"Canadian World War I poster" by unknown (circa 1917). Courtesy the Library of Congress.

I got back here in one of those rushes of work that come in wartime when fighting is near. At first no car could be spared to meet me at Boulogne in France, so I had to wait at the Hôtel Maurice for two or three days. I didn't mind much as I met such a lot of English friends and also visited some interesting hospitals. However, I knew by the thousands of wounded coming in that things must be busy at the front, and this made me ready to chomp at the bit.

The Canadians and English who poured in from Ypres were terribly damaged. The asphyxiating poison gas seems to have been simply diabolical. It was awful to see human beings so mangled. I never get one bit accustomed to it. The streets were full of British soldiers, and the hospitals swarmed with wounded. I went to visit the Casino one. The bright sun streamed through lowered blinds on hundreds of beds, and on stretchers lying between them.

Many Canadians were there and rows of British. How they were knocked about! The vast rooms echoed with cries of pain. The men were vowing they could never face shells and hand grenades any more. They were so newly wounded, poor boys, but they come up smiling when their country calls again.

But it isn't right. This damage to human life is horrible. It is madness to slaughter these thousands of young men. Almost at last, in a rage, you feel inclined to cry out against the sheer stupidity of it. Why bring lives into the world and shell them out of it with jagged pieces of iron, and knives thrust through their quivering flesh? The pain of it is all too much. I am sick from seeing suffering.

On Thursday, April 29, Mr. Cooper, and another man came for us, and we left Boulogne. At Dunkirk we could hardly believe our eyes—the place had been shelled that very afternoon! I never saw such a look of bewilderment and horror as there was on all faces. No one had ever dreamed the place could be hit by a German gun, yet here were houses falling as if by magic. No one knew for a moment where on earth or in heaven the shells were coming from. Some people said they came from the sea, but the houses I saw hadn't been hit from the sea, which lies north, but from the east. Others talked of an armored train, but armored trains don't carry 15-inch shells. So all anyone could do was to gape in sheer astonishment.

Dunkirk, that safest of places, the haven to which we were all to fly when Furnes or La Panne were bombarded! Everybody contradicted each other, of course, when someone declared that no naval gun had been at work, but the fact remains that a long-range, field-piece had been hidden at Leke, and Dunkirk was shelled for three days. As far as I know, it may be shelled again. The inhabitants have all fled. The shops are not even shut. You could help yourself to anything! The *"état major"* [staff] has left, and so have all the officials—23,000 tickets have been taken at the railway station, and the road to Calais is blocked with fleeing refugees.

It was rather odd that the day I left here and passed through Furnes, it was being shelled, and we had to wait a little while before we could get through. When I arrived at Dunkirk the bombardment was just over. A huge shell hole prevented us passing down a certain road.

Well, I got back to my work at Adinkerke in the midst of the fighting, reaching it just as the sun was setting. What a scene at the station where I stopped before arriving home to leave the chairs and things I had bought for the hospital there! They were bringing in civilians wounded at Ypres and Poperinghe, which also has been shelled (and yet we say we are advancing!), and there were natives also from Nieuport.

One whole ambulance was filled with wounded children. I think King Herod himself might have been sorry for them. Wee things in splints, or with their curly heads bandaged; tiny mites, looking with wonder at their hands swathed in linen; babies with their tender flesh torn, and older children crying with terror. There were two tiny things seated opposite each other on a big stretcher playing with dolls, and a little Christmas-card sort of baby in a red hood had its mother and father killed beside it. Another little mite belonged to no one at all. Who could tell whether its parents had been killed or not? I am afraid many of them will never find their relatives again. In the general scrimmage, everyone gets lost. If this isn't frightfulness enough, God in heaven help us!

On the platform was a row of women lying on stretchers. They were decent-looking, brown-haired matrons for the most part. It looked unnatural and ghastly to see them lying there. One big railway compartment was slung with their stretchers, and some young men in uniform nursed the babies. I shall never forget that railway compartment as long as I live. A man in khaki appeared, thoughtful, as our people always are, and brought a box of groceries with him and cookies for the children, and other things. Thank Heaven for the English!

"Gas attack in Liévin" by A.Y. Jackson, Canadian war artist (1918). Courtesy Wikimedia Commons.

At the hospital it was really awful. The doctors were working in shifts of 24 hours at a time.

I left my tables, chairs, trays, etc., for the hospital at the station and returned early the next day since numerous wounded were still coming in. I wanted slippers for everyone, but my Belgian helpers had given a hundred pairs of mine away in my absence. They were overworked a little, I think, so I overlooked the fact that they lost their tempers rather badly. Besides, I will not quarrel. In a small kitchen it would be too ridiculous. The three little people fight among themselves, but I don't think I was made for that sort of thing.

There was nothing but work for some time. My *"éclopés"* [lame ones] had been entirely neglected. No one had even bothered to buy vegetables for the men.

On Sunday, May 2, I went to see Dr. de Page's hospital. I saw a baby three weeks old with both his feet wounded. His mother came in one mass of wounds and died on the operating table—a young mother and a pretty one.

"French cyclist soldiers at the beginning of World War I," by *Bain News Service*, (circa 1915). Courtesy the Library of Congress.

A young man, with tears in his eyes looked at the baby, and then said, "A jolly good shot at 15 miles." They can't help making jokes.

There were two Scots lying in a little room—both gunners, who had been hit at Nieuport. One (Ochterlony from Arbroath) had an eye shot away, and some other wounds; the other (McDonald) had seven bad injuries. Ochterlony talked a good deal about his eyes, until McDonald rolled his head around on the pillow, and remarked briefly, "I'd swop my stomach for your eyes."

Sunday wasn't such a nasty day like I usually have. In fact, Sunday never is. But that station, with its glaring hot platform, its hotter kitchen, and its smells, takes a bit of sticking. I have discovered one thing about Belgium. Everything smells exactly alike. Today there have been presented to my nose four different things purporting to have different odors, drains, some cheese, tobacco, and a bunch of lilac. There was no difference at all in the smells!

I am much struck by the feeling of sheer weariness and disgust at the war that prevails at present. People are "soul sick" of it.

The Strange Side of War: A Woman's WWI Diary

"British Army recruiting poster for bicycle troops for the South Midland Divisional Cyclist Company" by unknown (circa 1914 to 1918). Courtesy Wikimedia Commons.

A man told me last night he longed to be wounded so he might go home honorably. Among all the volunteer corps I notice the same thing. "Fed up" is the expression they all use, fed up with the suffering they see, fed up even with red crosses and khaki. When you think of primrose woods at home, and birds singing, and apple-blossom against blue sky, and the park with its flowerbeds newly planted, and the fresh-watered streets, and women in pretty dresses—but you mustn't!

May 6:
War Game

Mrs. Guest arrived here to stay yesterday, and her chauffeur, Mr. Wood, dined here. It is nice to be no longer quite alone. Last night we were talking about how horrible war is. Mrs. Guest told me of a sight she had herself seen. Some men, horribly wounded, were being sent away by rail in a *"fourgon"* covered wagon. One man had only his mouth left in his face. He was raving mad—

raging up and down the van, trampling on other men's wounded and broken limbs. Certainly war is a pretty game, and we must go on singing "Tipperary" and saying what fun it is. A young friend of mine at home gave me a pamphlet (price 2d.) written by a spinster friend of hers who had never left England, proving what a good thing this war was for us all. When I said I saw another aspect of it, the kind, soothing suggestion was that I must be a little over-tired.

May 7:
Madness

They say La Panne, near the French border, is to be bombarded today. The Queen of Belgium has left. Some people fussed a good deal, but if you bothered your poor head about every rumor of this sort (mostly "dropped from a German airplane") where would you be?

I was much touched when some people at home pitched in their money and sent me out a little car a short while ago. But, alas, it had not been chosen with judgment and is no use. It has been rather a bother to me, and now it must go back. Mr. Carlisle drove it up from Dunkirk, and it broke down six times. Then it had to be left in a ditch while he got another car to tow it home. Since then it has sat at the station.

I can't get anyone to come and inspect it. The extraordinary habit which prevails here of saying "No" to every request makes things difficult, for no privileges can be bought. Sometimes, when I hear people ask for the salt, I think the answer will be: "Certainly not." Two of our own chauffeurs live quite close to the station. They say they are busy, and can't look at my car. You smile, and say: "When you have time I shall be so grateful, etc." Inwardly you are feeling that if you could roar just for once it would be a relief.

Sometimes at home I have felt a little embarrassed by the love people have shown me—as if I have somehow deceived them into thinking I was nicer than I really am.

Out here I have to try to remember that I have a few friends! In London I couldn't understand it when people praised me or said kind things. There is only one straight tip for Belgium—have a car and understand it yourself. Never did I feel so helpless without one. But the roads are too bad and too crowded to begin to learn to drive, and there are difficulties about a garage.

This evening Mr. Wood and I went to Hoogstadt, and towed that corpse—my car—up to La Panne for an inspection. The whole Belgian army seemed to gather around us as we proceeded on our toilsome journey, with breaking tow ropes (for the "corpse" is heavy) and has defective steering gear. They were amused. I was just weighed down with fatigue. Needless to say, ____ didn't come. As the car was a present I can't send it back without the authority of a chauffeur. If I keep it any longer they will say I used it and broke it....

There were some terribly bad cases at Hoogstadt today. We were touched to see an old man sitting beside his unconscious son and keeping the flies off him, while he sobbed in great gusts. One Belgian officer told us the hardest thing he had to do in the war was to give the order to fire on a German regiment which was advancing with Belgian women and children in front of it. He gave the order and saw these helpless creatures shot down before his eyes. At the Yser the other night, two German regiments got across the river and found themselves surrounded. When one regiment surrendered, the men of the other coolly turned their guns on it and shot their comrades down.

Some of our corps was evacuating women and children the other day. One man, seeing his wife and daughter stretched out on the ground, went mad, running up and down the field screaming. We see a lot of madness.

May 8:
The Crucifix Undamaged

The guns sound rather near this morning, and the windows shook. You never know what is happening until the wounded come in.

"Undamaged crucifix in a ruined church in Fromelles on the Western Front," by *Bain News Service* (1915). Courtesy the Library of Congress.

I sat with my watch in my hand and counted the sound of bursting shells. There were 32 in a minute. The firing is continuous, and very loud, and living men are under this fire at this moment, "mown down," "wiped out," as the horrible terms go. I loathe even the sound of a bugle now. This carnage is too horrible. If people can't "realize" let them come near the guns.

They were shelling Furnes again when I was at Steenkerke the other day. It was a strange sound to hear the shells whizzing over the peaceful fields. You hear them coming, and they passed overhead to fall on the old town. Under them the brown cattle fed unheeding, and old women hoed undisturbed, and the sinking sun threw long shadows on the grass. And then a busy ambulance would fly past on the road. You caught a glimpse of blood-covered forms. "Yes, a few wounded, and two or three killed."

Old women are the most courageous creatures on this earth. When everyone else has fled from a place you can see them sitting by their cottage doors or hoeing turnips in the line of fire.

It was touching to see a little family of terrified children sheltering with their mother in a roadside Calvary [shrine] when the shells were coming over. The poor young mother was holding up her baby to Christ on his cross.

There is something that seems almost more than a coincidence, and one which has been too often remarked to be ignored. That is, in the midst of ruins almost totally destroyed, the figure of Christ in some niche often remains untouched. I have seen it myself, and many writers have commented on the fact. Sometimes it is only a crucifix on some humble wall, or it may be a shrine in a church. The solitary figure remains and stands—often with arms raised to bless. At Neuve Chapelle, you learn that, although the havoc is like that wrought by an earthquake, and the very dead have been uprooted there, a crucifix stands at the crossroads at the north end of the village, and the pitiful Christ still stretches out his hands. At his feet lie the dead bodies of young soldiers. At Nieuport, I noticed a shrine over a doorway in the church standing peacefully among the ruins. And at Pervyse also one remained, until the tower reeled and fell with an explosion from beneath, which was deliberately ordered to prevent accidents from falling masonry.

I had to go to Dunkirk this afternoon. While I was there I heard that the *RMS Lusitania* ocean liner had been torpedoed and sunk with 1,600 souls on board her. What change will this make in the situation? Is America any use to us except in the matter of supplies, and are we not getting these through as it is? A nation like that ought to have an army or a navy.

Dunkirk was nearly deserted due to the bombardment. It was difficult to find a shop open to buy vegetables for my soup kitchen. Still, I enjoyed my afternoon. There was a chance that shelling might begin again at any time, and a bitter wind blew up clouds of prickly dust and sand. But it was a great relief to be out in the open away from smells and have your view no longer bounded by a line of train rails. God help us! What a year this has been! It tires me even to think of being happy again, cheerfulness has become such an effort.

May 10:

I went to see my Scottish gunner at the hospital today. He said, "I can't forget that night," and burst out crying. "That night" he had been wounded in seven places and then had to crawl to a "dugout" by himself for shelter.

Strong healthy men lie inert in these hospitals. Many of them have face and head wounds. I saw one splendid young fellow, with a beautiful face, and straight clear eyes of a sort of forget-me-not blue. He won't be able to speak again, as his jaw is shot away. The man next him was being fed through the nose.

The matron told me today that last night a man came in from Nieuport with the base of a shell ("the bit they make into ash trays," she said) embedded in him. His clothing had been carried in with it. He died, of course.

One of our friends has been helping with stretcher work, removing civilians. He was carrying away a girl shot to pieces and with her clothing in rags. He took her head, and a young Belgian took her feet, and the Belgian looked around and said quietly, "This is my fiancée."

May 11:

The Lusitania

Today being Madame's washing day—we ring the changes on the "*nettoyage*" [cleaning], "*le grand nettoyage*," and "*le lavage*" [washing]— everything was late. The newspaper came in and was full of such words as "horror," "resentment," "indignation," about the *Lusitania*. But that won't give us back our ship or our men.

The Strange Side of War: A Woman's WWI Diary

"Passengers aboard the *Lusitania*," by Bain News Service (circa 1910 to 1915). Courtesy the Library of Congress.

I wish we could do more and say less, but the press must talk and always does so "with its mouth." M. Rotsartz came to breakfast. The guns had been going all night long. There was a sense of something in the air. I worried against platitudes in French and Madame's washing. At last, I got away and went to the sea front as the sound of bursting shells had become tremendous.

It was a sort of British morning, with a fresh British breeze blowing our own blessed waves. And there, in its gray grandeur, stood off a British man-of-war, blazing away at the coast. The Germans answered by shells, which fell a bit wide, and must have startled the fishes (but no one else) by the splash they made. There were long, swift torpedo boats, with two great white wings of cloven foam at their bows, and a great flourish of it in their wake, moving along under a canopy of their own black smoke. It was the smoke of good British coal, from pits where grimy workmen dwell in the black country, and British sweat has to get it out of the ground. Our gray lady was burning plenty of it. When she had done her work, she put up a banner of smoke and steamed away with a splendid air of dignity across the white-flecked sea. You knew the men on board her! Probably not a heartbeat quicker by a second for all the German shells, probably dinner was served as usual, and men got their tubs and had their clothes brushed when it was all over.

I went down to my kitchen a little late, but I had seen something that Drake never saw—a bit of modern sea fighting. And in the evening, when I returned, my gray mistress had come back again. The sun was westering now, and the sea had turned to gold. The gray lady looked black against the glare, but the fire of her guns was brighter than the evening sunset. She was a spitfire, after all, this dignified queen, and she, "let 'em have it," too, while the long, lean torpedo boats looked on.

I went to the kitchen: I gave out jam, I distributed socks, I heard the fussy importance of minor officials, but I had something to work on since I had seen the gray lady at work. In the evening I dined quietly on the barge with Miss Close and Maxine Elliott. We played a game of bridge—a thing I had not seen for a year and more (the last time I played was down in Surrey at the Grange!). The little gathering on the old timbered barge was pleasant.

Some terrible stories of the war are coming through from the front. An officer told us that when they take a trench, the only thing that describes what the place is like is strawberry jam. Another said that in one trench the sides were falling and the Germans used corpses to make a wall, and kept them in with piles fixed into the ground. Hundreds of men remain unburied.

Some people say that the German gunners are chained to their guns. There were six Germans at the station today—two wounded and four prisoners. Individually I always like them. It is useless to say I don't. They are all polite and grateful. I thought today when the prisoners were surrounded by a gaping crowd, they conducted themselves very well. After all, you can't expect a whole nation of mad dogs. A Scotchman said: "The ones opposite us (i.e., in the trenches) were a very respectable lot of men." The German prisoners' letters contain news that battalions of British suffragettes have arrived at the front, and they warn officers not to be captured by these!

May 12:

Today, when I got to the station, I was asked to remove an old couple who sat there, hand in hand, covered with blood. The old woman had her arm blown off, and the man's hand was badly injured. We took them to de Page's hospital. The firing has been continuous for the last few days. Men coming in from Ypres, Dixmude, and Nieuport say the losses on both sides have been enormous. There were four Belgian officers who lived opposite my villa, whom I used to see going in and out. Last night all were killed.

At Dixmude the other day, the Duke of Westminster went to the French bureau to get his passport visa. The clerks were just leaving, but he begged them to remain a minute or two and to do his little business. They did so and came to the door to see him out, but a shell came hurtling in and killed them both as well a woman standing near, there was literally nothing left.

Last night, ___ and I were talking about the gossip, which would fill 10 unpublishable volumes out here. Why do these people come out to the front? Give me men for war, and no one else except nuns. Things may be all right, but the Belgians are horrified. I hate them to "say things" of the English. The grim part of it is I don't believe I personally hear one half of what goes on and what is being said. They are afraid of shocking me, I believe.

The craze for men baffles me. I see women, dead tired, perk up and begin to be sparkling as soon as a man appears. And when they are alone, they just seem to sink back into apathy and fatigue. Why won't these mad creatures stop at home? They are the exception, but war seems to bring them out. It really is intolerable, and I hate it for women's sake, and for England's. The other day, I heard some ladies having a rather forced discussion on moral questions, loud and frank. Shades of my modest ancestresses! Is this wartime (and in a room filled with men and smoke and drink) are women in knickerbockers discussing such things? Beautiful women and fast women should be chained up. Let men meet their God with their conscience clear. Most of them will be killed before the war is over. Surely the least we can do is not to offer them temptation. Death and destruction, and horror and wonderful heroism, seem so near and so transcendent, and then, quite close at hand, you find evil doings.

May 14:
Unbelievable Stories

I heard two little stories today. One was of a British soldier limping painfully through Poperinghe with a horrid wound in his arm and thigh.

"You seem badly wounded," a friend of mine said to him. "Yus," said the soldier, "there was a German, and he wounded me in three places, but," he drew from under his arm a treasure, and his poor dirty face was transformed by a delighted grin, "I got his bloody helmet."

Another story was of an English officer telephoning from a church tower. He gave all his directions clearly and distinctly, and never even hinted that the Germans had taken the town and were approaching the church. He just went on talking, until at last, as the tramp of footsteps sounded on the belfry stairs, he said: "Don't take any notice of any further information. I am going." He went—all the brave ones seem to go—and those were the last words he spoke.

William Barnard Rhodes-Moorhouse, of the Royal Flying Corps, flew low over the German lines the other day to bombard the German station at Courtrai, southwest of Ghent. He flew down to 300 feet and became the target for a hundred guns. In the murderous fire, he was wounded and might have descended, but he was determined not to let the Germans have his machine. He flew down to 100 feet in order to gather speed. At this elevation, he was hit again and mortally wounded, but he flew on alone to the British lines—like a shot bird heading for its own nest.

"British Red Cross orderly escorts a captured wounded German soldier, who has spent several days in the trenches, to a field hospital for treatment," by *Central News Photo Service*, (circa 1914 to 1918). Courtesy the Library of Congress.

He didn't even stop at the first aerodrome he came to, but sailed on—always alone—to his base, made a good landing, handed over his machine, and died.

In the hospitals what heroism you find! One splendid fellow of 6 feet 2 inches had both his legs and both his arms amputated. He turned round to the doctor and said, smiling, "I won't have to complain of beds being too short now!" And when someone came and sat with him in his deadly pain, he remarked in his gentle way, "I am afraid I am taking up all your time." His old father and mother arrived after he was dead.

Ah, if you could hear more, surely you would do more! But this hole-and-corner way of doing warfare damps all enthusiasm and stifles recruiting. Why are we allowed to know nothing until the news is stale? Yesterday I heard firsthand about the treatment of some civilians by Germans, and I visited a village to hear from the people themselves what had happened.

"Algerian soldiers at a train station during World War I," by *Bain News Service*, (circa 1914 to 1915). Courtesy the Library of Congress.

My work isn't so heavy now, and, much as I want to be here when the "forward movement" comes, I believe I ought to use the small amount of kick I have left in me to give lectures on the war to men in ammunition works at home. They all seem to be slacking and drinking. I believe you might rouse them if you went yourself, and told stories of heroism and tales of the front. The British authorities out here seem to think I ought to go home and give lectures at various centers. I have heard from Vickers-Maxim's people that they want me to come.

I think I'll arrive in London around June 1. There is a much to arrange, and I have to see the heads of departments. You have to forget all about parties in politics, and get help from Lloyd George himself. I only hope the lectures may be of some use.

May 16, 1915
To Mrs. ffolliott,
Villa les Chrysanthemes, La Panne, Belgium

Darling Old Poot,

One line, to wish you with all my heart a happy birthday. I won't forget you on the 22nd. Will you buy yourself some little thing with the enclosed check?

This war becomes a terrible strain. I don't know what we shall do when four nephews, a brother-in-law, and a nephew to be are in the field.

I get quite sick with the loss of life that is going on. The whole land seems under the shadow of death. I shall always think it an idiotic way of settling disputes to plug pieces of iron and steel into innocent boys and men. But the bravery is simply wonderful. I could tell you stories that are almost unbelievable of British courage and fortitude.

I am coming home soon to give some lectures, and then I hope to come out here again.

Bless you, dear Poot,
Your loving Sarah

May 17:
Vision

I saw a most curious thing today. A soldier in the Pavilion St. Vincent showed me five 5-franc pieces he had in his pocket when he was shot. A piece of shrapnel had bent the whole five until they were welded together. The shrapnel fitted into the silver exactly. Actually it was silvered by the scrape it had made against the coin. I would have liked to have it, but the man valued his souvenir, so I didn't want to offer him money for it.

A young Canadian found a comrade of his nailed to a door, and stone dead, of course. When did he die? A Belgian doctor told Mrs. Wynne that in looking through a German officer's knapsack he found a quantity of children's hands—a pretty souvenir! I write these things down because they must be known. If I go home to lecture to munitions workers I suppose I must tell them of these barbarities.

Meanwhile, the German prisoners in England are getting country houses placed at their service, electric lights, baths, etc. They say girls are allowed to come and play lawn tennis with them. The ships where they are interned are costing us £86,000 a month. Our own men imprisoned in Germany are starved, beaten, and spat on. They sleep on moldy straw, have no sanitation, and, in winter weather their coats and sometimes even their tunics were taken from them. Fortunately, reprisals need not come from us. Talk to Zouaves and Turcos and the French. God help Germany if they ever penetrate to the Rhine. A young man—Mr. Shoppe—is occupied in flying over low to take a photograph of the gun that is bombarding Dunkirk

It seems to me a great deal to ask of young men to give their lives when life must be so sweet, but no one seems to hold a grudge at all. Of some, you hear touching and splendid stories. Others, you know, die all alone, gasping out their last breath painfully, with no one at hand to give them even a cup of water. No one has a tale to tell of them. God, perhaps, heard a last prayer or a last groan before death came with its merciful hand and put an end to the intolerable pain.

How much can a man endure? A Frenchman at the Zouave Poste au Secours looked calmly on while the remains of his arm were cut away the other night. Many operations are performed without chloroform (because they take a shorter time) at the French hospital.

I heard from R. today. He says the story about the town of Mons is true. The English were retreating, and the German General Alexander von Kluck was following hard after them.

"View along one of a network of underground communication galleries that supply ammunition for Belgian fire trenches," *The Illustrated War News*, (March 21, 1917). Belgian trench lines along the front held by King Albert's Army in Western Flanders extend between Ypres and the sea near Nieuport and protect from infantry attacks. Shells hurtle across daily overhead from one side to another.

He wired to the Kaiser that he had "got the English," but this is what men say happened. A cloud came out of a clear day and stood between the two armies, and in the cloud men saw the chariots and horses of a heavenly host. Kluck turned back from pursuing, and the English went on unharmed. This may be true, or it may be the result of men's fancy or of their imagination. But there is one vision which no one can deny, and which each man who cares to look may see for himself. It is the vision of what lies beyond sacrifice. In that bright and heavenly atmosphere we shall see—we may, indeed, see today—the forms of those who have fallen. They fight still for England, unharmed now and forever more, warriors on the side of right, captains of the host that no man can number, champions of all we hold good. They are marching on ahead, and we hope to follow. When we all meet and the roll is called, we shall find them still cheery, I think, still unwavering, and answering to their good English names, which they carried unstained through a score of fights, at what price God and a few comrades know.

Chapter 8
Last Days in Flanders

"A French sergeant and a dog wear gas masks on their way to the front line trenches," by *National Photo Co.* (circa 1915). Courtesy the Library of Congress.

May 19, 1915:

Life & Death

In order to get material for my lecture to munitions workers, I was very anxious to see more of the war for myself than is possible at a soup kitchen.

I asked at the British Mission if I might be given permission to go into the British lines. Major ___ gave me a flat refusal, was a little pompous and important I thought, and he said it was impossible to get near the British.

Today I lunched on the barge with Miss Close. We took her car and drove to Poperinghe. I hardly like to write this even in a diary, I am so seldom naughty! But I really did something very wrong for once. And the amusing part of it was that military orders made going to Poperinghe so impossible that no one bothered us! We passed all the sentries with a flourish of our green papers and drove out to the typhoid hospital with only a few Tommies gaping at us.

I was amazed at the pleasure that wrongdoing gives and regretted my desperately strict past life! Oh, the freedom of that day in the open air! The joy of seeing trees after looking at one wretched line of rails for nine months! Lilacs were abloom in every garden, and buttercups made the fields look yellow. The air was misty—you could hardly have gone to Poperinghe except in a mist, as it was being so constantly shelled.

But in the mist, the trees had an odd light on them which made the early green look a deeper and stronger color than I've ever seen it. There appeared to be a sort of glare under the mist. The fresh wet landscape, with its top-heavy sky, radiated with some light of its own. Oh, the intoxication of that damp, wet drive, with a fine rain in our faces, and the car bounding under us. If I am interned until the end of the war I don't care a bit! I have had some fresh air and been away for one whole day from the smell of soup and drains.

How describe it all? The dear sense of guilt first, and then the still dearer British soldiers, all ready with some cheery, cheeky remark as they sat in carts under the wet trees. They were our brethren—blue-eyed and fair-haired, and with their old clumsy ways, which I seemed to be seeing plainly for the first time, or, rather, recognizing for the first time. It was all part of England and a day out. The officers were exercising, of course, with dogs and in the rain. We are never less than English! Tomorrow we may be killed, but today we will put on thick boots and take the dogs for a run in the rain.

Poperinghe was deserted, of course. Its busy cobbled streets were quite empty except for a few strolling soldiers in khaki. Just here and there was the same toothless old woman who is always the last to leave a doomed city.

At the typhoid hospital, we gravely offered the cases of milk, which we had brought as sign of our good conduct. But even the hospital was nearly empty. However, a secretary offered us a cup of tea. In the dining room we found Belgian Countess Maria van den Steen, who had just returned to take up her noble work again. She was at Dinant, at her own château, when war broke out. She was very interesting and able to tell me things firsthand. The German methods are pretty well known now, but she told me a great deal which only women talking together could discuss. When a village or town was taken, the women inhabitants were quite at the mercy of the Germans.

Continuing, Madame van den Steen said that all the filthiness that could be thought of was committed—the furniture, cupboards, flowerpots, and even bridge tables, were damaged by these brutes. Your pen won't write more. The horrors upset you too much. All the babies born about that time died; their mothers had been so shocked and frightened.

Of Ypres, Madame said: "It smells of lilac and death." Some Englishmen were looking for the body of a comrade there, and failed to find it among the ruins of the burning and devastated town. By chance they opened the door of a house, which still stood, and found in a room inside an old man of 86, sitting calmly in a chair. He said, "How do you do?" and invited them be seated. When they exclaimed, aghast at him still being still in Ypres, he replied that he was paralyzed and couldn't move, but he knew God would send someone to take him away. He smiled gently at them and was taken away in their ambulance.

Madame gave me a shell case and asked Mr. Thompson if he would bring in his large piece to show us. He wheeled it across the hall, as no one could lift it. This was only the base of a 15-inch shell. It was picked up in the garden of the hospital and had traveled 15 miles!

The other day I went to see for myself some of the poor refugees at Coxide. There were 25 people in one small cottage. Some were sleeping in a cart.

"Countess Elisabeth de Riquet Caraman-Chimay," by Philip Alexius de László (1905). Courtesy Wikimedia Commons.

One weeping woman, wearing the little black woolen cap which all the women wear, told me she and her family had to flee from their little farm at Lombaertzyde because it was being shelled by the Germans. But afterwards, when all seemed quiet, they went back to their home to save the cows. Alas, the Germans were there! They made this woman (who was expecting a baby) and all her family stand in a row, and one girl of 20, the eldest daughter, was shot before their eyes. When the poor mother begged for the body of her child it was refused her.

The *Times* list of atrocities is too frightful, and all the evidence has been sifted and proved to be true.

May 20:

Yesterday I arranged with Major du Pont about leaving the station to go home and give lectures in England. Then I had a good deal to do, so I abandoned my plan of visiting refugees with Etta Close and stayed on at the station. At 5:30 I came back to La Panne to see Belgian Countess Elisabeth de Riquet Caraman-Chimay, the dame d'honneur of the Queen of the Belgians. Then I went to dine with the nurses at the "Ocean." Here I heard that Adinkerke, which I had just left, was being shelled. Fortunately, with the train station being there, I hope the inhabitants got away, but it was unpleasant to hear the sound of guns so near. I knew the three Belgian Sisters would be all right, as they have a good cellar at their house, and I could trust Lady Bagot's staff to look after her. All the same, it was a horrible night, full of anxiety. There seems little doubt that La Panne will be shelled any day. My one wish is—let's all behave well.

I watched the sunset over the sea, and longed to be in England. But, naturally, you mean to stick it, and not leave at a nasty time.

May 21:
Socks

Yesterday at the station, there was a poor fellow lying on a stretcher, battered and wounded, as they all are, an eye gone and a foot bandaged. His toes were exposed. I went and got him a rather a bright pair of socks to pull on over his *"pansement"* [dressing]. He gave me a twinkle out of his remaining eye, and said: "Madame, in those socks I could take Constantinople!"

The work is slow for the moment, but a great attack is expected at Nieuport. They say the Kaiser is behind the lines there. His presence hasn't brought luck so far, and I hope it won't this time.

I went to tea with Miss Close on the barge. Afterwards we picked up Monsieur de la Haye, and went to see an old farm, which filled me with joy. The buildings here, except at the larger towns, are not interesting or beautiful, but this lovely old house was evidently once a summer palace of the bishops (perhaps of Bruges). It is called Beau Garde and lies off the Coxide road. You enter what must once have been a splendid courtyard, but is now filled indiscriminately with soldiers and pigs. The chapel still stands, with the Bishops' Arms on the wall. There are Spanish windows in the old house and a curious dog kennel built into the wall.

"French wounded convalescents nicknamed "the Cripples" (éclopés) about to return to the front," by *Underwood & Underwood*, (circa 1915). Courtesy the Library of Congress.

Over the gateway, some massive beams have been roughly painted in dark blue. These, covered in ivy and with old dim-toned bricks above, make a scheme of color that is simply enchanting. Some wind-torn trees and sand dunes, piled in miniature mountains, form a delicious background to the old place.

I also went with Etta Close to visit some of the refugees for whom she has done so much. In the sweet spring sunshine, I took a little walk in the fields with de la Haye, so altogether it was a real nice day. There were so few wounded that I was able to have a chat with each of them, and the poor *"éclopés"* were happy gambling in the garden of the St. Vincent.

In the evening, I went up to the Kursaal to dine with Mrs. Wynne. Our two new warriors, who came out with ambulances, have stood this absolutely quiet time for three days and are now leaving because it is too dangerous! The shells at Adinkerke never came near them, as they were deputed to drive to Nieuport only. (Mrs. Wynne continues to drive there every night!) Eight men of our corps have become depressed, no women.

I am going to take a week's rest before going home in the hope that I won't arrive looking as ill as I usually do. I hardly know how to celebrate my holiday, as it is the first time since I came out here that I haven't gone to the station except on Sundays.

May 23, Sunday:
War Souvenirs

I went to Morning Service at the "Ocean" today, then walked back with Prince Alexander. In the evening, we drove to the Hoogstadt hospital. The King of the Belgians was just saying goodbye to the staff, after paying a surprise visit. He has a splendid face. The simplicity of his plain dark uniform makes the strength and goodness of it all the more striking.

As I was waiting at the hospital, the Germans began firing at a little village a mile off. It is always strange to hear the shells whizzing over the fields. We drove out to see the Yser and the floods, which have protected us all the winter. With binoculars you could have seen the German lines.

Spring is coming late and with a marvel of green. A wind blows in from the sea, and the lilacs nod from over the hedge. The tender corn rustles its soft little chimes. All across it the wind sends arpeggio chords of delicate music, like a harp played on silver strings. A great big horse-chestnut tree, carrying its flowers proudly like a bouquet, showers the road with petals. The shy hedges put up a screen all laced and decorated with white may. It just seems as if Mother Earth had become young again, and was tossing her babies up to the summer sky, and the wind played hide-and-seek or some other ridiculous game with them, and made the summer babies as glad and as mischievous as himself. Only the guns boom all the time. My poor little French Marines, who drink far too much and have the manners of princes, come in on ambulances in the evening, or at the *"poste"* a hole is dug for them in the ground, and they are laid down gently in their dirty coats.

Mother Earth, with her newborn babies, stops laughing for a moment, and says to me: "It's all right, my dear; they have to come back to me, as all my children and all their works must do. Why make any complaint? For a time they are happy, playing and building their little castles, and making their little books, and weaving stories and wreaths of flowers; but the stories, the castles, the flowers I gave them, and they themselves, all come back to me at last—the leaves next autumn, and the boy you love perhaps tomorrow."

Oh, Father God, Mother Earth, as it was in the beginning will it be in the end? Will you give us and them a good time again? Will the spring burst into singing in some other country? I don't know. I don't know.

Only I do know this—I am sure of it now for the first time, and it is worth while spending a long, long winter within the sound of guns in order to know it—that death brings release, not release from mere suffering or pain, but in some strange and unknown way it brings freedom. Soldiers realize it. They have been more terrified than their own mothers will ever know, and their very spines have melted under the shrieking sound of shells. Then comes the day when they "don't mind." Death stalks just as near as ever, but his face is suddenly quite kind. A stray bullet or a piece of shell may come, but what does it matter? This is the day when the soldier learns to stroll when the shrapnel is falling, and look up and laugh when the murderous bullet pings close by.

War souvenirs! There are heaps of them. I hate them all: pieces of jagged shell, helmets with bullets through them, pieces of burnt airplanes, scraps of clothing torn by a bayonet.

Yesterday, at the station, I saw a sick Zouave nursing a German summer *casquette* [hat]. He said quietly, being very sick: "The burgomaster *chez moi* wanted one. Yes, I had to kill a German officer for it. *Ce n'est rien de quoi* [this is nothing]. I got a ball in my leg too, *mais mon burgomaster sera très content d'avoir une casquette d'un boche.* [My burgomaster will be very happy to have a cap of a Boche.]"

"A Scottish soldier stands on a street corner in a Belgian village," British Parliament Recruiting Committee poster (1914). Courtesy the Library of Congress.

Our own men leave their trenches and go out into the open to get these horrible things, with their battered exterior and the suggestion of pomade inside.

Yesterday, by chance, I went to the "Ierlinck" to see Mr. Clegg. I met Mr. Hubert Walter, lately arrived from England, and asked him to dine. So both he and Mr. Clegg came, and Madame van der Gienst. It was so like England to talk to Mr. Walter again and learn news of everyone. We actually sat up until 10:30 p.m. and had a great powwow.

Mr. Walter attaches great importance to the fact that the Germans are courageous in victory, but their spirits go down at once under defeat. He thinks that even one decisive defeat would do wonders in the way of bringing the war to an end. The Russians are preparing for a winter campaign. I look at all my "woolies," and wonder if I had better save some for 1916. What new horrors will have been invented by that time? I hear the Germans are throwing vitriol [sulfuric acid] now! In their results I hate hand grenades more than anything. The poor burnt faces wounded by them are hardly human sometimes. And in their bandages they have a suggestion of something tragically grotesque.

May 26:
Gas Poisoning

We had a great day—rather, a glorious day—at the station yesterday. In the morning I heard that *"les Anglais"* were arriving there. Although the news was a little startling, I couldn't go early to Adinkerke because I felt so seedy. However, I got off at last in a *"camion"* [truck]. When I arrived I found the little station hospital, the sale, and Lady Bagot's hospital crowded with men in khaki.

We don't know yet all that it means. The fighting has been fierce and awful at Ypres. Are the hospitals at the base all crowded? Is there no more room for our men? What numbers of them have fallen? Who is killed, and who is left?

All questions are idle for the moment. Only I have a postcard to say that Colin is at the front, so I suppose until the war is over I shall go on being very sick with anxiety. At night I say to myself, as the guns boom on, "Is he lying out in the open with a bullet through his heart?" In the morning I say, "Is he safe in hospital, and wounded, or is he still with his men, making them follow him (in the way he has) wherever he likes to lead them?" God knows, and the War Office, and neither tells us much.

The men at the station were nearly all cases of asphyxiation by gas. Unless you have actually seen the immediate results you could hardly believe it. In a day or two, the soldiers may leave off twitching and shuddering as they breathe and may be able to draw a breath fairly. But an hour or two after they have inhaled the deadly German gas is an awful time to see your men. Most of them yesterday were in bed, but a few sat on canvas chairs around the empty stove in the salle, and all slept, even those in deadly pain. Sleep comes to these tired soldiers like a death. They succumb to it. They are difficult to rouse. They are oblivious and want nothing else. They are able to sleep anywhere and in any position, but even in sleep they twitch and shudder, and their sides heave like those of spent horses.

It struck me very forcibly that what was immediately needed was a long drink for each of them of some clean, simple stimulant. I went and bought them red wine. I could see this seemed to do good. I went to the barge and got bottles of whisky and a quantity of distilled water, and we dosed the men. It seemed to do them a wonderful lot of good, and in some way acted as an antidote to the poison. Also, it pulled them together, and they got some quieter sleep afterwards.

Towards the afternoon, indeed, all but one Irishman seemed to be better, and then we began to be cheery. The scene at the station became intensely alive. The khaki-clad forms roused themselves, and (of course) wanted a wash. Also, they sat on their beds and produced pocket combs, and ran them through their hair. In their dirt and rags these poor battered, breathless men began to try to be smart again. It was a tragedy and a comedy all in one. A Highlander, in a shrunk kilt and with long bare legs, had his head bound about with bandages until it looked like a great melon, and his sleeve dangled empty from his greatcoat. Others of the Seaforths, and mere boys of the Highland Territorials, wore khaki shirts over their tartan, and these were bullet-torn and hanging in great shreds. And some boys still wore their caps jauntily with the wee dambrod pattern [of large, square solid-colored checks]. Some had no caps to wear. Some were all daubed about with white bandages stained crimson, and none had hose, and few had brogues. They had breathed poison and received shrapnel. None of them had slept since Sunday night. They had an "awful doing," and no one knew how the battle at Ypres had gone, but these were men yet—walking upright when they could, always civil, undismayed, intelligent, and about as like giving in as a piece of granite.

Only the young Scottish boys—the children of 17 who had sworn in as 19—were longing for Loch Lomond's side and the falls of Inversnaid. I believe the Loch Lomond lads believed the white burn that falls over the rocks near the pier has no rival (although they have heard of Niagara and the Victoria Falls), and it's *"oor glen"* and *"oor country"* with them all. And one boy wanted his mother badly and said so. But oh, how ready they were to be cheery! How they enjoyed their day! And, indeed, we did our best for them.

Lady Bagot's hospital was full. We called it her garden party when we all had tea in the open air there. We fed them, we got them handkerchiefs, our good du Pont got them tubs, the cook heaped more coal on the fire, although it was very hot, and made soup in buckets. Then began a curious stage scene I shall never forget. It was on the platform of the station. A band appeared from somewhere, and as a compliment to the English, played "God Save the King." All the dirty bandaged men stood at attention. As they did so an armored train backed slowly into the station and an airplane swooped overhead. At Drury Lane one would have said that the staging had been overdone, that the clothes were too ragged, the men too gaunt and too much wounded, and that by no stretch of imagination could a band be playing "God save the King" while a square painted train called "Lou-lou" steamed in, looking like a child's giant gaudy toy, and an airplane fussed overhead.

Everyone had stories to tell, but I think the best of them concerned the arrival of the wounded last night. All the beds in Lady Bagot's little hospital were full. The Belgians, who occupied them, insisted on getting up and giving their places to the English. They lay on the floor or stood on their feet all night. Someone told me that even very sick men leapt from their beds to give them to their Allies.

God help us, what a mixture it all is! Here were men talking of the very sound of bayonets on human flesh; here were men not only asphyxiated by gas, but blinded by the pepper that the Germans mix with it; and here were men determined to give no quarter—yet they were babbling of Loch Lomond's side and their mothers, and fighting as to who should give up their beds to each other.

Of course, the day ended with the exchange of souvenirs. The soldiers pulled buttons off their coats and badges out of their caps. And when it was all over, every mother's son of them rolled around and went to sleep. Most of them, I thought, had a curious air of innocence about them as they slept.

May 27:
What Matters

I took a great bundle of newspapers and magazines to the "Jellicoe" men today. English current literature isn't a waste out here. I often wonder why people don't buy more. They all fall upon my tableful.

The war news, even in the ever-optimistic English press, is not good, but not nearly as bad as what seems to me the real condition of affairs. The shortage of high explosives is very great. At Nieuport yesterday, Mrs. Wynne said to a French officer: "Things seem quiet here today." He laughed and said, "I suppose even Germans will stop firing when they know you have no ammunition."

In France, the armament works are going night and day. The men work in shifts of 24 hours—even the women only get one day off in a week. While in Glasgow the men are sticking out for strict labor conditions, "slacking" from Friday night until late on Tuesday morning, and then demanding extra pay for overtime. And this in the face of the bare facts that since October the Allies have lost ground in Russia; in Belgium they remain as they were; and in France they have advanced a few miles. At Ypres, the Germans are now within a mile of us, and the losses there are terrible. Whom shall we ever see again?

"Admiral Sir John Jellicoe, the new First Sea Lord of the Admiralty at Whitehall," *The Illustrated War News*, (Dec. 6, 1916). Jellicoe was a British naval officer who commanded a fleet against the Germans.

Men come out to die now, not to fight. One order from a sergeant was: "You've got to take that trench. You can't do it. Get on!"

A captain was heard saying to a gunner subaltern: "We must go back and get that gun." The subaltern said, "We shall be killed, but it doesn't matter." The captain echoed heavily, "No, it doesn't matter," and they went back.

Sir William Ramsay [a British chemist who won the Nobel Prize in 1904], speaking about the war, says that half the adult male population of Europe will be killed before it is over. Those who are left will be the feeble ones, the slackers, the unfit, and the cowards. It is good to be left to breed from such stock!

It is odd to me how confusing is the lack of difference that has come to pass between the living and the not living. Cottages and little towns seem to be part of nature. You regret their destruction almost as you regret the loss of life. They have a tragic look, with their disheveled windows and stripped roofs and skeleton frames. Life has become so cheap that cottages seem almost as valuable. "It doesn't matter"—nothing matters. I dread going back to London because there things may begin to seem important and you will be in bondage again. Here our men are going to their death laughing because it doesn't matter.

There is a proud humility about my countrymen that few people have yet realized. It is the outcome of nursery days and public schools. No one is allowed to think much of himself in either place, so when he dies, "It doesn't matter."

God help the boys! If they only knew how much it mattered to us! Life is over for them. We don't even know for certain that they will live again.

But their spirit, as I know it, can never die. I am not sure about the survival of personality. I care, but I do not know. But I do know that by these simple, glorious, uncomplaining deaths, some higher, purer, more splendid place is reached, some release is found from the heavy weight of foolish, sticky, burdensome, contemptible things.

These heroes do "rise," and we "rise" with them. Could Christ himself desire a better resurrection?

May 28:
Larks

I am busy getting things prepared for going home—my lecture, two articles, etc. I did not go to the station today, but worked until 3 o'clock. I then walked over to St. Idesbald, a hamlet along the North Sea. How I wish I could have been outdoors more since I came here. It is such a wonderful country, all sky. No wonder there are painters in Belgium.

During the winter it was too wet to see much, and I was always in the kitchen. But now I could kiss the very ground with the little roses on it among the dunes. Larks and nightingales sing at St. Idesbald. Some fine night I mean to walk out there and listen.

"A bird perched on the fuse of a German shell along the Western Front," by unknown in *The Sketch*, (Aug. 11, 1915).

May 29:
The Grave of a City

Today, as promised, Mr. Bevan took me into Nieuport. It was very difficult to get permission to go there, but Mr. Bevan got it from the British Mission on the plea that I was going to give lectures at home.

"The worst of going to Nieuport," said Major Tyrell, "is that you won't be likely to see home again."

Mr. Bevan called at 10 o'clock with the faithful MacEwan. First we went to the Cabour hospital, which I always like so much, and where the large grounds make things healthy and quiet for the patients. Then we had a tire problem and had to go to Dunkirk, where I met Mr. Sarrel and his friend Charles Hanson, Vice-Consul at Constantinople. They lunched with us while the car was being repaired.

"View (left) from British airplane of German positions in clearly defined trenches near Ypres, Belgium, with a similar scene of same positions soon after British bombardment," *The Illustrated War News* (July 12, 1916). According to the official account: "The whole place had become a mass of craters some 15 feet deep in which it is impossible to recognize the former features of the ground."

At last, we started towards Nieuport. Before we got there we found a car in a ditch, and its owner with a cut on his head and his arm broken. So we had to pick him up and take him to Coxide. It was a clear, bright day with all the trees swishing the sky. Mr. Bevan and MacEwan did nothing all the time, but tell me how dangerous it was. They pointed out every place on the road where they had picked up dead men or found people blown to pieces. This was lively for me. The amusing part of it was that I think they did it from a belated sense of responsibility.

It is as difficult to find words to describe Nieuport as it is to talk of metaphysics in slang. The words don't seem invented to convey that haunting sense of desolation, that supreme quiet under the shock of continually firing guns. Hardly anything is left now of the little homely bits that, when I saw the place last autumn, reminded you this was once a city of living human beings. Then I saw a few interiors—exposed, it is true, and damaged, but still of this world. Now it is one big grave, the grave of a city, and the grave of many of its inhabitants. Here, at a corner house, nine ladies lie under the piled-up debris that once made their home. There some soldiers met their death, and some crumbling bricks are heaped over them too. The houses are all fallen—some outer walls remain, but I hardly saw a roof left. Everywhere there are empty window frames and skeleton rafters.

I never knew so surely that a town can live and can die, and it gets you wondering whether life means a thing as a whole and death simply disintegration. A perfect crystal, chemists tell us, has the elements of life in it and may be said to live. Destruction and decay mean death. Separation and disintegration mean death. In this way we die, a crystal dies, a flower or a city dies.

Nieuport is dead. There isn't a heartbeat left to throb in it. Thousands and thousands of shells have fallen into it. At night the nightingale sings there, and by day the river flows gently under the ruined bridge. Every tree in a wood nearby is torn and beheaded; hardly one has the top remaining.

The new green pushes out among the blackened trunks. You speak low in Nieuport, the place is so horribly dead.

Mr. Bevan showed me a shell hole 42 feet across that was made by one single "soixante-quinze" [75] shell. Every field is pitted with holes. Where there are stretches of pale-colored mud, the round pits dotted all over it gives you the impression of an immense Gruyère cheese. The streets (heaped with debris and with houses fallen helplessly forward into their midst) were full of sunshine. From ruined cottages—whose insecure walls tottered—you saw here and there some Zouaves or a little French *"marin"* appear. Most of these ran out with letters in their hands for us to mail. Heaven knows what they can have to write about from that grave!

Some beautiful pillars of the cathedral still stand. The tower, full of holes, has not yet bent its head. Lieutenant Shoppe, of the Royal Navy, sits up there all day and takes observations, with the shells knocking gaily against the walls. One day the tower will fall or its stones will be pierced, and then Lieutenant Shoppe will be killed, as the Belgian *"observateur"* was killed at Oostkerke the other day. He still hangs there across a beam for all the world to see. His arms are stretched out and his body lays head downwards. No one can go near the dead Belgian because the tower is too unsafe now. One day perhaps it will fall altogether and bury him.

Meanwhile at Nieuport, in the tower of the ruined cathedral sits Shoppe in his shirtsleeves, with his telephone beside him and his observation instruments. His small staff is with him. They are immensely interested in the range of a gun and the accuracy of a hit. I believe they think of nothing else. No doubt the tower shakes a great deal when a shell hits it, and no doubt the number of holes in its sides is daily becoming more numerous. Each morning that Shoppe leaves home to spend his day in the tower he runs an excellent chance of being killed. And in the evening he returns and eats a good dinner in rather an uncomfortable hotel.

"Destruction of an avenue of trees in France on the Western Front," by unknown in *The Illustrated War News* (April 4, 1917).

In the cathedral, and among its crumbling battered aisles, a strange peace rests. The pitiful columns of the church stand here and there. The roof has long since gone. On its most sheltered side is the little graveyard, filled with crosses, where the dead lie. Here and there a shell has entered and torn a corpse from its resting place and bones lie scattered. On other graves a few simple flowers are laid.

We went to see the dim cellars forming the two *"postes au secours"* [places for assistance]. In the inner recess of one a doctor has a bed, in the outer cave some soldiers were eating food. There is no light even during the day except from the doorway. At Nieuport, the Germans put in 3,000 shells in one day. Nothing is left. If there ever was anything to loot, it has been looted. You don't know what lies under the debris. Here you see the inside of a piano and a few twisted strings, and there a metal umbrella stand. I saw one wrought-iron sign hanging from the falling walls of an inn.

Mr. Bevan and I wandered around in the unearthly quiet, which persisted even when the guns began to blaze away close by us, whizzing shells over our heads. We walked down to the river and saw the few boards remaining of the bridge. Afterwards a German shell landed with its unpleasant noise in the middle of the street, but we had wandered up a byway and so escaped it by a minute or less.

In a little burned house, where only a piece of blackened wall remained, I found a little crucifix which impressed me very much—it stood out against the smoke-stained walls with a sort of grandeur of pity about it. The legs had been shot away or burned, but "the hands were stretched out still."

As we came away, firing began all round about. We saw the toss of smoke as the shells fell.

May 31:
Nightingales

We went to Steenkerque yesterday. We called on Mrs. Knocker and saw a terrible infirmary, which must be put right. It isn't fit for dogs. At the station today our poor Irishman died. Ah, it was terrible! His lungs never recovered from the gas, and he breathed his last difficult breath at 5 o'clock. In the evening, a Zeppelin flew overhead on its way to England.

There is a nightingale in a wood near here. He seems to sing louder and more purely the heavier the fighting that is going on. When men are murdering each other, he loses himself in a rapture of song, recalling all the old joyous things I used to know.

The poetry of life seems to be over. The war songs are forced and foolish. There is no time for reading, and no one looks at pictures, but the nightingale sings on—and the long-ago spirit of youth looks out through time's strong bars and speaks of evenings in old, dim woods at home, and of girlish, splendid drives home from some dance where "he" was, when we watched the dawn break, and saw our mother sleeping in the carriage, and wondered what it would be like not to "thrill" all the time, and to sleep when the nightingale was singing.

Later there came the time when the song of the throbbing nightingale made you impatient because it sang in intolerable silence. You ached for the roar of things and for the clash of endeavor and strain of purpose. Peace was at a discount then, and struggle seemed to be the eternal good. The silent woods had word for you, the nightingale was only a mate singing a love song, and you wanted something more than that.

And afterwards, when the struggle and the strain were given to you in abundant measure, the song of the nightingale came in the lulls that occurred in your busy life. You grew to connect it with coffee out on the lawn in some houses of surpassing comfort, where (years and years ago) you dressed for dinner, and a crinkly housemaid brought hot water to your room. The song went on above the smug comfort of things, and the amusing conversation, and the smell of good cigars. Within we saw some pleasant drawing room with lamps and a big table set with candles and cards. We felt the nightingale provided a very charming orchestra. We listened to it as we listened to amusing conversation, with a sense of comfortable enjoyment and rest. Why talk of the time when it sang of breaking hearts and high endeavor never satisfied, and things which no one ever knew or guessed except yourself?

It sings now above the sound of death and of tears. Sometimes I think to myself that God has sent his angel to open the prison doors when I hear that bird in the little wood close beside the tramway line.

On Thursday, June 3, I drove in the "bug" to Boulogne and took the steamer to England. I went through a nasty time in Belgium, but now a good deal of strange affection is shown to me, and I believe they all really like me in the corps.

"Pile of human bones in a ghastly memento of the Battle of Verdun," by unknown (1916). Courtesy the Library of Congress.

[NOTE: Sarah saved the following article from an unknown newspaper that described her work in soup kitchens in Belgium and sent it home to a friend in England.]

"It was dark when my car stopped at the little station of Adinkerke, where I had been invited to visit a soup kitchen established there by a Scotchwoman

[Macnaughtan]. In peace she is a distinguished author; in war she is being a mother to such of the Belgian Army as are lucky enough to pass her way. I can see her now, against a background of big soup boilers and cooking-stoves, handing out woolen gloves and mufflers to the men who were to be on sentry duty along the line that night. It was bitterly cold, and the comforts were gratefully received.

"For a long time this most versatile lady made every drop of the soup that was prepared for the men herself, and she has, so a Belgian military doctor says, saved more lives than he has with her timely cups of hot, nourishing food.

"It is only the most seriously wounded men who are taken to the field hospital, the others are carried straight to the railway station, and have to wait there, sometimes for many hours, until a train can take them on. Even then trains carrying the wounded have constantly to be shunted to let troop trains through.

"But, thanks to the enterprise and hard work of this clever little lady, there is always a plentiful supply of hot food ready for the men who, weak from loss of blood, are often besides faint with hunger."

Chapter 9
Britain: At Home

"Victoria District railway station," by Bernard Meninsky, who served with the Royal Fusiliers in Palestine until he was commissioned as a war artist to create this for the British Ministry of Information (1918). Courtesy Wikimedia Commons.

October 1915:

Former Things

So much has happened since I came home from Flanders in June. I have not had one moment in which to write of it. I found my house occupied when I returned, so I went to the St. Petersburg Hotel and stayed there, going out of London for Sundays.

Everyone I met in England seemed absorbed in pale children with adenoids. No one cared much about the war. Children in houses nowadays require food at weird hours, not roast mutton and a good plain Christian pudding, but, "You will excuse our beginning, I know, dear, Jane has to have her massage after lunch, and Tom has to do his exercises, and baby has to learn to breathe." This one has its ears strapped, and that you are "nervous" and must be "understood."

"British World War I recruitment poster," by unknown (1915). Courtesy the Library of Congress.

Nothing is talked of but children. My mother would never have a doctor in the house; "nervousness" was called bad temper and was gotten rid of, while stooping was called "a trick" and smacked. The children I now see eat far too much, and when they finish lunch with gravy drunk out of tumblers it makes me feel very unwell.

I went to the Breitmeyers, at Rushton Hall, Kettering. It's a fine place, but I was too tired to enjoy anything but a bed. The next Sunday I stayed at Chenies, with the Louise, the Duchess of Bedford—always a favorite resort of mine. Another week I went to Welwyn.

I met a few old men at these places, but no one else. Everyone is at the front. The houses generally have wounded soldiers in them, who play croquet with a nurse on the lawn, or smoke in the sun. None of them want to go back to fight. They seem tired and talk of the trenches as *"proper 'ell."*

There is always a little too much walking around at a "weekend." You feel tired and stiff on Monday. I well remember last summer having to take people three times to a distant water garden—talking all the time, too! People are so kind in making it pleasant that they wear you out.

All the time I was in London, I was preparing my campaign of lecturing. I began with Vickers-Maxim works at Erith, on Wednesday, June 9. On the 8th, I went to stay with the Cameron-Heads. There was great bustle and preparation for my lecture. Press people in the house at all hours of the day, and so on. A great bore for my poor friends, but they were so good about it, and I loved being with them.

The lecture was a red-letter occasion for me, everyone praising, the Press very attentive, etc., etc. The audience promised well for future things, and the emotion that was stirred nearly bowled myself over. In some of the hushes that came you could hear men crying. The Scott-Gattys and a few of my own friends came to "stand by," and we all drove down to Erith in cars and returned to supper with the Vickers at 10:30.

The next day old Vickers sent for me and asked me to name my own price for my lectures, but I couldn't mix money up with the message. So I refused all pay and am happy I did so. I can't and won't profit by this war. I'd rather lose—I am losing—but that doesn't matter. Nothing matters much now. The former things are swept away, and all the old barriers are disappearing. Our old gods of possession and wealth are crumbling. Class distinctions don't count. Even life and death are pretty much the same thing.

The Jews say the Messiah will come after the war. I think He is here already—but on a cross as of yore!

I went up to Glasgow to make arrangements there, and my task wasn't an easy one. Somehow I knew I must speak, that I must arouse slackers, and tell rotters about what is going on. You go forth (led in a way) and only then do you realize you are going in unasked to shipbuilding yards and munitions sheds and docks, and that you are quite a small woman, alone, and up against a big thing.

"British Parliamentary Recruiting Committee poster," by unknown (1915). Courtesy the Library of Congress.

Always the answer I got was the same: "The men are not working; 40% are slackers. The output of shells is not what it ought to be, but they won't listen!"

In the face of this I arranged 7 meetings in 7 days to take place early in August. Then I went back to give my lecture in the Queen's Hall, London. I took the large hall because if you have a message to deliver, you had better deliver it to as many people as possible. It was rather a breathless undertaking, but people turned up splendidly, and I had a full house. Sir Francis Lloyd gave me the band of the Coldstream Guards, and things went with a good swing.

I am still wondering how I did it. The whole "campaign" has already got rather an unreal atmosphere about it. Often, after crowded meetings, I have come home and lain in the dark and have seen nothing but a sea of faces, and eyes all turned my way. It has been a most curious and unexpected experience. But England did not realize the war, and she did not realize the wave of heroism sweeping over the world, and I had to tell about it.

Well, my lectures went on—Erith, Queen's Hall, Sheffield (a splendid meeting, 3,000 people inside the hall and 300 turned away at the door!), Barrow-in-Furness. I gave two lectures at Barrow, at 3 p.m. and 7:30. They seemed very popular. In the evening quite a demonstration—pipe band playing "Auld lang syne," and much cheering. After that Newcastle, and back to the south again to speak there. Everywhere I took my image projector and showed my pictures. I told "good stories" to attract people to the meetings although my heart was, and is, nearly breaking all the time.

Then I began the Glasgow campaign—Parkhead, Whiteinch, Rosebank, Dumbarton, Greenock, Beardmore's, Denny's, Armour's, etc., etc. Everywhere there were big audiences. Although I would have spoken to two listeners gladly, I was still gladder to see the halls filled. The cheers of workmen when they are really roused just get me by the throat until I can't speak for a minute or two!

At one place, I spoke from a truck during the dinner hour. All the men, with blackened faces, crowded round the car. Others swung from the iron girders, while some perched, like queer bronze images, on pieces of machinery. They were all very intent, and very polite and courteous, no interruptions at any of the meetings. A great interest was shown in the war pictures, and the cheers were deafening sometimes.

After Glasgow, I went to dear Clemmie Waring's at Lennel and found her house full of convalescent officers. She herself very happy with them and her new baby. I really wanted to rest, and meant to enjoy five days of repose; but I gave a lecture the first night. Then I had a sort of breakdown and took to my bed. However, that had to be gotten over, and I went down to Wales at the end of the week. The Butes gave me their own rooms at Cardiff Castle, and a nice housekeeper looked after me.

There followed a strange fortnight in that ugly old fortress, with its fine stonework and the execrable decorations covering every inch of it. The days passed oddly. I did a little writing, and I saw my committee, whom I like. Colonel Dennis is an excellent fellow, and so are Mr. Needle, Vivian Reece, and Mr. Harrison. Mr. Howse acted as secretary.

The first day I gave a dock-gate meeting, and spoke from a truck. That night I had my great meeting at Cardiff. Sir Frank Younghusband [a British Army officer and explorer] came down for it, and the mayor took the chair. The audience was enthusiastic, and every place was filled. At one moment they all rose to their feet, and holding up their hands swore to fight for the right until right was won. It was one of the scenes I shall always remember.

Everyday after that, I used to have tea and an egg at 5 o'clock, and a vehicle would come with one of my committees to take me to different places of meeting. It was generally up the Rhondda Valley that we went. I came to know well that westward drive, with the sun setting behind the hills and turning the Taff river to gold.

Every night, we went a little further and a little higher—Aberdare, Aberystwyth, Tonypandy, Tonepentre, etc. I gave 14 lectures in 13 days. Generally, I spoke in chapels and from the pulpit. This seemed to give me the chance I wanted to speak all my mind to these people, and to ask them and teach them what power, and possession, and freedom really meant. Oh, it was wonderful! The rapt faces of the miners, the hush of the big buildings, and then the sudden burst of cheering!

At one meeting there was a proud-looking man, with a bald head, whom I remember. He took up his position just over the clock in the gallery. He listened critically, talked a good deal, and made remarks. I began to speak straight at him, without looking at him, and quite suddenly I saw him, as I spoke of our men at the war, cover his face and burst into tears.

The children were the only drawback. They were attracted by the idea of the image projector and used to come to the meetings and keep older people out.

My lectures were not meant for children. I had to adopt the plan of showing the pictures first, then telling the youngsters to go, and settling down to a talk with the older ones, who always remained behind voluntarily.

"British Parliamentary Recruiting Committee poster of women," by unknown (1915). Courtesy the Library of Congress.

We had some times which I can never forget. Nor can I forget those dark drives from far up in the hills, and the mists in the valley, and my own aching fatigue as I got back about midnight. From 5 p.m. until 12.30 a.m. every night I was on the stretch. During the daytime, I used to wander round the garden. You always meet someone you know. I had lunch with the Tylers one day, and tea with the Plymouths. It was still, bright autumn weather. The trees were gold in the ugly garden with the black river running through it. I got a few lessons in driving, and I spoke at the hospital one afternoon. I took the opportunity of getting a dress made at a good tailor's, and time passed in a manner quite solitary until the evenings.

Never before have I spent a year of so much solitude, and yet I have been with people during my work. I think I know now what thousands of men and women living alone and working are feeling. I wish I could help them. There won't be many young marriages now. What are we to do for girls all alone?

Aug. 31, 1915
To Mrs. Keays-Young
Cardiff Castle, Cardiff

Dearest Baby,

Many thanks for your letter, which I got on my way through London. I spent one night there to see about some work I am having done in the house.

I have a drawer full of press clippings, and I do not know what is in any of them. It is difficult to choose anything of interest, as they are all a good deal alike, and all sound my trumpet very loudly; but I enclose one specimen.

We had meetings every night in Glasgow. They were mostly badly organized and well attended. Here I have an agent arranging everything, and two of my meetings have been enormous. The first was at the dock-gates in the open air, and the second in the Town Hall. The band of the Welch Regiment played, and Mr. Glover conducted, but nothing is the same, of course. Alan is at Porthcawl, and came to see me this morning.

The war news could hardly be worse, and yet I am told by men who get sealed information from the Foreign Office that worse is coming.

Poor Russia! She wants help more than anyone. Her wounded are quite untended. I go there next month.

The King of the Belgians has made me Chevalier de l'Ordre de Léopold.

Love to all.
Yours ever,
S.

"Shop for machining 15-inch shells at the Singer Manufacturing Co. in Clydebank, Glasgow," by Anna Airy (1918). Courtesy Wikimedia Commons.

Newspaper clip, below, was enclosed with Sarah's letter.

"STORIES OF THE WAR"

CARDIFF LECTURE BY MISS MACNAUGHTAN

AUTHORESS'S APPEAL

TESTING-TIME OF NATIONAL CHARACTER

A large and enthusiastic audience assembled at the Park-hall, Cardiff, on Monday evening, to hear and see Miss Macnaughtan's "Stories and Pictures of the War." Miss Macnaughtan is a well-known authoress, whose works have attained a worldwide reputation, and, in addition to her travels in almost every corner of the globe, she has had actual experience of warfare at the bombardment of Rio, in the Balkans, the South African War, and, since September last, in Belgium and Flanders. In her capacity as ministrant to wounded soldiers she has gained a unique experience of the horrors of war, and to bring home the realities of the situation, at the instigation of Lady Bute, she consented to address a number of meetings in South Wales.

At the meeting on Monday night the Lord Mayor (Alderman J.T. Richards) presided, and in introducing Miss Macnaughtan to the audience announced that for her services in Belgium the honor of the Order of Leopold had been conferred upon her. (Applause.) We were engaged, he said, in fighting a war of right. We were not fighting only for the interests of England and our Empire, but we were fighting for the interests of humanity at large. ("Hear, hear.")

Miss Macnaughtan, in the course of her address, referred to the origin of the war, and how suddenly it came upon the people of this nation, who were, for the most part, engaged in summer holidays at the time. She knew what was going on at the front, and knew what the Welch Regiment had been doing, and "I must tell you," she added, "of the splendid way in which your regiment has behaved, and how proud Cardiff must be of it." We knew very well now that this war had been arranged by Germany for many years. The Germans used to profess exceeding kindness to us, and were received on excellent terms by our Royal House, but the veil was drawn away from that nation's face, and we had it revealed as an implacable foe. The Germans had spoken for years in their own country about "The Day," and now "The Day" had arrived, and it was for everyone a day of judgment, because it was a test of character. We had to put ourselves to the test. We knew that for some time England had not been at her best. Her great heart was beating true all the time, but there had crept into England a sort of national coldness and selfishness, and a great deal too much seriousness in the matter of money and money getting. Although this was discounted in great measure by her generosity, we appeared to the world at large as a greedy and money-getting nation.

However this might be, in all parts of the world the word of an Englishman was still as good as his bond. ("Hear, hear.")

Yet England, with its strikes and quarrels and class hatred, and one thing and another, was not at its best. It was well to admit that, just as they admitted the faults of those they loved best.

Had any one of them failed to rally round the flag? Had they kept anything back in this great war? She hoped not. The war had tested us more than anything else, and we had responded greatly to it; and the young manhood had come out in a way that was remarkable. We knew very well that when the war was begun we were quite unprepared for it; but she would tell them this, that our army, although small, was the finest army that ever took the field. (Applause.)

Miss Macnaughtan then related a number of interesting incidents, one of which was, that when a party of wounded Englishmen came to a station where she was tending the Belgian wounded, every wounded Belgian gave up his bed to accommodate an English soldier. The idea of a German occupation of English soil, she said, was the idea of a catastrophe that was unspeakable. People read things in the papers and thought they were exaggerated, but she had seen them, and she would show photographs of ruined Belgium which would convince them of what the Germans were now doing in the name of God. However unprepared we were for war, the wounded had been well cared for, and she thought there never was a war in which the care of the wounded had been so well managed or so efficient. (Applause.)

They had to be thankful that there had been no terrible epidemic, and she could not speak too highly of the work of the nurses and doctors in the performance of their duties. This was the time for every man to do his duty, and strain every nerve and muscle to bring the war to an end and get the boys home again. (Applause.)

Sir Francis Younghusband, K.C.I.E., spoke of Miss Macnaughtan as a very old friend, whom he had met in many parts of the Empire. In this crisis she might well have stayed at home in her comfortable residence in London, but she had sacrificed her own personal comforts in order to assist others. They must realize that this war was something much more than a war of defense of their homes. It was a fight on behalf of the whole of humanity. A staggering blow had been dealt by our relentless enemy at Belgium, which had been knocked down and trampled upon, and Germany had also dealt blow after blow at humanity by the use of poison gas, the bombardment of seaside towns, and bombs thrown on defenseless places by Zeppelins. She had thrust aside all those rights of humanity which we had cherished as a nation as most dear to our hearts. What we were now fighting for was right, and he would put to them a resolution that we would fight for right until right had won. In response to an appeal for the endorsement of his sentiments the audience stood en masse, and with upraised hands shouted "Aye." It was a stirring moment, and must have been gratifying to the authoress, who has devoted so much of her time and energy to the comfort of the wounded soldiers.

The Lord Mayor then proposed a vote of thanks to Miss Macnaughtan for her address, and this was carried by acclamation.

Miss Macnaughtan briefly responded, and then proceeded to illustrate many of the scenes she had witnessed by slides, showing the results of bombardments and the ruin of some of the fairest domains of Belgium and France.

"British Parliamentary Recruiting Committee," by unknown (1917). Courtesy the Library of Congress.

The provision of stewards was arranged by the Cardiff Chamber of Trade, under the direction of the President (Mr. G. Clarry). During the evening the band of the 3rd Welch Regiment, under the conductorship of Bandmaster K.S. Glover, gave selections.

A statement having been made that Miss Macnaughtan was the first to discover a remedy for the poison gas used by the Germans, a Western Mail reporter interviewed the lady before the lecture on her experiences in this direction. She replied, that when the first batch of men came in from the trenches suffering from the effects of the gas, the first thing they asked was for something to drink, to take the horrible taste out of their mouths. She obtained a couple of bottles of whisky from the barge of an American lady, and some distilled water, and gave this to the soldiers, who appeared to be greatly relieved. Whenever possible, she had adopted the same course, but she was unaware that the remedy had been applied by the military authorities. Even this method of relieving their sufferings, however, was rejected by a large number of young soldiers, on the ground that they were teetotalers, but the Belgian doctors had permitted its use among their men.

SHOULD THE GERMANS COME
FORETASTE OF HORRORS FURNISHED BY BELGIUM

During the dinner hour Miss Macnaughtan gave an address to workmen at the Bute Docks. An improvised platform was arranged at the back of the Seamen's Institute, and some hundreds of men gathered to hear the story that Miss Macnaughtan had to give of the war.

Colonel C.S. Denniss presided, and among those present were Messrs. T. Vivian Rees, John Andrews, W. Cocks, A. Hope, S. Fisher, and Robinson Smith. Colonel Denniss, in a few introductory remarks, referred to Miss Macnaughtan's reputation as a writer, and stated that since the outbreak of war she had devoted herself to the noble work of helping the wounded soldiers in Belgium and France. She had come to Cardiff to tell the working-men what she had seen, with the object, if possible, of stimulating them to help forward the great cause we were fighting for.

Miss Macnaughtan said she had been speaking in many parts of the country, but she was especially proud to address a meeting of Welsh workingmen. Besides coming of a long line of Welsh ancestors, her brother-in-law, Colonel Young, was in command of the 9th Welch Battalion at the front, and she had also four nephews serving in the Welch Regiment. Only the day before Colonel Young had written to her: "The Welshman is the most intensely patriotic man that I know, and it is always the same thing, 'stick it, Welch.' His patriotism is splendid, and I do not want to fight with a better man." Miss Macnaughtan then explained that she was not asking for funds, and was not speaking for employers or owners. She simply wished to tell them her experiences of the war as she had seen it, and to describe the heroism, which was going on at the front. If they looked at the war from the point of view of men going out to kill each other they had a wrong conception of what was going on. She had been asked to speak of the conditions which might prevail should the Germans reach this country. She did not feel competent to speak on that subject, as the whole idea of Germans in this country seemed absolutely inconceivable. If the Germans were to land on our shores all the waters that surrounded this isle would not wash the land clean. She knew what the Germans were, and had seen the wreck they had made of Belgium and part of France. She knew what the women and children had suffered, and how the churches had been desecrated and demolished. It was said that this was a war of humanity, but she believed it was a war of right against wrong; and if she were asked when the war would finish, she could only say that we would fight it right to the end until we were victorious.

The Germans were beaten already, and had been beaten from the day they gave up their honor. She spoke of the heroism of the troops, and stated that since September last she had been running a soup kitchen for the wounded. In this humble vocation she had had an opportunity of gauging the spirit of the soldiers. She had seen them sick, wounded, and dying, but had never known them give in. Why should humble villages in France without soldiers in them be shelled? That was Germany, and that was what they saw. The thing was almost inconceivable, but she had seen helpless women and children brought to the hospitals, maimed and wounded by the cruel German shells. After this war England was going to be a better country than before. Up to now there had been a national selfishness, which was growing very strong, and there was a terrible love of money, which, after all, was of very little account unless it was used in the proper direction. She could tell them stories of Belgians who had had to fire upon their own women and children who were being marched in front of German troops. The power of Germany had to be crushed. The spirit of England and Wales was one in this Great War, and they would not falter until they had emerged triumphant. (Applause.)

Mr. Robinson Smith said the clarion call had been sounded, and they were prepared, if necessary, to give their last shilling, their last drop of blood, and their very selves, body, soul, and spirit, to fight for right until right had won. (Applause.)

Cheers were given for the distinguished authoress, and the proceedings terminated.

Mid-October 1915:

After Cardiff (and a most cordial send off from my committee) I came back to London, and lectured at Eton, at the Polytechnic, and various other places, while all the time I was preparing to go to Russia, and I was also writing.

In the year that has passed, my time has been fully occupied. To begin with, when the war broke out I studied district nursing in Walworth for a month. I attended committees and arranged to go to Belgium, got my kit, and had a good deal of business to arrange in the way of house-letting, etc.

"U.S. Army military intelligence photo of Ypres, Belgium," by W.L. King (1919). Courtesy the Library of Congress.

Afterwards, I went to Antwerp, until the siege and the bombardment; then followed the flight to Ostend; after that a further flight to Furnes. Then came the winter of my work, day and night at the soup kitchen for the wounded, a few days at home in January, then back again and to work at Adinkerke until June, when I came home to lecture.

During the year, I have brought out four books, I have given 35 lectures, and written both stories and articles. I have gone from town to town in England, Scotland, and Wales. I have had a good deal of anxiety and much business at home. I have paid a few visits, but not restful ones. I have written all my own correspondence since I have not secretary. I collected funds for my work and sent off scores of begging letters. Often I have begun work at 5:30 a.m., and I have not rested all day. As I am not very young this seems to me a pretty strenuous time!

Now I have rented my house again and am off "into the unknown" in Russia! I shouldn't really mind a few days' rest before we begin any definite work. Behind everyone I suppose at this time lurks the horror of war, the deadly fear for your dearest; and, above all, you feel—at least I do—that you are always, and quite palpably, in the shadow of the death of youth—beautiful youth, happy and healthy and free.

Always I seem to see the white faces of boys turned up to the sky. I hear their cries and see the agony which joyous youth was never meant to bear. They are too young for it, far too young. But they lie out on the field between the trenches, and bite the mud in their frenzy of pain; and they call for their mothers, and no one comes, and they call to their friends, but no one hears. There is a roar of battle and of bursting shells. Who can listen to a boy's groans and his shrieks of pain? This is war.

A nation or a people want more seaboard or more trade, so they begin to kill youth, and to torture and to burn, and God himself may ask, "Where is my beautiful flock?"

No one answers. It is war. We must expect a "list of casualties."

"The Germans have lost more than we have done."

"We must go on, even if the war lasts 10 years."

"A million more men are needed."

Thus the fools called men talk! But youth looks up with haggard eyes, and youth, grown old, learns that death alone is merciful.

You see even in soldiers' jokes that the thought of death is not far off. I said to one man, "You have had a narrow squeak."

He replied: "I don't mind if I get there first so long as I can stoke up for those Germans."

Another, clasping the hand of his dead captain, said, "Put plenty of sandbags round heaven, sir, and don't let a German through."

The other day, when the forward movement was made in France and Belgium, Charles's Regiment, the 9th Welch, was told to attack at a certain point, which could only be reached across an open space raked by machine-gun fire.

"Parliamentary Recruiting Committee," by Henry Jenkinson Ltd., (1915). Courtesy the Library of Congress.

They were not given the order to move for 12 days, during which time the men hardly slept. When the charge had to be made, the roar of guns made speaking quite impossible, so directions were given by sending up rockets. When the rockets appeared, not a single man delayed an instant in making the attack. One young officer, in the trench where Charles was, had a football and flung it over the parapet, and shouting, "Come on, boys!" He and the men of the regiment played football in the open and in front of the guns. Right across the gun-raked level they kicked the ball, and when they reached the enemy's lines only a few of them were left.

Charles wrote, "I am too old to see boys killed."

Colonel Walton, with a handful of his regiment, was the only officer to get through the three lines of the enemy's trenches. He and his men dug themselves in. Just in front of them where they paused, he saw a fine young officer come along the road on a bicycle, carrying dispatches. The next minute a high-explosive shell burst, and, to use his own words: "There was not enough of the young officer to put on a three penny bit."

"British infantry men from the Worcester Regiment Going into Action," (circa 1914 to 1918). Courtesy the Library of Congress.

Always men tell me there is nothing left to bury. One minute there is a splendid piece of upstanding, vigorous manhood, and the next there is no finding one piece of him to lay in the sod.

The Turks seem to have forsaken their first horrible and devilish cruelties towards English prisoners. They have been taught a lesson by the Australians, who took some prisoners up to the top of a ridge and rolled them down into the Turks' trenches like balls, firing on them as they rolled. Horrible, but after that Turkish cruelties ceased.

We "censor" this or that in the newspapers, but nothing will censor men's tongues, and there is a terrible and awful tale of suffering and death and savagery going on now.

Like a ghastly dream we hear of trenches taken, and the cries of men go up, "Mercy, comrade, mercy!" Sometimes they plead, poor caught and trapped and pitiful human beings, that they have wives and children who love them.

The slaughter goes on, the bayonet rends open the poor body that someone loved, then comes the internal gush of blood, and another carcass is flung into the burying trench, with some lime on the top of it to prevent a smell of rotting flesh.

"French soldiers prepare to leave trench just before zero hour attack," by Keystone View Co. (circa 1914 to 1918). Courtesy the Library of Congress.

My God, what does it all mean? Are men so mad? And why are they killing all our best and bravest?

Our first army is gone, and surely such a company never before took the field! Outmatched by 20 to 1, they stuck it at Mons and on the Aisne, and saved Paris by a miracle.

All my old friends fell then—men near my own age, whom I have known in many climes—Eustace Crawley, Victor Brooke, the Goughs, and other splendid men.

Now the sons of my friends are falling fast—Duncan Sim's boy, young Wilson, Neville Strutt, and scores of others. I know one case in which four brothers have fallen; another, where twins of 19 died side by side; and this one has his eyes blown out, and that one has his leg torn off, and another goes mad; and boys, creeping back to the base holding an arm on, or bewildered by a bullet through the brain, wander out of their way until a piece of shrapnel or torn edge of shell finds them, and they fall again, with their poor boyish faces buried in the mud!

Mr. ___ dined with us last night. He had been talking of his brother who was killed, and he said: "I think it makes a difference if you belong to a family which has always given its lives to the country. We are accustomed to make these sacrifices."

Thus, bravely in the light of day. But when evening came and we sat together, then we knew just what the life of the boy had cost him. They tell us—these defrauded broken-hearted ones—just how tall the lad was, and how good to look at! That seems to me so sad—as if you reckoned your love by inches! And yet it is the beauty of youth I mourn also and its horribly lonely death.

"They never got him further than the dressing station," Mr. ___ said, "but, he would always put up a fight, you know. He lived for four days. No, there was never any hope. Half the back of his head was shattered. But he put up a fight. My brother would always do that."

Chapter 10
1915: The Eastern Front
BY NOËL FLETCHER

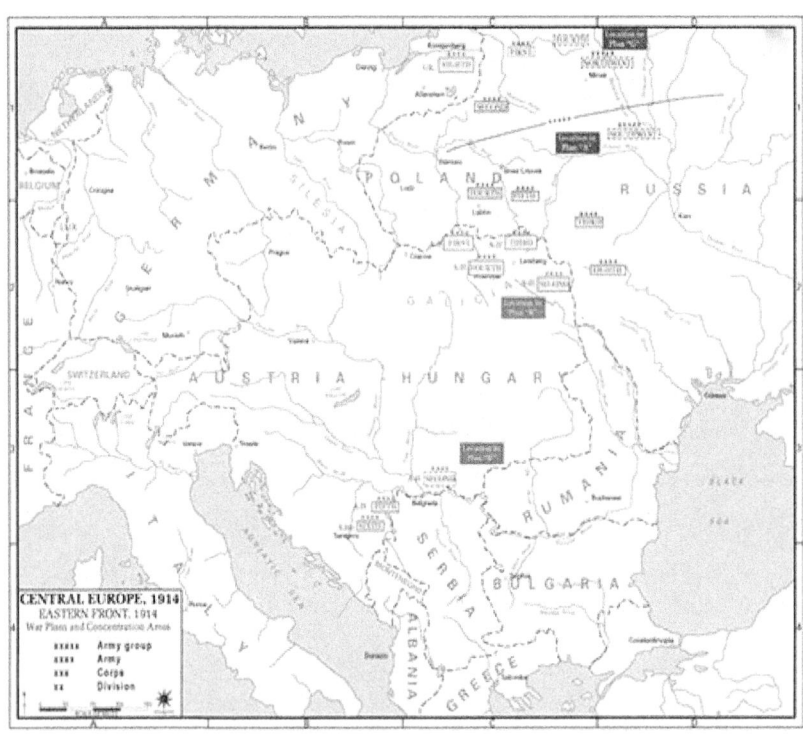

"Map of the Eastern Front in 1914," by History Department of the US Military Academy West Point. Courtesy Wikimedia Commons.

Unlike the trench warfare in the Western Front, military operations in the Eastern Front spanned vast territories flanked on one side by Romania and Russia. The other side bordered Bulgaria, Austria-Hungary and Germany.

Germany had declared war in July 1914 on Russia. One month later, Austria-Hungary's declared war on Russia, which had pledged to protect Serbia from Austrian invasion. At the outbreak of war, Russia's Imperial military was 4.1 million strong in reservists and volunteers. It was led by Czar Nicholas II.

"Bulgarians burying dead after battle in Turkey," by Bain News Service (circa 1915). Courtesy the Library of Congress.

In 1915, Germany concentrated efforts in the Eastern Front against Russian. That year also witnessed the expansion of international hostilities among various nations:

- May 23: Italy declared war on Austria-Hungary.
- June 3: San Marino declared war on Austria-Hungary.
- August 20: Italy declared war on Turkey.
- October 14: Bulgaria declared war on Serbia.
- October 15: Britain declared war on Bulgaria.
- October 19: Russia and Italy declared war on Bulgaria.

Chapter 11
St. Petersburg

"Russian Red Cross soldiers," in *Harper's Pictorial Library of the World War*, Vol. II (1920).

May 19, 1915:

Mrs. Wynne, Mr. Bevan, and I left London for Russia on Oct. 16, 1915. We are attached provisionally to the Anglo-Russian hospital, with a stipulation that we are free to proceed to the front with our ambulances as soon as we can get permission. We understand that the Russian wounded are suffering terribly, and getting no doctors, nurses, or field ambulances. We crossed from Newcastle to Christiania in a Norwegian boat, the *S.S. Bessheim*. It was thought that traveling in this ship posed less risk of being stopped, torpedoed, or otherwise inconvenienced.

We reached Christiania after a wonderfully calm crossing, and went to the Grand Hotel at 1 a.m. No rooms were available, so we went to the Victoria—a good old house, not fashionable, but with a nice air about it and some solid comforts.

"British recruiting poster flags (left) of Great Britain, France, Russia, and Belgium," by the British Parliamentary Recruiting Committee (1915). Courtesy the Library of Congress.

We left on Wednesday, Oct. 20, at 7 a.m. This was something of a feat, as we have 24 boxes with us. I only claim four and feel as if I might have brought more, but everyone has a different way of traveling, and luggage is often objected to.

Indeed, I think this matter of traveling is one of the most curious in the world. I cannot understand why it is that to get into a train or a boat causes men and women to forget about restraint and act in a primitive way. Why should the companionship of the open road be the supreme test of friendship? Why should you feel a certain fear of getting to know people too well on a journey? The last friends I traveled with were very careful indeed. We used to add up accounts and divide the price of a bottle of *"vin ordinaire"* [wine] equally. My friends today seem inclined to enjoy themselves and scatter generosity everywhere.

October 21:
A Sojourn in Sweden

After a long day in the train we reached Stockholm yesterday evening and went to the usual "Grand Hotel." This time it is very "grand" and very expensive. Mr. Bevan has a terrible pink boudoir-bedroom, which costs £3 per night. I have a small room without a bath on the 4th floor, which costs 17s. 6d.

"The then-Crown Prince and Princess Margaret of Sweden," by *Bain News Service*. Princess Margaret died in 1920 before her husband, who ascended the throne in 1950. Courtesy the Library of Congress.

There is a nice courtyard in the middle of the house with flowers, a band and tables for dinner, but the sight of everyone enjoying themselves very well always makes me feel a little sick. The wines and liqueurs, and the big cigars at two shillings each, and the look of repletion on men's faces as they listen to the band after being fed, somewhat disgust me.

My instinct is to dislike luxury, but in wartime it seems horrible. We ourselves will probably have to rough out it badly soon, so I don't mind, but it's a side of life that seems to me as beastly as anything I know. Fortunately, the luxury of a hotel is minimized by the fact that there are no "necessaries," and you live in an atmosphere of open trunks and bags, with things pulled out of them, which counterbalances crystal electric fittings and marble floors.

We rested all this morning and ate lunch out. In the afternoon went to have tea with the Crown Prince Gustaf VI Adolf and Princess Margaret of Sweden. They were very delightful.

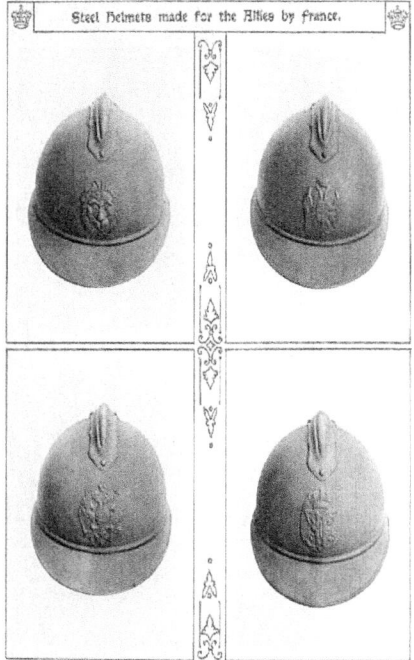

"The Battle Headdress of the Four Armies: Belgian, Serbian, Russian and Romanian (left to right)," in *Illustrated War News* (Dec. 13, 1916). Similar steel helmets were being made in Russia for troops along the Eastern Front. Some 12 million "casque Adrian" helmets, made from 18,000 tons of steel, had been distributed since May 1915.

The British Minister's wife, Lady Isabel Howard, went with us. The Princess had just finished reading my *"Diary of the War,"* and was very nice about it. The children, who came in to tea, were the prettiest little creatures I have ever seen, with curly hair and faces like the watercolor pictures of 100 years ago. The Princess herself is most attractive and reminds you of the pictures of Queen Victoria as a young woman. Her sensitive face is full of expression, and her color comes and goes as she speaks of things that move her.

This afternoon we went to tea at the British Legation with the Howards. The house is charmingly situated on the lake, with lovely trees all about it. It isn't quite finished yet, but will be very delightful.

October 22:

It is very strange to find yourself in a country where war is not going on. The absence of guns and Zeppelins as well as the well-lit streets and the peace of it all are quite striking. But the country is pro-German almost to a man! And it has been a narrow squeak to prevent war. Even now I suppose one wrong move may lead to an outbreak of hostilities, and the recent German victories may yet bring in other countries on her side. Bulgaria has been a glaring instance of siding with the one she considers the winning side, and Greece is still wondering what to do! Thank God, I belong to a race that is full of primitive instincts! Poor old England still barges in whenever there is a fight going on, and gets her head knocked, and goes on fighting just the same, and never knows that she is heroic, but blunders on—simple-hearted, stupid, sublime!

October 24:
Love and Pain

I went to the English church this morning with Lancelot Hugh Smith, but there was no service as the chaplain had chicken pox! So I came home and packed. Then lunched with Eric Hambro, Lancelot Smith, and Mr. __, all rather interesting men at this crisis, when four nations at least are undecided what to do in the matter of the war. [Hambro and Smith were both bankers from the British Delegation in Sweden.]

About 6 o'clock, we and our boxes got away from Stockholm. Our expenses for the few days we spent there were £60, although we had very few meals in the hotel.

We had a long journey to the river town of Haparanda near the Finnish border, where we stopped for a day. The cold was terrible. We spent the day (my birthday) on a sort of luggage barge on the river. On my last birthday we were bolting from Furnes in front of the Germans, and the birthday before that I was on the top of the Rocky Mountains.

Talking of the Rockies reminds me (did I need reminding) of Elsie Northcote, my dear friend, who married and went to live there. The other night some friends of mine gave me a little "send off" before I left London—dinner and the Palace Theatre, where I felt like a ghost returned to earth. All the old lot were there as of yore—Viola Tree [English actress], Lady Diana Manners, Harry Lindsay, the Raymond Asquiths, etc. I saw them all from quite far away. Lord Stanmore was in the box with us, and he it was who told me of Elsie Northcote's sudden death. It wasn't the right place to hear about it. Too many are gone or are going. My own losses are almost stupefying; and something dead within myself looks with sightless eyes on death; with groping hands I touch it sometimes, and then I know that I am dead also.

There is only one thing you can never renounce and that is love. Love is part of you, and can't be given up. Love can't be separated from you, even by death. It comes once and remains always. It is never fulfilled. The fulfillment of love is its crucifixion; but it lives on forever in a passion-week of pain until pain itself grows dull; and then you wish you had been born quite a common little soul, when you would probably have been very happy.

October 28:
Football under Fire

We arrived at midnight last night at St. Petersburg. Ian Malcolm was at the hotel and had remained up to welcome us. Today we have been unpacking and settling down into rather comfortable, very expensive rooms. My little box of a place costs 26 shillings a night.

We lunched with two Russian officers and Ian Malcolm, and then I went to the British Embassy, where the other two joined me.

"Sir George Buchanan, appointed in 1910 as the British ambassador to Russia," by unknown (1915). He was known as a helper of the allied cause in St. Petersburg. Courtesy Wikimedia Commons.

Sir George Buchanan, our Ambassador, looks overworked and tired. His wife, Lady Georgina, and I got on well together.

The day wasn't quite satisfactory, but you must remember an odd spirit is evoked in wartime that is very difficult to analyze. Primarily there is "a right spirit renewed" in every one of us. We want to be among those involved in the great sacrifice which war involves. We offer and present ourselves, our souls and bodies in great causes, only to find there is some strange unexplained quality of resistance meeting us everywhere.

Mary once said to me in her quaint way, "Your duty is to give to the Queen's Fund as becomes your position and to get properly thanked."

This lady-like behavior, combined with check writing on a large scale, is always popular. It can be repeated and again repeated until check writing becomes automatic. Then from nowhere springs a strange class of people you have never heard of before, with skins of invulnerable thickness and with wonderful self-confidence. They claim almost extraordinary powers in matters of "organization" and generally require sympathy for being overworked. For a time their names are on everyone's lips but afterwards you don't hear very much about them. Florence Nightingale would have had no distinction nowadays. It is doubtful if she would have been allowed to work. Some quite inept person in a high position would have intentionally prevented it. Most people are on the offensive against "high-souled work" and prepared to put their foot down heavily on anything so presumptuous as heroism except of the orthodox kind, and even the right kind is often not understood. There is a story I try to tell, but something gets stuck in my throat, and I tell it in spurts as I can.

It is the story of the men who played football across the open between the enemy's line of trenches and our own when it was raked by fire. When I had finished, a friend of mine, evidently waiting for the end of a pointless story, said: "What did they do that for?" (Oh, ye gods, have pity on men and women who suffer from fatty degeneration of the soul!)

Still, in spite of it all, the voice comes, and has to be obeyed.

October 30:
Spies and Slackers

We at lunch at the British Embassy yesterday to meet the Grand Duchess Viktoria Feodorovna. She is a striking-looking woman, tall and strong, and she wore a plain dark blue cloth dress and a funny little blue silk cap along with a splendid string of pearls. At the front she does very fine work so we offered our services to her. I have begun to write a little, but after my crowded life during the daytime, I feel curiously empty. Lady Heron-Maxwell came to call.

We were telling each other spy stories the other night. Some of them were very interesting. The Germans have lately adopted the plan of writing letters in English to English prisoners of war in Germany.

These, of course, are quite simple, and pass the censor in England, but, once on the other side, they go straight to Government officials. Whereas "Dear Bill" may mean nothing to us, it is part of a German code and conveys some important information. Mr. O.S. Philpotts at the British Legation in Stockholm discovered this trick.

On the Russian front, a soldier was found with his jaw tied up, speechless and bleeding. A doctor tried to persuade him to take cover and get attention. However, shook his head and signified by actions that he was unable to speak due to his damaged jaw. The doctor, shoving him into a dugout, kindly said: "Just let me have a look at you." On stripping the bandages off there was no wound at all, and the German in Russian uniform was given a cigarette and shot through the head.

In Flanders, we used to see companies of spies led out to be shot—first a party of soldiers, then the spies, after them the burying party, and then the firing party—marching stolidly to some place of execution.

How awful shellfire must be for those who really can't stand it! I heard of a colonel the other day—a man who rode to hounds and seemed quite a sound sort of fellow—and when the first shell came over, he leapt from his horse and lay on the ground shrieking with fear. With every shell that came over, he yelled and screamed. He had to be sent home, of course. Some people say this sort of thing is purely physical. That is never my view of the matter.

Miss Edith Cavell's execution has stirred us all to the bottom of our hearts. [Convicted of treason, she was a 49-year-old British nurse shot by a German firing squad in occupied Belgium for helping Allied soldiers escape.] The mean trickiness of her trial, the refusal to let facts be known, and then the cold-blooded murder of a brave English woman at 2 a.m. on a Sunday morning in a prison yard! It is too awful to think about. She was not even technically a spy, but had merely assisted some soldiers to get away because she thought they were going to be shot.

"British nurse Edith Cavell," by *Bain News Service* (circa 1915). She was executed by a German firing squad. Courtesy the Library of Congress.

A rumor reached the American and Spanish Legations that she had been condemned and was to be shot at once. They instantly called on the telephone to know if this was true. The Military Court, which had tried and condemned her, informed them that the verdict would not be pronounced until three days later. But the two Legations, still unsatisfied, protested that they must be allowed to visit the prisoner. This was refused. The English Anglican chaplain was at last permitted to enter the prison. He saw Miss Cavell and gave her the sacrament. She said she was happy to die for her country. They led her out into the prison yard to stand before a firing-party of soldiers, but on her way there she fainted. An officer took out his revolver and shot her through the head.

"Nicolai Bridge, named after Czar Nicholas I, in St. Petersburg," by *Bain News Service* (circa 1915). Courtesy the Library of Congress.

St. Petersburg! the stage of romance, and the subject of dazzling pictures, is one of the most commonplace towns I have ever been in. It has its one big street—the Nevski Prospect—where people walk and shop as they do in Oxford Street. And it has a few cathedrals and churches, which are not very wonderful. The roadways are a mass of slush and are seldom swept. There are tramways, always crowded and hot, and many rickety little victorias [light horse-drawn carriages] with damp cushions, in which you go everywhere. Even in the evening we go out in these; and the colds in the head that follow are chronic.

The English colony seems to me as provincial as the rest of St. Petersburg. The town and its people disappoint me greatly. The Hôtel Astoria is a would-be fashionable place, and there is an unusual crowd of people listening to the band and eating, as surely only in Russia they can eat. It is all wrong in wartime. I hate being one of the people here.

Note—Write "Miss Wilbraham" as soon as possible and write it in gusts. Call one chapter "The Diners," and try to convey the awful solemnity of meals—the grave young men with their goblets of brandy, in which they slowly rotate ice, the waiter who hands the bowl where the ice is thrown when the brandy is cool enough, and then the final gulp, with a nose inside the large goblet. Shade of Heliogabalus! If the human tummy must indeed be distended four times in 24 hours, need it be done so solemnly, and with such a pig-like love of the trough? If they would even eat what there is with joy you wouldn't mind, but the talk about food, the once-enjoyed food, the favorite food, is really too tiresome.

"Where to dine" becomes a sort of test of true worth. Grave young men give the names of four or five favored places in London. Others, hailed and acknowledged as really good judges, name half-a-dozen more in Paris where they "do you well." The real toff knows that Russia is the place to dine. We earnestly discuss blue-point oysters and caviar, which, if you "know the man," you can get sent fresh on the *Vienna Express* from Moscow.

I once asked Bernard Shaw to dinner, and he replied on a postcard: "Never! I decline to sit in a hot room and eat dead animals, even with you to amuse me!"

I always seem to be sitting in hot rooms and eating dead animals, and then paying amazing high prices for them.

November 5:
"Charity" and War

Yesterday we lunched with the English chaplain, Mr. Lombard. He and I had a great talk walking home on a dark afternoon through the slush after we had been to call on the Maxwells. I think he is one of the "exiles" you meet all over the world, one of those who don't transplant well. I am one myself!

And Mr. Lombard and I nearly wept when we found ourselves in a street that recalled the Marylebone Road. We pretended we were in sight of Euston Station and talked of taking a Baker Street bus until our voices grew choky.

How absurd we islanders are! London is a poky place, but we adore it. St. James's Street is about the length of a good big ship, yet we don't feel we have lived until we get back to it! And as for Piccadilly and St. Paul's, well, we see them in our dreams.

Our little unit has not found work yet. I was told before I joined it that it had been accepted by the Russian Red Cross Society.

I have been hearing many things out here, and thinking many things. There is only one way of directing Red Cross work. Everything should be—and must be in future—put under military authority and used by military authority. "Charity" and war should be separate. It is absurd that the Belgians in England should be housed and fed by a government grant, and our own soldiers are dependent on private charity for the very socks they wear and cigarettes they smoke. Airplanes had to be instituted and prizes offered for them by a newspaper, and ammunition wasn't provided until a newspaper took up the matter. To be mob-ridden is bad enough, but to be press-ridden is worse!

Now, war is a military matter and should be controlled by military authorities. Mrs. Wynne, Mr. Bevan, and I should not be out here waiting for work. We ought to be sent where we are needed and so should all Red Cross people. This would put an end, you hope, to the horrid business of getting "soft jobs."

November 7:

Whenever I am away from England I rejoice in the passing of each week that brings me nearer to my return. I had hardly realized today was the 7th, but I am thankful I am one week nearer the gray little island and all the nice people in it.

Yesterday I went to Lady Georgina Buchanan's soup kitchen and helped feed Polish refugees. In the barracks where they lodge everyone crowds in. There is no division of the sexes, babies are yelling, and families are sleeping on wooden boards. The places are heated, but not aired, and the smell is horrid; but they seem to revel in "frowst." All the women are dandling babies or trying to cook things on little oil stoves. At nighttime things are awful, I believe, and the British Ambassador has been asked to protect the girls who are there.

November 8:
Visions of Peace

This afternoon I went to see Mrs. Bray, and then I had an unexpected pleasure, for I met Johnnie Parsons, who is Naval Attaché to Admiral Richard Phillimore, British liaison to the Imperial Russian Headquarters, and we had a long chat. When you are in a strange land, or with people who know you but little, these encounters are wonderfully nice.

The other night I dined with the Heron-Maxwells, and had a nice evening and a game of bridge. Some Americans, called de Velter, were there. I think most people from the States regret the neutrality of their country.

Everyone brings in different stories of the war. Some say Germany is exhausted and beaten. Others say she is flushed with victory, and with enormous reserves of men, food, and ammunition. I try to believe all the good I hear. Even when children or fools tell me the war will soon be over, I want to embrace them. I don't care whether they are talking nonsense or not. Sometimes I seem to see a great hushed cathedral, and us returning thanks for peace and victory, and the vision is too much for me. I must either work or be chloroformed until that time comes.

November 9:

I think there is only one thing I dislike more than sitting in a hotel bedroom and learning a new language, and that is sitting in a hotel bedroom and nursing a cold in my head. Lately I have been learning Russian—and now I am sniffing. My own fault. I would sleep with my window open in this unhealthiest of cities, and smells and marsh produced a feverish cold.

Out in the square, the soldiers drill all the time in the snow—lying in it, standing in it, and dressed for the most part in cotton clothing. Wool can't be bought, so a close cotton web is made, with the inside teased out like flannelette. This is all they have. The necessities of life are being "cornered" right and left, mostly by the commercial houses and the banks. The other day 163 railway trucks of sugar were discovered in a siding, where the owners had placed it to await for a price hike. Meanwhile, sugar has been almost unprocurable.

Everyone from the front describes the condition of the refugees as being most wretched. They are camping in the snow by the thousand and still tramping from Poland.

And here we are in the Astoria Hotel. There is one pane of glass between us and the weather; one pane of glass between us and the peasants of Poland; one pane of glass dividing us from poverty, and keeping us in the horrid atmosphere of this place, with its evil women and its squeaky band! How I hate money!

I hope soon to join a train going to Dvinsk [today known as Daugavpils, Latvia] with food and supplies.

November 13:
Brothers

I have felt very brainless since I came here. It is the result, I believe, of the St. Petersburg climate. Nearly everyone feels it. I had a little book in my head that I thought I could "dash off," and that writing it would fill up these waiting days, but I can't write a word.

The Strange Side of War: A Woman's WWI Diary　　225

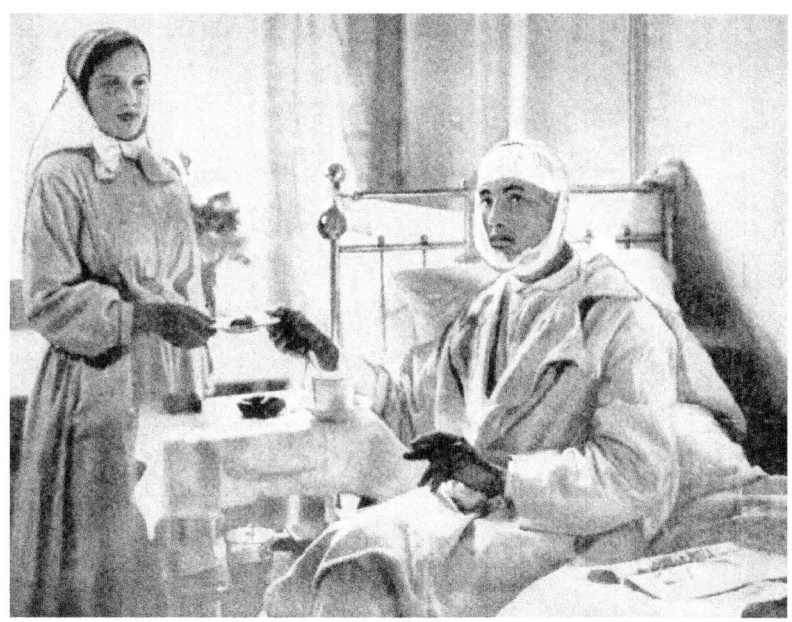

"Cossack officer, wounded in the mouth by a Hussar lance, in a Russian hospital,"(unknown). Courtesy *Harper's Pictorial Library of the World War,* Vol. 7, 1920.

The war news is not good, but the more territory that Germany takes, the more the British rub their hands and cry victory. Their courage and optimism are wonderful.

Today I spent with the Maxwells. I met a nurse, newly returned from Galicia, who had interesting tales to tell. One about some Russian airmen touched me. There had been a fierce fight overhead. Suddenly a German airplane began to wheel round and round like a leaf, when it was learned that the machine was on fire. One of the airmen had been shot, and the other burnt to death.

The Russians refused to come look at the remains even of the airplane, and said sadly, "All we men of the air are brothers." They gave the dead Germans a military funeral, and then sailed over the enemy's lines to drop a note saying that all honor had been done to the brave dead.

"Russian artillery," by *Bain News Service*, (circa 1914 to 1918). Courtesy the Library of Congress.

I met Monsieur Jecquier, who was full of the political situation. He said Bulgaria would have joined us any day if we had promised to give her Bukowina; and blamed Pyotr Bark, the Russian Finance Minister, for the terms of England's loan (the loan is for 30 million; repayment is promised in a year, which is manifestly impossible, and the situation may be strained). He also said Motono Ichiro, the Japanese Ambassador to Russia, is by far the finest politician here, and while Russia ought to have been protecting the road to Constantinople she was quarreling about what its new name was to be, and had decided to call it "Czareska."

Now, I suppose, the Germans are already there. Lloyds has been giving £100 at a premium of £5 that King Ferdinand I of Romania won't be on his throne next June. The premium has gone to £10, which is good news. If Ferdie is assassinated the world will be rid of an evil fellow who has played a mean and degraded part in this war.

We dined at the British Embassy last night. I was taken in to dinner by

George Lloyd, who was full of interesting news. I had a nice chat with Lady Georgina.

November 20:
Stagnation

It has been like hanging on ever since I wrote last, nothing settled and nothing to do. No one ever seems at their best in St. Petersburg. It is a crossroads and a common place. I never understood Tolstoy until I came here. On all sides you see the same insane love of money and love of food.

A restaurant here disgusts me as nothing else ever did. From a menu a foot long, no one seems able to choose a meal, but something fresh must be ordered. The prices are quite silly, and, oddly enough, people seem to revel in them. They still eat caviar at 10 shillings a head; the larger the bill the better they are pleased.

Joseph, the Napoleon of the restaurant, keeps an eye on everyone. He is yellow and pigeon-breasted, but his voice is like grease, and he speaks caressingly of food, pencils entries in his notebook, and stimulates jaded appetites by signaling the *"voiture aux hors d'oeuvres"* to approach. The rooms are far too hot for anyone to feel hungry, the band plays, and the leader of it grins all the time, and capers about on his little platform like a monkey on an organ.

Always in this life of restaurants and gilt and rubles, I am reminded of the fact that the only authentic picture we have of hell is of a man there who all his life had eaten good dinners.

I have been busy seeing all types of people to try and get work to do. I hear of suffering, but I am never able to locate it or to do anything for it. No distinct information is forthcoming. When I go to one high official, he gives me his card and sends me to another. Nothing is even decided about Mrs. Wynne's cars, although she is offering a gift worth some thousands of pounds. I go to Lady Georgina's work-party on Mondays and meet the

English colony. On Wednesdays and Saturdays, I distribute soup; but it is an unsatisfactory business.

The days go by and you get nothing done. You aren't even storing up health, because this is rather an unhealthy place, so altogether we are feeling a bit low. I can never again be surprised at Russian *"laissez faire,"* or want of push and energy. It is all the result of the place itself.

I feel in a dream and wish with all my heart I could wake up in my own bed.

November 21:

Sunday, and I have slept late. At home I begin work at 6 a.m. Here, like everyone else, I only wake up at night. And the "best hours of the day," as we call them, are wasted, à la Watts' hymn, in slumber.

If it was possible you would organize your time a bit, but hotel life is the very mischief for that sort of thing. There are no facilities for anything. You must telephone in Russian or spend rubles on messengers if you want to get into touch with anyone. I took a taxi out to lunch one day. It cost 16 rubles—i.e., 32s.

Dear old Lord Radstock used to say in the spring, "The Lord is calling me to Italy," and a testy parson once remarked, "The Lord always calls you at very convenient times, Radstock." I don't feel as if the Lord had called me here at a very convenient time.

I called on Princess Hélène Scherbatoff yesterday, and found her and her people at home. Her mother runs a hospital train for the wounded amid intervals of hunting wolves. Her son has been dead for some months, and she says she hasn't had time to bury him yet! You assume he is embalmed! Yet I can't help saying they were charming people to meet, so we must suppose they are somewhat cracked. The daughter is lovely, and they were all in deep mourning for the unburied relative.

"Liquid fire used in trenches by Germans," (August 1915). Courtesy the Library of Congress.

November 24:
Wounded Russians

This long wait is very hard for us. There is literally nothing to do. We arrange pathetic little programs for ourselves. Today I shall lunch with Mr. Cunard, and see the lace he has bought. Yesterday I did some shopping with Captain Smith: one day I sew at Lady Georgina's work-party.

Heavens, what a life! I realize that for years I have not drawn rein, and I am sure I don't require holidays. Moses was a wise man, and he knew that one day in seven is rest enough for most humans. I always "keep the Sabbath," and it is all the rest I want. Even here I might write and get on with something, but there is something paralyzing about the place. My brain won't work. I can't even write a diary! Everyone is depressed and everyone wants to be out of St. Petersburg. Today we hear that the Swedes have closed the Haparanda line, and Archangel is frozen, so here we are.

Now I have got to work at the hospital. There are 25,000 amputation cases in St. Petersburg. The men at my hospital are mostly convalescent, but, of course, their wounds require dressing. This is never done in their beds, as the English plan is, but each man is carried in turn to the *"salle des pansements"* [dressing room], where he is laid on an operating table, has fresh dressings put on, and is then carried back to bed again. It is a good plan, I think. The hospital keeps me busy all the morning. Once more I begin to see severed limbs and gashed flesh. The old question arises, "Why, what evil hath he done?" This war is the crucifixion of the youth of the world.

In a way, I am learning something here. For instance, I have always disliked "explanations" and "speaking your mind," more than I can say. I must say I have chosen the path of least resistance in these matters. Here you must speak out sometimes and speak firmly. It isn't all "being pleasant." One girl has been consistently rude to me. Today, poor soul, I gave her a second sermon on our way back from church. Indeed she has numerous opportunities in this war and she is wasting them all on gossip, prejudices, and petty jealousies. So we had a straight talk, and I hope she didn't hate it. At any rate, she has promised amendment of life. You hear of men that "this war gives them a chance to distinguish themselves." Women ought to distinguish themselves, too.

"Hesper! Venus! were we native to their splendor, or in Mars,
We should see this world we live in, fairest of their evening stars.
Who could dream of wars and tumults, hate and envy, sin and spite,
Roaring London, raving Paris, in that spot of peaceful light?
Might we not, in looking heavenward on a star so silver fair,
Yearn and clasp our hands and murmur, 'Would to God that we were there!'"

The Strange Side of War: A Woman's WWI Diary 231

"German troops pursuing Russians along a roadway with a column of troops proceeding from the left toward the center and mounted troops on the roadway in the foreground moving toward the right," by unknown (1915). Courtesy the Library of Congress.

Always when I see war, and boys with their poor dead faces turned up to the sky, and their hands so small in death, and when I see wounded men, and hear of soldiers going out of the trenches with a laugh and a joke to cut wire entanglements, knowing they will not come back, then I am ashamed of meanness and petty spite. So my poor young woman got a "fair dose of it" this morning, and when she had gulped once or twice I think she felt better.

Yesterday I saw enough to stir me profoundly and enough to make small things seem small indeed! It was a fine day at last, after weeks of black weather and skies heavy with snow. Although the cold was intense the sun was shining. I got into one of the horrid little droshkys, in which you sit on very damp cushions, and an *"izvoztchik"* in a heavy coat takes you to the wrong address always!

The weather has been so thick, the rain and snow so constant, I had not yet seen St. Petersburg. Yesterday, out of the mists appeared golden spires, and beyond the Neva, all sullen and heavy with ice, I saw towers and domes I hadn't seen before. I stamped my feet on the shaky little carriage and begged the izvoztchik to drive a little quicker. We had to be at the Finnish station at 10 a.m., and my horse, with a long tail that embraced the reins every time the driver urged speed, seemed incapable of doing more than to trot over the frozen roads. I picked up Madame Takmakoff, who was taking me to the station, and we went together.

At the station there was a long wooden building and, outside, a platform, all frozen and white, where we waited for the train to come in. Madame Sazonoff, a fine well-bred woman, the wife of the Minister for Foreign Affairs Sergei Dmitriyevich Sazonov, was there and "many others," as the press notices say. The train was late. We went inside the long wooden building to shelter us from the bitter cold beside the hot-water pipes. As we waited we heard the train coming in. It came slowly and carefully alongside the platform with its crunching snow, almost with the creeping movement of a woman who carries something tenderly. Then it stopped. Its windows were frozen and dark, so that you could see nothing.

I heard a voice behind me say, "The blind are coming first." From the train there came groping you by one, young men with their eyes shot out. They felt for the step of the train and waited bewildered until someone came to lead them. Then, with their sightless eyes looking upwards more than ours do, they moved stumbling along. Poor fellows, they'll never see home, but they turned with smiles of delight when the band, in its gray uniforms and fur caps, began to play the national anthem.

These were the first wounded prisoners from Germany, sent home because they could never fight again—quite useless men, too sorely hurt to stand once more under raining bullets and hurtling shell-fire—so back they came, and like dazed creatures they got out of the train, carrying their little bundles, limping, groping, but home.

After the blind came those who had lost limbs—one-legged men, men still in bandages, men hobbling with sticks or with an arm round a comrade's neck, and then the stretcher cases. There was one man carrying his crutches like a cross. Others lay twisted sideways. Some never moved their heads from their pillows. All seemed to me to have about them a splendid dignity, which made the long, battered, suffering company into some great pageant. I have never seen men so lean as they were. I have never seen men's cheekbones seem to cut through the flesh just where the close-cropped hair on their temples ends. I had never seen such hollow eyes. But they were Russian soldiers, Russian gentlemen, and they were home again!

In the great hall, we greeted them with tables laid with food, and spread with wine and little presents beside each place. They know how to do this, the princely Russians, so each man got a welcome to make him proud. The band was there, and the long tables, the hot soup and the cigarettes. All the men had washed at Torneo, and all of them wore clean cotton waistcoats. Their hair was cut, too, but their faces hadn't recovered. You knew they would never be young again. The Germans had done their work. Semi-starvation and wounds had made old men of these poor Russian soldiers. All was done that could be done to welcome them back, but no one could take it in for a time. A sister in black distributed some little Testaments, each with a cross on it, and the soldiers kissed the symbol of suffering passionately.

They filed into their places at the tables. The stretchers were placed in a row two deep up the whole length of the room. In the middle of it stood an altar, covered with silver tinsel, and two priests in tinsel and gold stood beside it. Upon it was the sacred icon, and the everlasting Mother and Child smiled down at the men laid in helplessness and weakness at their feet.

A General welcomed the soldiers back; and when they were thanked in the name of the Emperor for what they had done, the tears coursed down their thin cheeks. It was too pitiful and touching. I remember thinking how quietly and sweetly a Sister of Mercy went from one group of soldiers to another, silently giving them handkerchiefs to dry their tears. We are all mothers now, and our sons are so helpless, so much in need of us.

Down the middle of the room were low tables for the men who lay down all the time. They saluted the icon, as all the soldiers did, and some service began which I was unable to follow. I can't tell what the soldiers said, or of what they were thinking. About their comrades they said to Madame Takmakoff that 25,000 of them had died in two days from neglect. We shall never hear the worst perhaps.

There were three officers at a table. One of them was shot through the throat and bandaged. I saw him put all his food on one side, unable to swallow it. Then a high official came and sat down and drank his health. The officer raised his glass gallantly, and put his lips to the wine, but his throat was shot through, he made a face of agony, bowed to the great man opposite, and put down his glass.

Some surgeons in white began to go about, taking names and details of the men's condition. Everyone was kind to the returned soldiers, but they had suffered too much. Some day they will smile perhaps, but yesterday they were silent men returned from the dead, and not yet certain that their feet touched Russia again.

Chapter 12
Waiting in Moscow

"Russian emperor Nicholas II standing next to a car with Russian general Grand Duke Nikolay Nikolayevich Romanov, standing in the car, at the front during World War I," *Bain News Service* (circa 1914 to 1915). Courtesy the Library of Congress.

Nov. 29, 1915:

We paid our heavy bills and left St. Petersburg on Monday, November 29. There was great fuss at the station, as our luggage and the guide had disappeared together. A comfortable, slow journey, and Colonel Malcolm met us at Moscow station and took us to the Hôtel de Luxe—a shocking bad pub, but the only one where we could get rooms. We went out to lunch. I had a plate of soup, two faens (little wheat cakes), and the fifth part of a bottle of Graves wine. This modest meal cost 16 shillings per head. We left the Luxe Hotel the following day, and came to the National Hotel of, Moscow, where 400 people were waiting to get in. But our guide Grundy had influence and managed to get us rooms. It is quite comfortable.

"Nikolay Nikolayevich Romanov, Grand Duke of Russia, Commander in Chief," (circa 1914). Courtesy the Library of Congress.

None of us was sorry to leave St. Petersburg, and that is putting the case mildly. People there are very depressed. It was a case of "she said" and "he said" all the time. Everyone was trying to snuff everyone else out. "I don't know them"—and the lips pursed up finished many a reputation. I heard more about money and position than I ever heard in my life before. "Bunty" and I used to say the world was inhabited by "nice people and very nice people," and once she added a third class, "fearfully nice people." That is a world you used to inhabit. I suppose you must make the best of this one!

December 2:
The Kremlin

Mrs. Hilda Wynne was rather feverish today and lay in bed. So I had a solitary walk about the Kremlin. I saw a fine view from its splendid position.

But, somehow, I am getting tired of solitude. I suppose the war gives us the feeling that we must hold together, and yet I have never been more alone than during this last 18 months.

December 3,
To Sarah's Sisters
Crédit Lyonnais, Moscow

My Dears,

I have just heard there is a man going up to St. Petersburg tonight who will put our letters in the Embassy bag, so there is some hope of this reaching you. It is really my Christmas letter to you all, so may it be passed around, please, although there won't be much in it.

We are now at Moscow, en route for the Caucasus via Tbilisi, Georgia, and our base will probably be Julfa, Iran. We have been chosen to go there by the Grand Duchess Cyril (Victoria Melita), but the reports about the roads are so conflicting that we are going to see for ourselves. When we get there it will be difficult to send letters home, but the banks will always be in communication with each other. So I shall get all you send to Crédit Lyonnais, St. Petersburg.

So far we have been waiting for our cars all this time. They had to come by Archangel and left long before we did, but they have not arrived yet. There are six ambulance cars on board three different ships (for safety) and no news of any of them yet.

Now, at least, we have got a move on. Barring accidents, we shall be in Tbilisi next week. It's rather a fearsome journey as the train only takes us to the foot of the mountains in four days. Then we must ride or drive across the passes, which they say are too cold for anything.

You must imagine us like Napoleon in the "Retreat from Moscow" picture.

St. Petersburg is a singularly unpleasant town, where the sun never shines, and it rains or snows every day. The river is full of ice, but it looks sullen and sad in the perpetual mist.

There are many English people there, but you are supposed to know the Russians, which means speaking French all the time. Moscow is a far superior place and is really most interesting and beautiful, and very Eastern, while St. Petersburg might be Liverpool. I filled up my time there in the hospital and soup kitchen.

The price of everything gets worse, I do believe! Even a glass of filtered water costs one shilling and three pence! I have just left a hotel for which my bill was £3 for one night, and I was sick nearly all the time!

Now, my dears, I wish you all the best Christmas you can have this year. I am just longing for news of you, but I never knew such a far-off place as this for letters. Tell me about every one of the family. Write lengthy letters. When do people say the war will end?

Your loving,
Sarah Broom

"Towards the Megectski Castle in Tbilisi, located in former Russia now in Georgia," (circa 1900). Courtesy the Library of Congress.

December 12:
Tbilisi

It is evening and I have only just remembered it is Sunday, a thing I can't recollect ever having happened before. I have been ill in my room all day, which no doubt accounts for it.

We stayed at Moscow for a few days and my memory of it is of a great deal of snow and frequent shopping expeditions in cold little sleighs. I liked the place. It was infinitely preferable to St. Petersburg. Mr. Cazalet took us to the theatre one night, and there was rather a good ballet. These poor dancers! They, like others, have lost their nearest and dearest in the war, but they still have to dance. Of course they call themselves "The Allies," and I saw rather a stale ballet-girl in very sketchy clothes dancing with a red, yellow, and black flag draped across her. Poor Belgium! It was such a travesty of her sufferings.

Mr. Cazalet came to see us off at the station. We began our long journey to Tbilisi, but we changed our minds and took the local train from ___ to Vladikavkaz at the foothills of the Caucasus mountains, where we stayed one night rather enjoyably at a smelly hotel.

The following day we got a car and started at 7 a.m. for the pass. The drive did us all good. The great snow peaks were so unlike St. Petersburg and gossip! I had been very ill on the train, and got worse at the hotel and during the drive. So I was quite a poor Sarah when I reached Tbilisi. Still, the scenery had been lovely all the time, and we had funny little meals at rest houses.

When we got to Tbilisi, I went on being seedy for a while. I finished Stephen Graham's book on Russia, which he gave me before I left home. It is charmingly written. The line he chooses is mine also, but his is a more important book than mine.

December 22:
Batumi

We have had a really delightful time since I last wrote up the old diary! (A dull book so far.) We saw many important people at Tbilisi—Gorlebeff, the head of the Russian Red Cross, Prince Orloff, Prince Galitzin (a charming man), General Bernoff, etc.

Mrs. Wynne's and Mr. Ivor Bevan's cars are definitely accepted for the Tehran district. My own plans are not yet settled, but I hope they may be soon. People seem to think I look so delicate they are a little bit afraid of giving me hard work.

Yet I suppose there are not many women who get through more work than I do; but I believe I am looking like a rather a poor specimen, and my hair has fallen out. I think I am rather like those pictures on the covers of "appeals"—pictures of small children, underneath which is written: "This is Johnny Smith, or Eliza Jones, who was found in a cellar by one of our officers; weight—age—etc., etc."

"Both Workmanlike and Chic: Mrs. Wynne, of the Hector Munro Flying Ambulance," *The Sketch* (March 3, 1915). She was posing in two styles of service dress for duty at the front.

If I could have a small hospital north of Tehran it would be a good center for the wounded and a good place for the others to come to. Mr. Hills and Dr. Gordon (American missionaries) seem to think they would like me to join them in their work for the Armenians. These unfortunate people have been nearly exterminated by massacres, and it has been officially stated that 75% of the whole race has been put to the sword. This sounds awful enough, but when we consider there is no refinement of torture that has not been practiced upon them, then something within you gets up and shouts for revenge.

There are rumors of peace offers from Germany, but we must go on fighting now, if only for the sake of the soldiers, who will be the ones to suffer, but who can't be asked to give in. The Russians are terribly out of spirits, and very depressed about the war. The German influence at Court scares them, and there is, besides, the mysterious Rasputin to contend with! This extraordinary man seems to exercise a malign influence over everyone, and people are powerless to resist him. Nothing seems too strange or too mad to recount of this man and his dupes. He is by birth a moujik, or peasant, and is illiterate, a drunkard, and an immoral wretch. Yet there is hardly a great lady at Court who has not come under his influence, and he is supposed by this set of people to be a reincarnation of Christ. Rasputin's figure is one of those mysterious ones around which every sort of rumor gathers.

We left Tbilisi on Friday, December 17, and had a panic at the station since our passports had been left at the hotel, and our tickets had gone off to Baku. However, the unpunctuality of the train helped us, and we got off all right an hour late. The train was about a 1,000 years old and went at the rate of 10 miles an hour. We could only get 2nd-class ordinary carriages to sleep in! But morning showed us such lovely scenery that nothing else mattered. You found yourself in a semi-tropical country, with soft skies and blue sea, and palms and flowers, and with tea gardens on all the hillsides. When will people discover Caucasia? It is one of the countries of the world.

We had letters to Count Groholski, a most charming young fellow, who arranged a delightful journey for us into the mountains. Since we had not brought riding things, we began to search the small shops for riding boots and the like. Then in the evening we dined with Count Oulieheff and had an interesting pleasant time. Two Japanese were at dinner. Although they couldn't speak any tongue but their own, the Japanese always manage to look interesting. No doubt much of that depends upon being able to say nothing.

Early the next day, we drove out to the Count's Red Cross camp at ___. Here everyone was sleeping under tents or in little wooden huts. We met some good-mannered, nice soldier men, most of them Poles. The scenery was grand, and we were actually in the little known and wonderful old kingdom of Georgia. Very little of it is left. There are ruins all along the river of castles, fortresses, and old stone bridges now crumbling into decay.

"Batumi," (circa 1915). Courtesy the Library of Congress.

But of the country once so proud only one small dirty city remains, and that is Artvin [in northeastern Turkey], on the mountainside. It was too full of an infectious sort of typhus for us to go there, but we drove out to the hospital on the opposite side of the valley. The doctor in charge there gave us beds for the night.

On Sunday, December 19, I wandered around the hillside, found some well-made trenches, and saw some houses that had been shelled. The Turks were in possession of Artvin only a year ago, and there was a lot of fighting in the mountains. It seems to me that the population of the place is pretty Turkish still; and there are Turkish houses with small Moorish doorways, and little windows looking out on the glorious view. In all the mountains around here the shooting is fine and consists of toor (goats), leopards, bears, wolves, and on the Persian front, tigers also. Land can be had for nothing if you are a Russian.

On Sunday afternoon, we drove in a most painful little carriage to a village that seemed to be inhabited by good-looking cutthroats, but there was not much to see except the picturesque, smelly, old brown houses. We met a handsome Cossack carrying a man down to the military hospital. He was holding him upright, as children carry each other. The man was moaning with fever and had been stricken with the virulent typhus, which nearly always kills. But what did the handsome Cossack care about infection? He was a mountaineer and had eyes with a little flame in them as well as a fierce mustache. Perhaps tomorrow he will be gone. People die like flies in these unhealthy towns, and the Russians are supremely careless.

We went back to the hospital for dinner and out into the crisp, beautiful moonlight before driving back to the Red Cross camp. I had a little hut to sleep in, which had just been built. It contained a bed and two chairs, upon one of which was a tin basin! The cold in the morning was about as sharp as anything I have known, but everyone was jolly and pleasant, and we had a charming time.

The Count told us of the old proud Georgians when there was a famine in the country and a Russian governor came to offer relief to the starving inhabitants.

Their great men went out to receive him, and said courteously: "We have not been here, Gracious One, 100 or 200 years, but much more than a thousand years, and during that time we have not had a visit from the Russian government. We are pleased to see you, and the honor you have done us is sufficient in itself—for the rest we think we will not require anything at your hands."

On Monday, I drove with the others out to the ferry. Then I had to leave them, as they were going to ride 40 miles, which was thought too much for me. Age has no compensations, and it is not much use fighting it. One only ends by being "a wonderful old woman of 80": reminiscent, perhaps a little obstinate, and in the world to come—always 80?

I came back to Batumi with Count Stanislas Constant, and went for a drive with him to see the tea gardens.

"Field-marshal Sir John French, Commander in Chief, in France," by unknown (1915). He was also responsible for the land defense of the British Isles. Courtesy Wikimedia Commons.

Christmas Eve at Tbilisi, and here we are with cars still stuck in the ice 30 miles from Archangel, and ourselves just holding on and trying not to worry. But what a waste of time!

Also, fighting is going on now in Persia, and we might be a lot of use. We came back from Batumi in the hottest and slowest train I have ever been in. Still, Georgia delighted me, and I am glad to have seen it.

They have a curious custom there (the result of generations of fighting). Instead of saying "Good morning," they say "Victory." And the answer is: "May the victory be yours." The language is Georgian, of course; and then there is Tartar, and Polish, and Russian. I can't help thinking that the Tower of Babel was the poorest joke ever played on mankind. Nothing stops work so completely.

What will Christmas Day be like at home? I think of all the village churches, with the holly and evergreens, and in almost every one the little new brass plates to the memory of beautiful youth, dead and mangled, and left in the mud to await another trumpet than that which called it from the trenches.

"Field-marshal Sir Douglas Haig, Commander-in-chief of France from December 1915," by war artist Major Sir William Orpen, painted at General Headquarters (1917). He was the Commander-in-Chief of the British Army on the Western Front. Courtesy Wikimedia Commons.

There is nothing like a boy, and all the life of England and the prayers of mothers have centered round them. Your older friends died first, and now the boys are falling—from every little vicarage, from school-houses and colleges, the endless stream goes, all with their heads up, fussing over their little bits of packing, and then away to stand exploding shells and gas and bombs. No one except those who have seen knows the ghastly tale of human suffering that this war involves every day. Down here 550,000 Armenians have been butchered in cold blood. The women are either massacred or driven into Turkish harems.

Yesterday we heard some news at last in this most benighted corner of the world! England has raised 4 million volunteers. Hurrah! Over 1 million men volunteered in one week. Field Marshal Lord French takes command at home and General Sir Douglas Haig at the front.

"Russian prisoners of war during World War I," by *Bain News Service* (circa 1915). Courtesy the Library of Congress.

December 26
To Mrs. Charles Young,
Hotel Orient, Tbilisi

Darling J.,

It seems almost useless to write letters, or even to wire! Letters sometimes take 49 days to get to England, and telegrams are always kept two weeks before being sent. We have had great difficulty about the ambulance cars, as they all got frozen into the river at Archangel; however, as you will see from the newspapers, there isn't a great deal going on yet.

I do hope you and all the family are safe and sound. I wired to ____ for her birthday to ask news of you all, and I prepaid the reply, but, of course, none came, so I am sure she never got the wire. I have wired twice to ____, but no reply. At last you give up expecting any. I got some newspapers nearly a month old today, and I have been devouring them.

This is rather a curious place. The climate is quite good—no snow and a *good deal of pleasant sun, but the hills all round are very bare and rugged.*

I have had a cough, which I think equals your best efforts in that line. How it does shake you up! I had some odd traveling when it was at its worst: for the first night we were given a shakedown in a little mountain hospital, which was fearfully cold; and the next night I was put into a newly built little place, made of planks roughly nailed together, and with just a bed and a basin in it.

The cold was wonderful, and since then—as you may imagine—the Macnaughtan cough has been heard in the land!

Yesterday (Christmas Day) we were invited to breakfast with the Grand Duke Nicholas Nikolaevich Romanov. A Court function in Russia is the most royal that you can imagine—no half measures about it! The Grand Duke is an adorably handsome man, quite extraordinarily and obviously a Grand Duke. He measures 6 feet 5 inches and is worshipped by every soldier in the Army.

We went first into a huge anteroom, where a lady-in-waiting received us, and presented us to "Son Altesse Impériale," and then to the Grand Duke and to his brother, the Grand Duke Peter Nikolaevich. Some scenes seem to move as if in a play. I had a vision of a great polished floor, and many tall men in Cossack dress, with daggers and swords, most of them different grades of Princes and Imperial Highnesses.

A great party of Generals, ladies, and members of the household then went into a big dining room, where every imaginable hors d'oeuvre was laid out on dishes—dozens of different kinds—and we each ate caviar or something. Afterwards, with a great tramp and clank of spurs and swords, everyone moved to a larger dining room, where there were a lot of servants, who waited excellently. In the middle of the meal, the Grand Duke Nicholas got up as did everyone else at the same time, and they toasted us! The Grand Duke made a speech about our "gallantry," etc. Everyone raised glasses and bowed. Nothing in a play could have been more of a real fine sort of scene.

"Russian army officers," *Bain News Service* (circa 1915). Courtesy the Library of Congress.

And certainly S. Macnaughtan in her wildest dreams hadn't thought of anything so wonderful as being toasted in Russia by the Imperial Staff.

It's quite a thing to be tiresome about when you grow old!

In the evening we tried to be merry and failed. The Grand Duchess sent us mistletoe and plum pudding by the hand of M. Boulderoff. He took us shopping, but the bazaars are not interesting. Goodbye, and bless you, my dear.

Yours as ever,
S. Macnaughtan

Homesick

December 27

To Julia Keays-Young

Hotel D'Orient, Tbilisi, Caucasus, Russia

Darling Jenny,

I can't tell you what a pleasure your letters are. I only wish I could get some more from anybody, but not a line gets through! I want so much to hear about Bet and her marriage, and to know if the nephews and Charles are safe.

There seems to be the usual winter pause over the greater part of the war area. But around about here, there are the most awful massacres: 550,000 Armenians have been slaughtered in cold blood by the Turks, and with cruelties that pass all telling. You feel quite impotent.

I expect to be sent into Persia soon. Meanwhile I hope to join some American missionaries who are helping the refugees. Our ambulances are at last out of the ice at Archangel, and will be here in two weeks. But we are not to go to Persia for a month. "The Front" is always changing, and we never have any idea where our work will be wanted.

We are still asking when the war will end, but, of course, no one knows. You get pretty homesick out here at times. There was a chance I might have to go back to England for equipment, but that seems off at present.

Your always loving,

A. S.

"The Czar reviewing his troops," *Bain News Service* (circa 1915). Courtesy the Library of Congress.

December 29:

I have still got a horrid bad cough, and my big, dull room is depressing. We are all depressed, I am afraid. Being accustomed to have plenty to do, this long wait is maddening.

Whatever Russia may have in store for us in the way of useful work, nothing can exceed the boredom of our first seven weeks here. We are just anxious for work. I believe it is as bad as an illness to feel like this, and we won't be normal again for some time. Oddly enough, it does affect your health, and Hilda Wynne and I are both seedy. We are always trying to wire for things, but not a word gets through.

We were summoned to dine at the palace last night. Everyone was very charming.

December 31:

Prince Murat came to dine and play bridge. Count Groholski turned up for a few days. My doctor vetted me for my cold. Business done—none. No sailor ever longed for port as I do for home.

Chapter 13
Georgia & Armenia

"Imperial Russian World War I poster," (1916). Courtesy Wikimedia Commons.

Jan. 1, 1916:

Tbilisi

Kind wishes from the Grand Duke and everybody. Not such an aimless day as usual. I got into a new sitting room and arranged it. In the evening we went to Prince Orloff's box for a performance of "Carmen." It was very Russian and wealthy. At the back of the box were two anterooms, where we sat and talked between the acts. There tea, chocolates, etc., were served. They say the Prince has £200,000 a year. He is gigantically fat, with a real Cossack face.

Scandal is so rife here that it hardly seems to mean gossip. They don't appear to be so much immoral as non-moral. Everyone sits up late; then most of them, I am told, get drunk, and then the evening orgies begin. No one is ostracized; everyone is called upon and "known" whatever they have done. I suppose English respectability would simply make them smile—if, indeed, they believed in it.

January 2:
Ill-Bestowed Charity

I don't suppose I shall ever write an article on war charities, but I believe I ought to. Many facts about them have come my way, and I consider that the public at home should be told how the finances are being administered.

I know of one hospital in Russia which has, I believe, cost England £100,000. The staff consists of nurses and doctors, dressers, etc., all fully paid. The expenses of those in charge of it are paid for out of the funds. They live in good hotels and have "entertaining allowances" for entertaining their friends. Yet one of them herself volunteered the information that the hospital is not needed. The staff arrived weeks ago, but not the equipment. Probably the building won't be opened for some time to come, and when it is opened there will be difficulty in getting patients to fill it.

In many parts of Russia, hospitals are not wanted. In St. Petersburg there are 500 of them run by Russians alone.

Then there is a fund for relief of the Poles, which is administered by Princess ___. The ambulance which the fund owns is used by the Princess to take her to the theatre every night.

A great deal of money has been given for the benefit of the Armenians. Who knows how much this has cost the givers? Yet distribution of this large sum seems to be conducted on most haphazard lines. An open letter arrived the other day for the Mayor of Tbilisi. There is no Mayor of Tbilisi, so the letter was brought to Major ___. It said: "Have you received two checks already sent? We have had no acknowledgment." There seems to be no check on the expenditure, and there is no local organization for dispensing the relief. I don't say it is cheating: I only say as much as I know.

Some generous people in England sent numerous ambulances to Russia the other day. They were inspected by Royalty before being sent and arrived in the care of Mr. ___. When their engines were examined it was found they were tied together with bits of copper wire, and even with string. None of them could be made to work, and they were returned to England.

We are desperately hard up at home just now, and we are denying ourselves in order to send these charitable contributions to the richest country in the world. Gorlebeff himself (head of the Russian Red Cross Society) has £30,000 a year. The Armenians are literally rolling in money. It is common to find Armenian ladies buying hats at 250 Rs. (£25) in Tbilisi. The Poles are not ruined, nor do they seem to object to German rule, which is doing more for them than Russia ever did. Tbilisi people are now sending money for relief to Mesopotamia. Of the 300,000 Rs. sent by England, 70,000 Rs. have stuck to someone's fingers.

In Flanders there were many people living in comfort such as they had probably never seen before at the expense of the charitable public, and doing very little indeed all the time. Cars to go about in, chauffeurs at their disposal, gasoline without stint, and even their clothes (called uniforms) are paid for.

And the little half-crowns that come in to run these shows, "how hardly they are earned sometimes! With what sacrifices they are given!" A man in Flanders said to me one day: "We could lie down and roll in tobacco, and we all help ourselves to every blooming thing we want; and here is a note I found in a poor little parcel of things tonight: 'We are so sorry not to be able to send more, but money is very scarce this week.'"

My own cousin brought four cars over to France, and he told me he was simply an unpaid chauffeur at the command of young officers coming in to shop at Dunkirk. I am thankful to say that Mrs. Wynne, Mr. Bevan, and I have paid our own expenses ever since the war began, and given things too. And I think many of our own corps in Flanders used to contribute liberally and pay for all they had. People here tell us that their cars have all been commandeered for use by the wives of Generals, who never had entered one before and who proudly do their shopping in them.

"Russian Red Cross World War I poster," (1916). Courtesy Wikimedia Commons.

War must be a military matter, and these things must end, unless money is to find its way into the possession of the vultures who are always at hand when there is any carcass about.

January 5:
A Feeling about the Future

Absolutely nothing to write about. I saw Gorlebeff, Domerchekoff, and Count Tysczkievcz of the Croix Rouge about my plans. They suggest my going to Urumiyah in Persia, where workers seem to be needed. The only other opening seems to be to go to Count Groholski's new little hospital on the top of the mountains.

Mr. Hills, the American missionary, wants me first to go with him to see the Armenian refugees at Yerevan, but we can't get transportation for his gifts of clothing for them.

"Armenian orphans boarding barges for Greece at Constantinople with help from the Near East Relief workers," *Bain News Service* (circa 1915). Courtesy the Library of Congress.

Before I left England I had a very strange, almost an overwhelming presentiment that I had better not come to Russia. I had by that time promised Mrs. Wynne that I would come. I couldn't see that it would be the right thing to refuse her. I thought the work would suffer if I stayed at home since she might find it impossible to get any other woman who would pay her own way and agree to be away for so long a time. Our prayers are always such childish things—prayer itself is only a cry—and I remember praying that if I was "meant to stay at home" some substitute might be found for me. This all seems too absurd when I think of it in the light of what afterwards happened. My vision of "honor" and "work" seem for the moment ridiculous. Yet I know I was not so foolish as I seem, for I got a written statement from Mr. Hume-Williams (Mrs. Wynne's trustee), saying, "A unit has been formed, consisting of Mrs. Wynne, Miss Macnaughtan, etc., and it has been accepted by the Russian Red Cross." The idea of being in Russia and having to look for work never in my wildest moments entered my head—and this is the end of the "vision," I suppose.

"Seven men in Cossack clothing, posing as if at a feast in Georgia," (circa 1900). Courtesy the Library of Congress.

Russian Christmas Day

I took a car and went for a short drive into the country. Weather fine and bright. There is severe fighting in Galicia in East Central Europe. The rumor is that Urumiyah—the place to which I am going—has been evacuated.

My impression of Russia deepens—that it is run by beautiful women and rich men; and yet how charming everyone is to meet! Hardly anyone is not interesting, and half the men are good-looking. The Cossack dress is very handsome and nearly everyone wears it. When the color is dark red and the ornaments are of silver the effect is unusually good. They all walk well. You are among a primitive people, but a remarkably fine one!

January 10: Difficulties

I am taking French lessons. This would appear to be a simple matter, even in Russia, but it has taken me three weeks to get a teacher. The first to come required a rest, and must decline. The second was recalled by an old employer. The third had too many engagements. The fourth came and then holidays began, as they always do! First our Christmas, then the Russian Christmas, then the Armenian Christmas, leading on to three New Year Days! After that the Baptism of Jesus, with its holidays and its vigils.

There is only one sort of breakfast roll in this hotel soft enough to eat; it is not made on festivals, nor on the day after a festival. I can honestly say we hardly ever see one. With much fear and trembling I have bought a car. No work seems possible without it. The price is costly, but everyone says I will be able to get it back when I leave. All the same, I shake in my shoes—a chauffeur, tires, fuel, mean money all the time. You can't stop spending out here. It is like some fate from which you can't escape. Still the car is bought, and I suppose now I shall get work.

We are all in the same boat. Mrs. Wynne has waited for her ambulances for three months. I hear that even the Anglo-Russian hospital, with every name from Queen Alexandra's downwards on the list of its patrons, is in "one long difficulty." It is Russia. Nothing but Russia, that breaks us all. Everything is promised, nothing is done. The only hope of getting a something to move is by bribery, and you may bribe the wrong people until you find your way around.

January 13:

The car took us up the Kajour road, and behaved well; but the chauffeur drove us into a bridge on the way down, and had to be dismissed. Tried to go to Yerevan, but the new chauffeur mistook the road, so we had to return to Tbilisi. Another holiday was coming on, and he wanted to be at home. I actually used to like difficulties!

January 15:

Started again for Yerevan. All went well, and we had a lovely drive until about 6 p.m. The dusk was gathering and we were up in the hills, when "bang!" went something. Nothing on earth would make the car move. We unscrewed nuts, we lighted matches, we got out the "jack," but we could not discover what was wrong. So where were we to spend the night?

In a fold of the gray hills was a little gray village—just a few huts belonging to Muslim shepherds, but there was nothing to be done, but to ask them for shelter. Fortunately, Dr. Wilson knew the language, and he persuaded the "head man" to turn out for us. His family consisted of about 16 people, all sleeping on the floor. They gave us the clay-daubed little place. Fortunately it contained a stove, but nothing else. The snow was all round us. We made a fire and got some tea, which we carried with us, and finally slept in the little place while the chauffeur guarded the car.

In the morning nothing would make the car budge an inch. Seeing our difficulty, the Muslims made us pay a good deal for horses to tow the thing to the next village, where we heard there was a blacksmith. We followed in a hay cart. We got to a Malokand settlement about 5 o'clock, and found ourselves in an extraordinarily pretty little village, where we were given shelter in the very cleanest house I ever saw. The woman was a perfect treasure. She made us soup and gave us clean beds, and honey for breakfast. The chauffeur found that our shaft was broken, and the whole piece had to go back to Tbilisi.

It was a real blow to our trip. Now how were we to get on? The railway was 48 versts away, and the railway had to be reached. We hired one of those painful little carts, made of rough poles on wheels, and, clinging on by our eyelids, we drove as far as an Armenian village, where a snowstorm came on. We took shelter with a "well-to-do" Armenian family, who gave us lunch and displayed their wool-work. They were very friendly. From there we got into another cart of the painful variety, and jolted off for about 25 miles, until, as night fell, we came to the railway, where we were given two wooden benches to sleep on in a small waiting room. People came and went all night, and we slept with one eye open until 2 a.m., when the chauffeur took a train to Tbilisi. We sat up until 6 a.m., when the train, two hours late, started for Yerevan, where we arrived pretty well exhausted at 11 p.m.

"Armenian Catholic women in traditional dress," by Sergeĭ Mikhaĭlovich (circa 1905 to 1915). Courtesy the Library of Congress.

January 20:
Massacres

Last night's experiences were certainly very "Russian." We had wired for rooms, but although the message had been received nothing was prepared. The miserable rooms were an inch thick in dust, there were no fires, and no sheets on the beds! We went to a restaurant—fortunately no Russian goes to bed early—and found the oddest place, empty except for a band and a lady. The lady and the band were having supper. She, poor soul, was painted and dyed, but offered her services to translate my French for me when the waiters could understand nothing but Russian. I was thankful to eat something and go to bed under my fur coat.

Today we have been busy seeing the Armenian refugees. There are 17,000 of them in this city of 30,000 inhabitants. We went from one place to another.

Always you saw the same things and heard the same tales.

Since the war broke out I think I have seen the actual breaking of the wave of anguish which has swept over the world. (I often wonder if I can "feel" much more!). There was Dunkirk and its shambles, there was ruined Belgium, and there was, above all, the field hospital at Furnes, with its horrible courtyard, the burning heap of bandages, and the mattresses set on edge to drip the blood off them and then laid on some bed again. I can never forget it. I was helping a nurse once, and the whole time I was sitting on a dead man and never knew it!

And now I am hearing of 1 million Armenians slaughtered in cold blood. The pitiful women in the shelters were saying, "We are safe because we are old and ugly; all the young ones went to the harems." Nearly all the men were massacred. The surplus children and unwanted women were put into houses and burned alive. Everywhere you heard, "We were 4,000 in one village, and only 143 escaped;" "There were 30 of us, and now only a few children remain;" and "All the men are killed." These were things you saw for yourself, heard for yourself. There was nothing sensational in the way the women told their stories.

Russia does what she can in the way of "relief." She gives 4-1/2 Rs. per month to each person. This gives them bread, and there might be fires, for stoves are there, but no one seems to have the gumption to put them up. Here and there men and women are sleeping on valuable rugs, which look strange in the bare shelters. Most of the women knitted, and some wove on little "fegir" looms. The dullness of their existence matches the tragedy of it. The food is so plain it doesn't need cooking—being mostly bread and water. But sometimes a few rags are washed, and there is an attempt to try and keep warm. Yet I have heard an English officer say nothing pleases a Russian more than to ask, "When is there to be another Armenian massacre?"

The Armenians are hated. I wonder Christ doesn't do more for them considering they were the first nation in the world to embrace Christianity. But then, you wonder about so many things during this war. Oh, if we could stamp out the madness that seems to accompany religion, and just live sober, kind, sensible lives, how good it would be; but the Turks must burn women and children, alive, because, poor souls, they think one thing and the Turks think another! And men and women are hating and killing each other because Christ, says one, had a nature both human and divine, and, says another, the two were merged in one. And a third says that Christ was equal to the Father, while a whole Church separated itself on the question of Sabellianism, or "The Procession of the Son."

Poor Christ, once crucified, and now dismembered by your own disciples, are you glad you came to earth, or do you still think God forsook you, and did you, too, die an unbeliever? The crucifixion will never be understood until men know that its worst agony consisted in the disbelief which first of all doubts God and then must, by all reason, doubt itself.

January 21:
The White Jewel

Today, I drove out to Etchmiadzin with Mr. Lazarienne, an Armenian, to see that curious little place. It is the ecclesiastical city of Armenia—its little Rome, where the Catholics lives. He was ill, but a charming Bishop—Wardepett by name—with a flowing brown beard and long black silk hood, welcomed us and gave us lunch. Then he showed us the hospital—which had no open windows, and smelt horrible—and the lovely little third-century "temple." Then he took us round the strange, quiet little place, with its peaceful park and its three old brown churches, which mark what must once have been a great city and the first seat of a national Christianity. Now there are perhaps 300 inhabitants, but Mount Ararat dominates it, and Mount Ararat is not a hill. It is a great white jewel set up against a sheet of dazzling blue.

Hills and ships always seem to me to be alive, and I think they have a personality of their own. Ararat stands for the unassailable. It is like some great fact, such as that what is beautiful must be true. It is grand and pure and lovely. When the sun sets it is more than this, for then its top is one sheet of rose, and it melts into a mystic hill, and you know that whatever else may "go to Heaven" Ararat goes there every night.

We visited the old Persian palace built on the river's cliff, looked out over the gardens to the hills beyond, and saw the mosque, with its blue roof against the blue sky, and its wonderful covering of old tiles, which drop like leaves and are left to crumble.

January 24:
Despair

I left Yerevan on Sunday, January 23. It was cold and sharp, and the train was crowded. People were standing all down the corridors, as usual. Nothing goes quicker than eight miles an hour, nothing is punctual, nothing arrives. The stations are filthy, and the food is quite uneatable. I often despair of this country, and if the Russians were not our Allies I should feel inclined to say nothing would do them so much good as a year or two of German conquest. No one, after the first six months, has been enthusiastic over the war, and the soldiers want to get home. One young officer, 26 years old, has been loafing in Tbilisi for six months and has at last been arrested. Another took his ticket on eight successive nights to leave the place and never moved. At last he was locked in his room and a car ordered to take him to the station. He got into it and was not heard of for three days, when his wife appeared and found her husband somewhere in the town.

Mrs. Wynne and Mr. Bevan have gone on ahead to Baku, but I must wait for my damaged car. A young officer in this hotel shot himself dead this morning. No one seems to mind much.

"Prince Napoleon Murat, a descendant of Marshal Joachim Murat and an Imperial Russian army colonel," (circa 1918). Courtesy Wikimedia Commons.

January 25:
Russian Society

Last night I was invited to play bridge by one of the richest women in Russia. Her room was just a converted bedroom, with dirty wallpaper. The packs of cards were such as you might see railway men playing with in a lamp room. Our stakes were a few kopeks. Refreshments consisted of one tepid cup of tea, without either milk or lemon, and not a biscuit to eat. We all sat with shawls on, as our hostess said it wasn't worthwhile to light a fire so late at night. A nice little Princess Musaloff and Prince Napoleon Murat played with me. We were rich in titles, but our shoulders were cold.

I have not seen a single nice or even comfortable room since I left England. Although some women dress well, and have pretty cigarette cases from the renowned Faberge, other things about them are all wrong. The furniture in their rooms is covered with plush upholstery, and the ornaments (to me) suggest a head gardener's house at home with "an enlargement of mother" over the mantelpiece; or a Clapham drawing room, furnished during some happy year when cotton rose, or copper was popular. In this hotel the carpets have holes in the passages and there are few servants, but I don't think the people here notice things very much.

I went to see Mme. ___ one day in her new house. The rooms were large and handsome. There was a picture of a cow at one end of the drawing room, and a mirror framed in plush at the other!

I must draw a "character study" one day of the very charming woman who is absolutely indifferent to people's feelings. The fact that some humble soul has prepared something for her, or that a sacrifice has been made, or that one kind speech would satisfy, does not occur to her. These are the people who discard engagements when they get better invitations. I always seem to see them with expensive little bags and chains and Faberge enamels. Men will slave for such women—will carry things for them and serve them. They have "success" until they are quite old, and after they turn to makeup with rouge and paint. A tired woman hardly ever gets anything carried for her.

January 26:
Enforced Idleness

A day's march nearer home! This is the Feast of St. Nina. There is always a feast or a fête here. People walk around on the streets, they give each other rich cakes, and work a little less than usual.

This hotel still keeps its cripples. Prince Murat sits on his little chair on the landing. Prince Tschelikoff has his heart all wrong; there is the man with one leg. Now Mademoiselle Lepnakoff, the singer, Musaloff, in his red coat, and some heavy Generals are here. We have the same food every day.

Perhaps I was pretty near having a breakdown when I came abroad, and the enforced idleness of this life may have been providential (all my hair was falling out, and my eyes were very bad, and the war was wearing me down rather). But to sit in a hotel bedroom or to worry over small things in sitting rooms seems a poor sort of way of passing your time. To rest has always seemed to me very hard work. I can't even go to bed without a pile of papers beside me to work at during the night or in the early morning!

When the power of writing leaves me, as it does fitfully and without warning, I have a feeling of loneliness, which helps convince me of what I have always felt, that this power comes from outside, and can only be explained psychically. I asked a great writer once if he ever experienced the feeling I have of being "left." He told me sometimes during the time of desolation he had seriously contemplated suicide.

January 30:

I got a telephone message from Mr. Bevan last night. He says Baku is too horrible, and there is no news of the cars. People are telling me now that if instead of cars we had given money, we should have been honored, decorated and extolled to the skies; but then, where would the money have gone?

Last week the two richest Armenian merchants in this town were arrested for cheating the soldiers out of thousands of yards of stuff for their coats. A government official could easily be found to say that the cloth had been received. Meanwhile what has the soldier to cover him in the trenches?

Armenians are certainly an odious set of people, and their ingratitude is equalled by their meanness and greed. Mr. Hills, who is doing the Armenian relief work here, pays all his own expenses, and he can't get a truck to take his things to the refugees without paying for it. While he is often asked the question: "Why can't you leave these things alone?" Now that Mrs. Wynne has left, I am asked the same question about her.

Russia can "break" one very successfully. The weather has turned cold, and there is biting wind and snow.

"Russian soldiers in trenches along the Eastern Front," by *Bain News Service* (circa 1915). Courtesy the Library of Congress.

February 1:
Imaginary Ailments

"No," says I to myself, in a supremely virtuous manner, "I shall not be beaten by this enervating existence here. I'll do something—if it's only sewing a seam." So out came needles and cotton and mending and hemming, but, would it be believed, I am afflicted with two *"doigts blancs"* (festered fingers), and have to wear bandages, which prevent my doing even the mildest seam. Oddly enough, this illness is a sort of epidemic here. The fact is, the dust is full of microbes, and no one is too well nourished.

I am rather amused by those brave strong people who "don't make a fuss about their health." You hear from them almost daily that their temperature has gone up to 103 degrees, "but it's nothing," they say heroically, "or if it is, it's only typhoid, and who cares for a little typhoid?" Does a headache, there is "something very queer about it, but"—pushing back hair from a hot eyebrow—"no one is to worry about it."

"Merchant's Wife at Tea," by Boris Kustodiev (1918). Courtesy Wikimedia Commons.

It will be better tomorrow; or if it really is going to be fever, we must just try to make the best of it." A sty in the eye is cataract, "but lots of blind people are very happy;" and an attack of nausea is generally that mysterious, oft-recurring and interesting complaint "camp fever."

Cheer up, no one is to be discouraged if the worst happens! A thermometer is produced, shaken and applied. The temperature is too low now; it is probably only typhus, and we mean to be brave and get up.

February 3:

Last night we played bridge. All the princes and princesses moistened their thumbs before dealing. No one is above using a *"crachoir"* [spittoon] on the staircase!

Oh for one hour of England! In all my travels I have only found one foreign race which seemed to me to be well bred (as I understand it), and that is the native of India.

The very best French people come next; and the Spaniard knows how to bow, but he clears his throat in an objectionable manner. None of them have been licked! That is the trouble. An Eton boy of 15 could give them all points, and beat them with his hands in his pockets.

I am quite sure that the British nation is really superior to all others. Ours is the only well-bred race, and the only generous or hospitable nation. Fancy a foreigner keeping "open house"!

Here the entertainment is a glass of thickened tea, and the stove is frequently not lighted even on a chilly evening.

Since I have been in Russia I have had nothing better or more substantial given to me (by the Russians) than a piece of cake, except by the Grand Duke.

We brought heaps of letters of introduction, and people called, but that is all, or else they gave an "evening" with the very lightest refreshments I have ever seen. Someone plays badly on the piano, there is a little bridge, and a samovar!

"Lydia Lipkowska, famed soprano of the Imperial Russian Opera," *Musical America*, (April 30, 1921), 33-34.

February 6:

The queer epidemic of "gathered fingers" continues here. Having two, I am in the fashion. They make one awkward and more idle than ever. A lot of people come in and out of my sitting room to "cheer me up." Everyone wants me to tell their fortune. Mrs. Wynne and Mr. Bevan are still at Baku.

Last night I went to Prince Orloff's box to hear Lydia Lipkowska in "Faust."

My car has come back and is running well, but the weather has been cold and stormy, with snow drifting in from the hills. I took Madame Derfelden and her husband to Kajura today. Now that I have the car everyone wants me to work with them. The difficulty of transport is indescribable. Without a car it is like being without a leg. You simply can't get around. In order to get a seat on a train, people walk up the line and bribe the officials at the place where it is standing to allow them to get on board.

Chapter 14
1915: The War in Persia
BY NOËL FLETCHER

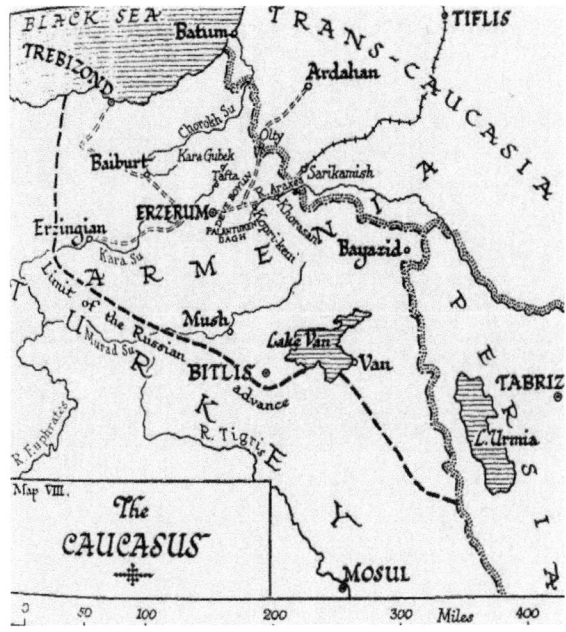

The Story of the Great War,"(1916), Vol. 5, P.F. Collier and Son.

At this time, Iran was called Persia and divided into three zones (Russian, British and neutral) by the 1907 Anglo-Russian agreement. Although Persia declared itself neutral during World War I, there were multiple battles there during World War I between British, Russian and Turkish forces.

"Russian soldiers in Persia," Bain News Service (circa 1915). Courtesy the Library of Congress.

Russia and Turkey fought across various numerous cities in Persia. Russian warships from the Black Sea blasted the northern Turkish coast for over a year.

In Turkey there had been massacres of thousands of Christian Armenians, with news coming from the Russian city Tiflis (present day Tbilisi, Georgia). Britain created a local military force called the South Persia Rifles in 1916 to protect its interests and prevent political and economic gains by German diplomats and agents.

"Map of the Russians in Persia" (left) and "Map of Persia and British forces (below)," in *The Story of the Great War*, (1916), Vol. 5, P.F. Collier and Son.

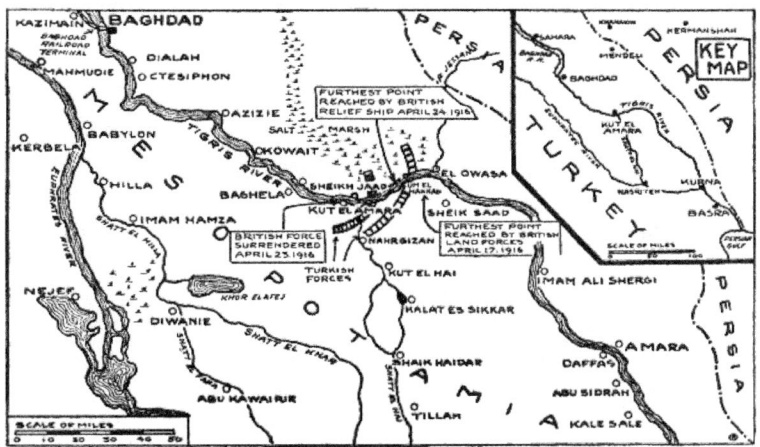

Chapter 15
Travels in 3 Cities

British Legation, Tehran

Feb. 8, 1916:

A repair shop having been found for my car, Pavel Ignatieff of the Red Cross and I started for Baku today. We found our little party at the Métropole Hotel. Went to the R. Ronald MacDonells to lunch. He is British Consul in Baku, Azerbaijan. They are quite charming people, and their little apartment was open to us all the time we were at Baku.

The place itself is wind-blown and flyblown and brown, but the harbor is very pretty, with its crowds of shipping, painted with red hulls, which make a nice bit of color in the general drab of the hills and the town. There are no gardens and no trees, and all enterprise in the way of town planning and the like is impossible owing to the Russian habit of cheating. They have tried for 16 years to start electric trolleys, but everyone wants too much for his own pocket. The morals become dingier and dingier as you get nearer Tartar influence, and no shame is thought of it. Most of the stories you hear would blister the pages of a diary. When a house of ill repute is opened, it is publicly blessed by the priest!

February 18:
Kasvin [Qazvin], Persia

We spent a week at Baku and grumbled all the time, although really we were not at all unhappy. The MacDonells were always with us and we had good games of bridge with Ignatieff in the evenings. We went to see the oil city at Baku. One day we drove to the much larger oil city further out. One of the directors, an Armenian, went with us, and gave us the very largest lunch at his house that I have ever seen. It began with many plates of *zakouska* (hors d'oeuvres), and went on to a cold entrée of cream and chickens' livers; then grilled salmon, with some excellent sauce, and a salad of beetroot and cranberries. This was followed by an entrée of kidneys. Then we came to soup, the best I have ever eaten. After soup was roast turkey, followed by chicken pilaf, sweets and cheese. It was impossible even to taste all the things, but the Georgian cook must have been a "cordon bleu."

On February 16, one of the long-delayed cars arrived. We were in ecstasies and took our places on the steamer for Persia; but the radiator had been broken on the way down. And Mrs. Wynne was delayed again. I started, as my car was arranged for, and had to go on board. Also, I found I could be useful to Ernest S. Scott of the Tehran Legation, who was going there. We traveled on the boat together and had an excellent crossing to Enzeli [Bandar-e Anzalī], a lovely little port. Then we took my car and drove to Rasht, where Mr. and Mrs. Charles Walter de Bois Maclaren, the Consul and his wife, kindly put us up. Their garden is quiet and damp; the house is damp too, and very ugly. There are only two other English people (at the bank) to form the society of the place, and it must be a bit lonely for a young woman. I found the situation a little tragic.

We drove on next day to Kasvin, and Mr. and Mrs. Goodwin were good enough to ask us to stay with them. [Goodwin worked at Britain's Imperial Bank of Persia.] The big fires in the house were very cheering after our cold drive in the snow. The moonlight was marvelous, and the mountain passes were beyond words picturesque. We passed a string of 150 camels pacing along in the moonlight and the snow. All of them wore bells which jingled softly. Around us were the weird white hills, with a smear of mist over them. The radiant moon, the snow, and the chiming camels I shall never forget.

Captain Rhys Rhys-Williams, acting Military Attaché at the British Legation, was also at the Goodwins. He was in very great anxiety to get to Hamedan. I offered to take him in my car, and let Mr. Scott do the last stage of the journey in the Legation car to Tehran. We were delayed one day at Kasvin, which was passed very pleasantly in the sheltered sunny compound of the house. My little white bedroom was part of the "women's quarters" of the old days, and with its bright fire at night and the sun by day it was a very comfortable place in which to perch.

February 24:
Arrival at Hamadan

Captain Williams and I left Kasvin at 8 a.m. on February 19. I had always had an idea that Persia was in the tropics. Where I got this notion I can't say.

As soon as we left sheltered Kasvin and got out to the plains, the cold was as sharp as anything I have known. Snow lay deep on every side, and the icy wind nearly cut you in two.

We stopped at a little *"tschinaya"* (tea house) and ate some sandwiches we had brought with us. I also had a flask of Sandeman's port, given to me last Christmas by Sir Ivor Heron-Maxwell [a British military intelligence officer]. I think a glass of this just prevented me from being frozen solid.

We drove onto the top of the pass and arrived there about 3 o'clock. We found some Russian officers having an excellent lunch, and we shared ours and had some of theirs.

The Strange Side of War: A Woman's WWI Diary

"Russian Red Cross field hospital during World War I," *Bain News Service* (circa 1914 to 1915). Courtesy the Library of Congress.

We saw a lot of game in the snow—great coveys of fat partridges, hares by the score, a jackal, two wolves, and many birds. The hares were very odd, for after twilight fell, and we lit our lamps, they seemed quite paralyzed by the glare, and used to sit down in front of the car.

We passed a regiment of Cossacks, extended in a long line, and coming over the snow on their strong horses. We began to get near war once more, and see transport and guns. Russian General Nikolai N. Baratoff wants us up here to remove wounded men when the advance begins towards Bagdad.

The cold was really as bad as they say after the sun had sunk. An icy mist enveloped the hills. We got within sight of the clay-built, flat Persian town of Hamadan about 10 p.m., but the car couldn't make any way on the awful roads. So I left Captain Williams at the barracks and came to the Red Cross hospital with two Russian officers, one a little the worse for drink.

With the genius for confusion which the Russians possess in a remarkable degree, no preparations had been made for me. Rather an unpleasant doctor came to the gateway with two nurses. The officers began to flirt with the girls and to give them compliments. Some young Englishmen, one of whom was the British Consul, then appeared on the scene, so we began to make progress a little (although it seemed to me that we stood about in the snow for a terribly long time, and I got quite frozen!). As it was then past midnight, I felt I had had enough, so I went to the American missionary's house, which was pointed out to me. He and his wife hopped out of bed, and, clad in curious gray robes, came downstairs and got me a cup of hot tea, which I had needed badly for many hours. There was no fireplace in my room. The other fires of the house were all out, but the old couple was kindness and goodness itself. In the end, I rolled myself up in my faithful plaid blanket and slept at their house.

The next day—Sunday, February 20—John Cowan, the young Consul, and a Mr. Lightfoot, came round and bore me off to the Consulate. On Monday I began to settle in, but even now I find it difficult to take my bearings, as we have been in a heavy mountain fog ever since I got here. There is a little English colony, the bank manager, J. A. MacMurray, and his wife—a capable, energetic woman, and an excellent working partner—Mr. McLean, a Scottish clerk, a Mr. McDowal, also a Scot, and a few other good folk; whom in Scotland you would reckon the farmer class, but none the worse for that, and never vulgar however humbly born.

On Monday, February 21, I called on the Russian element—Madame Kirsanoff, General Baratoff, etc. They were all cordial, but nothing will convince me that Russians take this war seriously. They do the thing as comfortably as possible. "My country" is a word you never hear from their lips, and they indulge in masterly retreats too often for my liking. The fire of the French, the dogged courage of the British, seem quite unknown to them. Literally, no one seems much interested. There is a good deal of fuss about a "forward movement" on this front; but I fancy that at Kermanshah and at ____ there will be very little resistance, and the troops there are only Persian gendarmerie.

The Strange Side of War: A Woman's WWI Diary

"Czar Nicholas II of Russia and Tsarevich Alexei Nikolaievich wearing the parade uniform of the 1st Ural Sotnia Squadron of the Combined Cossack Guards' Regiment," (1913). Courtesy Wikimedia Commons.

No doubt the most will be made of the Russian "victory," but compared with the Western Front, this is simply not war. I often think of the guns firing day and night, the Taubes overhead, and the burning towns of Flanders. And then I find myself living a peaceful life, with an occasional glimpse of a regiment passing by.

Feb. 23, 1916
To Mrs. Charles Percival,
British Vice-Consulate, Hamadan

My Dearest Tabby,

We are buried in snow, and every road is a dugout, with parapets of snow on either side. All journeys have to be made by road and generally over mountain passes, where you may or may not get through the snow.

You see "breakdowns" all along the routes. Everywhere we go we have to take food and blankets in case of a camp out. I have had to buy a car and got a very good one in Tbilisi, but they are so scarce you have to pay a ransom for them. I am hoping it won't be quite smashed up, and I will be able to sell it for something when I leave.

Transport is the difficulty everywhere in these vast countries, with their persistent lack of railways. The best way of helping the wounded is to remove them as painlessly and expeditiously as possible, but this can only be done with cars. Only one of Mrs. Wynne's ambulances has yet to arrive. In the end, I came here without her and Mr. Bevan. I had to give a member of the Legation at Tehran a ride; and, still more important, I had to bring an important soldier here. So long as you can offer a car, you are everybody's friend.

Yesterday I was requested to go up to a mountain pass and fetch two doctors, whose vehicle had broken down in the snow. The wind is often a hurricane, and I am told there will be no warm weather until May. I look at a light silk dressing gown and gauze underclothing, and wonder why it is that no one seems able to tell you what a climate will be like. I have warm things too, I am glad to say.

Although our luggage is now of the lightest type and is only what we can take in a car. The great thing is to be very independent. No one would dream of bringing heavy luggage or anything of that sort, except, of course, Legation people, who have their own transportation and servants.

On journeys, I am treated kindly by the few Scottish people (they all seem to be Scots) scattered here and there. Everywhere I go I find the usual Scottish couple trying to "have things nice," and longing for mails from home. One woman was newly married and had only one wish in life, and that was for acid drops [candy]. Poor soul, she wasn't well. I want to make her the best imitation I can and send them to her. They make their houses wonderfully comfortable, but the difficulty is getting things! Another woman had written home for her child's dress in August, but got it by mail on February 15. Cases of things coming by boat or train take far longer, or never arrive at all.

I will be working with the Russian hospital here until our next move. There are 25 beds and 120 patients. Of course, we are only waiting to push on further. The political situation is most interesting, but I must not write about it, of course. It is rather wonderful to have seen the war from so many quarters.

The long wait for the cars was quite maddening, but I believe it did me good. I was just about "through." Now I am in a bachelor's little house, full of terrier dogs and tobacco smoke. And when I am not at the hospital, I darn socks and play bridge.

Now that really is all my news, I think. Empire is not made for nothing, and you see some plucky lives in these out-of-the-way parts. I did not like my host at one house where we stayed and something made me think his wife was bullied and not very happy. A husband would have to be quite all right to compensate for exile, mud, and solitude.

Always my feeling is that we want far more people—especially educated people, of course—to run the world. Yet we continue to shoot down our best and noblest, and when shall we ever see their kind again?

Always, my dear,
Your loving S. Macnaughtan

I hope to get over to Tehran on my "transport service," and there I may find a mail. Some people called ____, living near Glasgow, had nine sons, eight of whom have been killed in the war. The ninth is delicate and doing Red Cross work.

"Fruit market in Persia [Iran]," *Bain News Service* (circa 1911). Courtesy the Library of Congress.

February 26:
Missionaries and Religion

On Tuesday, a doctor took my car by fraud so there had to be an enquiry made, and I don't feel happy about it yet. With Russians anything can happen. I have begun to suffer from the chilly temperatures I experienced getting here. I have a cold and also my mouth and chin are very bad; so I have had to lie doggo [quiet]. I see an ancient Persian doctor, who prescribed and talked of the mission field at the same time.

I am struck by one thing, which is so naïvely expressed out here that it is very humorous, and that is the firm and formidable attitude that the best sort of men show towards religion. To all of them it means missionaries and pious talk. To hear them speak you would imagine it was something between a dangerous disease and a disgrace. The best they can say of any clergyman (whom they loathe) or missionary is: "He never tried out the Gospel on me." A religious young man means a sneak, and a person who swears freely is generally rather a good fellow. When you live in the wilds I am afraid you often find that this view is the right one, although it isn't very orthodox; but the pi-jaw [pious talk] that passes for religion seems deliberately calculated to disgust the natural man, who shows his contempt for the thing wholesomely as becomes him. He intends to smoke, have a whisky when he can get it, and a game of cards when possible. His smoke is harmless, he seldom drinks too much, and he plays fair at all games, but when he finds that these harmless amusements keep him from a place in the Kingdom of Heaven he naturally—if he has the spirit of a mouse—says, "All right. Leave me out. I am not on in this show."

February 27:
How News Travels in Persia

On Sunday, I always think of home. I am rather inclined to wonder what my family imagines I am actually doing on the Persian front. No doubt some of my dear friends ascribe to me noble deeds, but I still seem unable to strike the "noble" tack. Even my work in the hospital has been stopped by a telegram from the Red Cross, saying, "Don't let Miss Macnaughtan work yet." A typhus scare, I think. Such rot. But I am now used to hearing all the British out here murmur: "What can be the good of this long delay?"

I am still staying at the British Consulate. The Consul, Mr. Cowan, is a good fellow, and Mr. Lightfoot, his chum, is a real backwoodsman, full of histories of adventures, fights, "natives," and wars in many lands. He seems to me one of those headstrong, straight, fine fellows whom you only meet in the wilds. England doesn't agree with them; they haven't always a suit of evening clothes. But in a tight place you know how levelheaded he would be. And as for tales there is no one better. He tells you a lot about this country, and he knows the Arabs like brothers. Their system of communicating with each other is as puzzling to him as it is to everyone else. News travels faster among them than any messenger or mail can take it.

"Aerial view of houses in the heart of the old city of Haroun El-Rashid in Baghdad," (circa 1920). Courtesy the Library of Congress.

At Bagdad they heard from these strange people of the fall of Basra, which is 230 miles away, within 25 hours of its having been taken. Mr. Lightfoot says that even if he travels by car Arab news is always ahead of him. Where he arrives with news it is known already. Telegraphy is unknown in the places he speaks of, except in Bagdad, of course, and Persia owns exactly one line of railway, 8 miles long, which leads to a tomb! More important than any man here are the dogs—Smudge, Jimmy, and the puppy. Most of the conversation is addressed to them. All of it is about them.

February 28:
A Day on the Persian Front

I wake early because it is always so cold at 4 a.m., and I generally boil up water for my hot-water bottle and go to sleep again. Then at 8 comes the usual

Resident Sahib's servant, whom I have known in many countries and in many climes. He is always exactly alike, and the Empire depends upon him! He is thin, he is mysterious. He is faithful and allows no one to rob his master but himself. He believes in the British. He worships British rule, and he speaks no language but his own, though he probably knows English perfectly, and listens to it at every meal without even the cock of an ear! He is never hurried, never surprised. What he thinks his private idol may know—no one else does. His master's boots—especially the brown sort—are part of his religion. He understands an Englishman and is unmoved by his behavior, whatever it may be. I have met him in India, in Kashmir, at Embassies, in Consulates, on steamers, and I have never known his conduct alter by a hair's breadth. He is piped in red, and let that explain him, as it explains much else that is British. Just a thin red line down the length of a trouser or around a coat, and the man thus adorned is part of the Empire.

The man piped in red lights my fire every morning in Persia and arranges my tub, and we breakfast very late because there is nothing to do on three days of the week—i.e., Friday, the Persian Sabbath, Saturday, the Jewish Sabbath, and Sunday, the Armenian Sunday. On these three days neither bazaars nor offices are open. Business is at a standstill. The Consulate smokes pipes, develops photographs, and reads old novels. On the four busy days we breakfast at 10 o'clock, and during the meal we learn what the dogs have done during the night—whether Jimmy has barked, or Smudge has lain on someone's bed, or the puppy "coolly put his head on my pillow."

About 11 o'clock I, who am acting as wardrobe-mender to some very untidy clothes and socks, get to work, and the young men go to the town and appear at lunchtime. We hear what the local news is, and what Mr. MacMurray has said and Mr. McLean thought, and sometimes one of the people from the Russian hospital comes in. About 3 p.m. we put on galoshes and take exercise single-file on the pathways cut in the snow. At 5 the samovar appears, and tea and cake, and we talk to the dogs and to each other. We dress for dinner because that is our creed; and we burn a good deal of wood, and go to bed early.

Travel really means movement. Otherwise, it is far better to stay at home. I am beginning to sympathies with the Americans who insist upon doing two cities a day. We got some papers today dated October 26, and also a few letters of the same date.

Unfinished Article on Persia found among Sarah's papers

THE YOUNG PERSIAN MOVEMENT

Persia is a difficult country to write about, for unless you color the picture too highly to be recognizable, it is likely to be uninteresting even under the haze of the summer sun, while in wintertime the country disappears under a blanket of white snow. Of course, most of us thought that Persia was somewhere in the tropics, and it gives us a little shock when we find ourselves living in a temperature of 8 degrees below zero. The rays of the sun are popularly supposed to minimize the effect of this cold, and a fortnight's fog on the Persian highlands has still left you a believer in this phenomenon, for when the sun does shine, it does it handsomely, and, according to the inhabitants, it is only when strangers are here that it turns sulky.

Be that as it may, the most loyal lover of Persia will have to admit that Persian mud is the deepest and blackest in the world, and that snow and mud in equal proportions to a depth of 8 inches make anything but agreeable traveling. Snow is indiscriminately shoveled down off the roofs of houses on to the heads of passersby, and great holes in the road are accepted as the inevitable accompaniment to winter traffic.

In the bazaars—narrow, and filled with small booths, where Manchester cotton is stacked upon shelves—the merchants sit huddled up on their counters, each with a cotton lahaf (quilt) over him, under which is a small brazier of ougol (charcoal). In this way he manages to remain in a thawed condition, while a pipe consoles him for his little trade and the horrible weather. Before him, in the narrow alleys of the bazaar, Persians walk with their umbrellas unfurled; and Russians have put the convenient bashluk (a sort of woolen hood) over their heads and ears. The Arab, in his long camel-skin coat, looks impervious to the weather, and women with veiled faces and long black cloaks pick their way through the mire. Throngs of donkeys, melancholy and overladen, their small feet sinking in the slush, may be with the foot passengers. Some stray dogs make a dirty patch in the snow. A troop of Cossacks, their long cloaks spotted with huge snowflakes, trot heavily through the narrow lanes.

But it is not only, nor principally, of climate that you speak in Persia at the present time.

Persia has been stirring, if not with great events, at least with important ones. At the risk of telling stale news, you must take a glance at the recent history of the country and its people. It is proverbial to say that Persia has been misgoverned for years. It is a country, and the Persians are people who seem fated by circumstances and by temperament to endure ill government. A ruler is either a despot or a knave, and frequently both. Any system of policy is liable to change at any moment. Property is held in the uneasy tenure of those who have stolen it. A long string of names of rulers and politicians reveals the fact that most of them have made what they could for themselves by any means, and that perhaps, on the whole, violence has been less detrimental to the country than weakness.

The worst of it is that no one seems particularly to want the Deliverer—the great and single-minded leader who might free and uplift the country. Persia does not crave the ideal ruler; he might make it very unpleasant for those who are content and rich in their own way. It is this thing, among many others, which helps to make the situation in Persia not only difficult, but almost impossible to follow or describe. It is, above all, the temperament of the Persians themselves which is the baffling thing in the way of Persian reform. Yet reform has been spoken of loudly, and again and again in the last few years, and the reformation is generally known as the Nationalist or Young Persian Movement. To follow this movement through its various ramifications would require a clue as plain and as clear as a golden thread, and the best we can do in our present obscurity is to give a few of the leading features.

The important and critical situation evident in Persia today owes its beginning to the disturbances in 1909, when the Constitutional Party came into power, forcibly, and with guns ready to train on Tehran, and when, almost without an effort, they obtained their rights, and lost them again with even less effort.

February 29:
Tombs and Dervishes

It is the last day of a long month. The snow falls without ceasing, blotting out everything that may be to be seen. Today, for the first time, I realized there are hills nearby. Mr. Lightfoot and I walked to the old stone lion that marks the gateway of Ekmadan—i.e., ancient Hamadan. I think the snow was rather thicker than usual today. Mr. Lightfoot and I went to Hamadan, plodding our way through little tramped-down paths, with snow 3 feet deep on either side. By way of being cheerful we went to see two tombs. One was an old, old place, where slept "the first great physician" who ever lived.

"Dervishes in Persia," by Bain News Service (1915). Courtesy the Library of Congress.

In it a dervish kept watch in the bitter cold, and some slabs of dung kept a smoldering fire not burning but smoking. These dervishes have been carrying messages for Germans. Mysterious, like all religious men, they travel through the country and distribute their whispers and messages. The other tomb is called Queen Esther's, though why they should bury her at Ekmadan when she lived down at Shushan I don't know.

We went to see Annie Montgomery the other day. She is an American Presbyterian missionary, who has lived at Hamadan for 33 years. She has schools, lives in the Armenian quarter, and devotes her life to her neighbors. Her language is entirely Biblical, and it sounds almost racy as she says it. There is nothing to record. Yesterday I cleaned out my room for something to do, and in the evening a smoky lamp laid it an inch thick in black. The pass here is quite blocked, and no one can come or go. The snow falls steadily in fine small flakes. My car has disappeared, with the chauffeur, at Kasvin. I hear of it being sent to the seaport Enzeli [Bandar-e Anzali]. But the whole thing is a mystery and is making me very anxious. There are no answers to any of my telegrams. I am completely in the dark.

"A French barber's trench dugout on the Somme front, with a customer being shaved and another waiting his turn outside," *The Illustrated War News* (Dec. 20, 1916). "Hair on the face, mustaches and short beards, are allowed, but only that. Beards must either be kept closely trimmed or else shaved off. The conditions of trench life made such an order necessary in the interests of the men... Health, not vanity, is the first consideration, and very properly so."

March 3:

I think that to be on a frozen hilltop, with fever, some boils, three dogs, and a blizzard, is about as near wearing down your spirits as anything I know.

March 5, Sunday:
Journey of the Brave

In bed all day, with the ancient Persian in attendance. This is not a story for Sunday afternoon. It is true for one thing, and Sunday afternoon stories are not, as a rule, true. They nearly all tell of the return of the prodigals, but they leave out the return of the pilgrims. That is why this parable is not for Sunday afternoon.

I write it because I never knew a true thing yet that was not of use to someone.

Most of us leave home when we are grown up. The people who never grow up stop at home. The journey and the outward-bound vision are signs of an active mind stirring wholesomely or unwholesomely as the case may be. The prodigal is generally thought of as someone those whose sane mind demands an outlet; but he lands in trouble, and gets hungry, and comes back penitent, as we have heard a thousand million times. The far country is always barren, the husks of swine are the only food to be had, and bankruptcy is inevitable.

The story has been accepted by many generations of men as a picture of the world, with its temptations, its sins, its moral bankruptcy, and its illusionary and unsatisfying pleasures. Preachers have always been fond of allusions to the husks and swine, and the desperate hunger which there is nothing to satisfy in the far country. The story is true; it gives many a man a wholesome fright, and keeps him at home. Its note of forgiveness for a wasted life has proved the salvation of many prodigals.

But there is another journey, far more often undertaken by the young and by all those who needs must seek—the brave, the energetic, the good. It is towards a country distant yet ever near, and it lies much removed from the far country where swine feed. Its minarets stand up against a clear and cloudless sky, its radiance shines from afar off. It is set on a hill, and the road thither is very steep and very long, but the pilgrims start out bravely. They know the way! They carry torches! They have the Light within and without, and "watchwords" for every night, and songs for the morning. Some walk painfully, with bleeding feet, on the path that leads to the beautiful country, and some run joyously with eager feet. Whatever anyone likes to say, it is a much more crowded path than the old trail towards the pigsty. At the first step of the journey stand Faith and Hope and Charity, and beyond are more wondrous things by far—Glory, Praise, Vision, Sacrifice, Heroism, sublime Trust, the Need-to-Give, and the Love that runs to help. And some of the pilgrims—most of them—get there.

But there is a little stream of pilgrims sometimes to be met with going the other way. They are returning, like the prodigal, but there is no one to welcome them. Some are very tragic figures, and for them the sun is forever obscured. But there are others—quite plain, sober men and women, some humorists, and some sages. They have honestly sought the country. They, too, have unfurled banners and marched on, but met with many things on the road which do not match the watchwords, and they have heard many wonderful things which, truthfully considered, do not always appear to them to be facts. They have called poverty beautiful, and they have found it very ugly; and they have called money naught [worthless], and they have found it to be power. They have found sacrifice accepted, and then claimed by the selfish and mean, and even love has not been all that was expected. The pilgrims return. Their poor tummies, too, are empty, but no calf is killed for them, there is no feasting and no joy. They stay at home, but neither elder son nor prodigal has any use for them. In the end they turn out the light and go to sleep, regretting—if they have any humor—their many virtues, which for so long prevented them enjoying the pleasant things of life.

March 1916
Memories of Home

I lie in bed all day up here among these horrible snows. The engineer comes in sometimes and makes me a cup of Benger's Food [a milk additive for babies and the sick]. For the rest, I lean up on my elbow when I can, and cook some little thing—Bovril [meat extract that can be diluted in hot water] or hot milk—on my Etna stove. Then I am too tired to eat it, and the sickness begins all over again. Oh, if I could leave this place! If only someone would send back my car, which has been taken away, or if I could hear where Mrs. Wynne and Mr. Bevan are! But no, the door of this odious place is locked, and the key is thrown away. I have lost count of time. I just wait from day to day, hoping someone will come and take me away.

"British World War I poster showing a bull approaching a recruiting station. Bovril is a brand name for beef extract," (1915). Courtesy the Library of Congress.

Though I am now getting so weak I don't suppose I can travel. You wonder whether there can be Providence in all this disappointment. I think not. I just made a great mistake coming out here, and I have suffered for it. What a winter it has been—disillusioning, dull, hideously and achingly disappointing!

It is too odd to think that until the war came I was the happiest woman in the world. It is too funny to think of my house in London, which people say is the only "salon"—a small "salon," indeed! But I can hardly believe now in my crowds of friends, my devoted servants, my pleasant work, the daily budget of letters and invitations, and the press notices in their pink slips. Then the big lectures and the applause—the shouts when I come in. The joy, almost the intoxication of life, has been mine.

Of course, I ought to have turned back at St. Petersburg! But I thought all my work was before me, and in Russia you can't go around alone without knowing the way and the language of the people. Permits are difficult, nothing is possible unless you is attached to somebody or an organization. And now I have reached the end—Persia! And there is no earthly use for us, and there are no roads.

Chapter 16
Last Journey Home

"What Greets the Eye when You Look Back at the Pilot," by Frank Johnston (1918). Courtesy Wikimedia Commons.

March 1916:
Illness at Kasvin

My car turned up at Hamadan on March 9. On March 13, I said goodbye to my friends at the British Consulate and left the place with a Tartar prince, who cleared his throat from the bottom of his soul, and spat luxuriously all the time. The mud was beyond anything you could imagine. There was a sea of it everywhere, and men waded knee-deep in slush. My poor car floundered bravely and bumped heavily, until at last it could move no more. Two wheels were sunk far past the hubs, and the step of the car was under mud.

The Tartar prince hailed a horse from some men and flung himself across it, and then rode off through the thick sea of mud to find help to move the car. His methods were simple. He came up behind men, and hit them over the head, or beat them with a stick, and drove them in front of him. Sometimes he took out a revolver and fired over the men's heads, making them jump; but nothing makes them really work. We pushed on for a mile or two, and then it became stuck again.

This time there were no men near. The prince walked on to collect some soldiers at the next station. It was a wicked, blowy day. I crept into a wrecked *"camion"* [bus] for shelter, ate some lunch, and slept a little. I wasn't feeling a bit well.

That night we only made 20 miles, and then we stayed at a little rest house, where the woman had 10 children. They all had colds and coughed all the time. She promised supper at 8 o'clock, but kept us waiting until 10 p.m., and then a terrible meal of batter appeared in a big tin dish. Everyone except me ate it, and everyone drank my wine. Then six children and their parents lay in one tiny room, while a nurse and I occupied the hot dining room. There we lay until the cold morning came, and I felt very ill.

So the day began, and it did not improve. I was sick all the time until I could neither think nor see. The poor prince could do nothing, of course.

At last we came to a rest house, and I felt I could go no further. I was quite unconscious for a time. Then they told me it was only two hours to Kasvin. Somehow they got me aboard the car, and the horrible journey began again. Every time the car bumped I was sick. Of course, we punctured a tire, which delayed us. When we got into Kasvin it was 9 o'clock. The Tartar lifted me out of the car. I had been told I might be able to stay in a room belonging to Dr. Smitkin, but where it was I had no idea. I knew there would be no one there. So I gathered up courage to go to the only English people in the place—the Goodwins, with whom I had stayed on my way up—and ask for a bed. This I did, and they let me spread my camp bed in his little sitting room. I was ill indeed, and aching in every bone.

The next day I had to go to Smitkin's room. It was an absolutely bare apartment, but someone spread my bed for me. There were some Red Cross nurses who all offered to do things. The one thing I wanted was food, and this they could only get at the soldiers' mess 2 miles away. So all I had was one tin of sweet Swiss milk. The day after this I decided I must leave, whatever happened, and get to Tehran, where there are hotels.

"Tartar women from the Caucasus," (circa 1900). Courtesy the Library of Congress.

After one night there I was taken to a hospital. I was alone in Persia, in a Russian hospital, where few people even spoke French!

On March 19 an English doctor rescued me. He heard I was ill and came to see me. He took me off to be with his wife at his own home at the British Legation. I will never forget it as long as I live—the blessed change from dirty glasses and tin basins and a rocky bed!

What does illness matter with a pretty room, and kindness showered on you, and everything clean and fragrant? I have a little sitting room, where my meals are served, and I have a fire, a bath, and a garden to sit in.

God bless these good people!

"A Voluntary Aid Detachment nurse lighting a cigarette for a patient inside an ambulance during World War I," by Olive Mudie-Cooke (circa 1916). Courtesy the Wikimedia Commons.

A Letter from Tehran
March 22, 1916
To Lady Clémentine Waring,
British Legation, Tehran

Darling Clemmie,

I am coming home, having fallen sick. Do you know, I was thinking about you so much the other night, since you told me that if ever I was really "down and out" you would know.

So I wondered if, about a week ago, you saw a poor small person (who has shrunk to about half her size!) in an empty room, feeling worth nothing at all, and getting nothing to eat and no attention!

Persia isn't the country to be ill in. I was taken to the Russian hospital—

which is an experience I don't want to repeat!—but now I am in the hands of the Legation doctor, and he is going to nurse me until I am well enough to go home.

There are no railways in this country, except one of 8 miles to a tomb! Hence we all have to flounder about on awful roads in cars, which break down and have to be dug out, and always collapse at the wrong moment, so we have to stay out all night.

You thought Persia was in the tropics? So did I! I have been in deep snow all the time until I came here.

I think the campaign here is nearly over. It might have been a lot bigger, for the Germans were bribing like made.

Ever, dear Clemmie,
Your loving
S. Macnaughtan

P.S. So nice to know you think of me, as I know you do.

March 26:

I am getting stronger, and the days are bright. As a great treat I have been allowed to go to church this morning, the first I have been to since St. Petersburg.

The Strange Side of War: A Woman's WWI Diary

"The Shah of Persia, Ahmad Shah Qajar," by Frank Johnston (1918). Courtesy the Library of Congress.

April 1
To Julia Keays-Young,
British Legation, Tehran

Darling Jenny,

In case you want to make plans about leave, etc., will you come and stop with me when first I get home, say about the 5th or 6th May, I can't say to a day? It will be nice to see you all and have a holiday, and then I hope to come out to Russia again.

Did I tell you I have been ill, but am now being nursed by a delightful English doctor and his wife, and getting the most ideal attention, and medicines changed at every change in the health of the patient. I've missed everything here.

"Palace attendant runners in Persia," by *Bain News Service* (circa 1918). Courtesy the Library of Congress.

I was to be presented to the Shah, etc., and to have gone to the reception on his birthday. All the time I've lain in bed or in the garden. Since I haven't felt up to anything else I haven't worried, and the Shah must do wanting me for the present.

The flowers here are just like England, primroses and violets and Lent lilies, but I'm sure the trees are further out at home.

Your most loving,
Aunt Sally

Convalescence
April 8
To Mrs. Keays-Young,
British Legation, Tehran

Dearest Baby,

I don't think I'll get home until the end of April, as I am not supposed to be strong enough to travel yet. My journey begins with a drive of 300 miles over fearful roads and a chain of mountains always under snow.

Then I have to cross the lumpy Caspian Sea. I shall rest at Baku two nights before beginning the four days journey to St. Petersburg.

After that the fun really begins, as you always lose all your luggage in Finland, and you finish up with the North Sea. What do you think of that, my cat?

Dr. Anthony R. Neligan is still looking after me quite splendidly, and I never drank so much medicine in my life. No fees or money can repay the dear man.

Tehran is the most primitive place! You can't, for instance, get one scrap of flannel, and if a bit of bacon comes into the town there is a stampede for it. People get their wine from England in two-bottle parcels.

Yours as ever,

S.

"Dead soldiers, possibly French, lying in a field," (circa 1915). Courtesy the Library of Congress.

April 1916:
Tehran

The days pass peacefully and even quickly, which is odd, for they are singularly idle. I get up about 11 a.m. and am pretty tired when dressing is finished. Then I sit in the garden and have my lunch there. After lunch I lie down for an hour. Presently tea comes; I watch the Neligans start for their ride, and already I wonder if I was ever strong and rode!

It is such an odd jump I have taken. At home I drifted on, never feeling older, hardly counting birthdays—always brisk, and getting through a heap of work—beginning my day early and ending it late. And now there is a great gulf dividing me from youth and old times, and it is filled with dead people whom I can't forget.

In the matter of dying, you don't interfere with Providence, but it seems to me that now would be rather an appropriate time to depart. I wish I could give my life for some boy who would like to live very much, and to whom all things are joyous. But alas! You can't swap lives like this—at least, I don't see the chance of doing so.

I should like to have "left the party"—quitted the feast of life—when all was gay and amusing. I should have been sorry to come away, but it would have been far better than being left until all the lights are out.

I could have said truly to the Giver of the feast, "Thanks for an excellent time."

But now so many of the guests have left, and the fires are going out, and I am tired.

END OF DIARY

The Final Days: Told by the Author's Niece Betty (Keays-Young) Salmon in 1918

"The H.M.S. 'Iron Duke,' the flag ship of the Grand Fleet of the British Royal Navy during World War I," by Bain News Service (circa 1915). The battleship was named after Arthur Wellesley, 1st Duke of Wellington. Courtesy the Library of Congress.

Sarah left Tehran in mid-April 1916. The Persian hot weather was approaching, and it would have been impossible for her to travel any later in the season. The long journey seemed a sufficiently hazardous undertaking for a person in her weak state of health, but in Dr. Neligan's opinion she would have run an even greater risk by remaining in Persia during the hot weather.

The Final Journey

Dr. Neligan's goodness and kindness to Sarah will always be remembered by my family. He seems to have taken an enormous amount of trouble to make arrangements for her journey home. He found an escort for her in an English missionary who was going to St. Petersburg and gave her a pass which enabled her to travel as quickly as possible. The authorities were not allowed to delay or stop her. She was much too ill to stop for anything, and drove night and day—even through a cholera village—to the shores of the Caspian Sea.

We know very few details concerning the journey home. I think my aunt herself did not remember much about it. You can hardly bear to think of the suffering it caused her. A few incidents stood out in her memory from the indeterminate recollection of pain and discomfort in which most of the expedition was mercifully veiled, and we learned them after she returned.

There was the occasion when she reached the port on the Caspian Sea one hour after the English boat had sailed. She called it the "English" boat, but whether it could have belonged to an English company, or was merely the usual boat run in connection with the train service to England, I do not know. A "Russian" vessel was due to leave in a couple of hours, but for some reason Sarah had to walk three-quarters of a mile to get permission to go by it. We can never forget her pitiful description of how she staggered and crawled to the office and back, so ill that only her iron strength of will could force her tired body to accomplish the distance. She obtained the necessary permission and started forth once more upon her way.

She stayed for a week at the British Embassy in St. Petersburg, where her escort had to leave her, so the rest of the journey was undertaken alone. We know nothing of how she got to Helsingfors in Sweden, but I believe it was there that she had to walk a great distance over a frozen lake to reach the ship. She was hobbling along, leaning heavily on two sticks. Just as she stumbled and almost fell, a young Englishman came up and offered her his arm.

In an old diary, written years before in the Argentine, during a time when Sarah was faced with what seemed overwhelming difficulties, and when she had in her care a very sick man, a kind stranger came to the rescue.

"People along London Bridge," by Bain News Service (circa 1915). Courtesy the Library of Congress.

Her diary entry for that day is one of heartfelt gratitude, and ends with the words: "God always sends someone."

Certainly at Helsingfors some Protecting Power sent help in a big extremity, and this young fellow—Mr. Seymour—devoted himself to her for the rest of the journey in a marvelously unselfish manner. He could not have been kinder to her if she had been his mother. He actually changed all his plans on arriving in England and brought her to the very door of her house in Norfolk Street. Without his help I sometimes wonder whether my aunt would have succeeded in reaching home, and her own gratitude to him knew no bounds. She used to say that, in her experience, if people were in a difficulty and wanted help, they ought to go to a young man for it. She said that young men were the kindest members of the human race.

May 8:
The End of Travels

It was on May 8 that Sarah reached home. Her travels were over for good and all. We were thankful that the last weeks of her life were not spent in a foreign land but among her own people, surrounded by all the care and comfort that love could supply. Two of her sisters were with her always, and her house was thronged with visitors, who had to wait their turn for a few minutes by her bedside, which, alas, was all her strength allowed.

She was nursed night and day by her devoted maid, Mary King, as she did not wish to have a professional nurse; but no skill or care could save her. The seeds of her illness had probably been sown some years before, during a shooting trip in Kashmir, and the hard work and strain of the first year of the war had weakened her powers of resistance. But it was the trip to Russia that killed her. Before she went there many of her friends urged her to give up the expedition. Her maid had a premonition that the effort would end in disaster and had begged her mistress to stay at home.

"I feel sure you will never return alive ma'am," she had urged. Sarah's first words to her old servant on her return were: "You were right, Mary. Russia has killed me."

Sarah rallied a little in June. She was occasionally carried down to her library for a few hours in the afternoon, but even that amount of exertion was too much for her. For the last weeks of her life she never left her room. Surely there never was a sweeter or more adorable invalid! I can see her now, propped up on pillows in a room filled with masses of most exquisite flowers. She always had things dainty and fragrant about her, and you had a vision of pale blue ribbons, soft laces, and lovely flowers. Then you forgot everything else as you looked at the dear face framed in such soft gray hair. She looked so fragile that you fancied she might be wafted away by a summer breeze, and I have never seen anyone so pale.

"French poster seeking support for National War Orphans Day for children who lost their parents in the war since 1914," (1916). Courtesy the Library of Congress.

There was not a tinge of color in face or hands, and you kissed her gently for fear that even a caress might be too much for her waning strength. Her patience never failed. She never grumbled or complained, and even in the smallest things her interest and sympathy were as fresh as ever. A new dress worn by one of her sisters was a pleasure, and she would plan it, and suggest and admire.

With joy, Sarah learned in June that she had received the honor of being chosen to be a Dame of Grace in the Order of St. John of Jerusalem. Any recognition of her good work was an unfailing source of gratification to her sensitive nature, sensitive alike to praise or blame. She was so strong in her mind and will that it seemed impossible in those long June days to believe she had such a little time to live. She managed all her own business affairs, personally dictated or wrote answers to her correspondence, and was full of plans to redecorate her house and plans for the future. I have only been able to obtain three of my aunt's letters written after her return to England. They were addressed to her eldest sister, Mrs. Ffolliott.

> Let there not be a man or a woman among us who, when the war is over, will not then be able to say:
>
> "I was not idle.
>
> "I took such part as I could in the greatest task which, in all the storied annals of our country, has ever fallen to the lot of Great Britain to achieve."
>
> **THE PRIME MINISTER.**
> May 4th 1915.

"A World War I recruiting poster," British Parliamentary Recruiting Committee(1915). Courtesy the Library of Congress.

Sarah's Last Letters

April 15, 1916

My Dearest Old Poot,

How good of you to write. I was awfully pleased to see a letter from you. I have been a fearful crock since I got home, and I have to lie in bed for six weeks and live on milk diet for eight weeks. The illness is of a tropical nature, and one of the symptoms is that you can't eat, so you get fearfully thin. I am something over six stone [84 pounds] now, but I was very much less.

We were right up on the Persian front, and I went to Tehran. I saw some most interesting phases of the war and met all the distinguished generals and such-like people. The notice you sent me of my little book is charming.

Your loving,

S. B. M.

June 9, 1916

Darling Poot,

I must thank you myself for the lovely flowers and your kind letters. I am sure that people's good wishes and prayers do me good. I so nearly died!

Your loving,

S. M.

"A country cottage in Kent, England," (circa 1905). Courtesy the Library of Congress.

June 17, 1916

Still getting on pretty well, but it is slow work. Baby and Julia are both in town, so they are constantly here. I am to get up for a little bit tomorrow. Kindest love. It was naughty of you to send more flowers.

As ever fondly,
Sarah

As the hot weather advanced it was hoped to move Sarah to the country. Her friends showered invitations on "dear Sally" to come and convalesce with them, but the plans fell through.

It became increasingly clear that the traveler was about to embark on that last journey from which there is no return. Indeed, towards the end, her sufferings were so great that those who loved her best could only pray that she might not have long to wait. She passed away in the afternoon of Monday, July 24, 1916.

A few days later the body of Sarah Broom Macnaughtan was laid to rest in the plot of ground reserved for her kinsfolk in the churchyard at Chart Sutton, in Kent.

It is very quiet there up on the hill, the great Weald stretches away to the south, and fruit trees surround the hallowed acre. But even as they laid earth to earth and dust to dust in this peaceful spot, the booming of the guns in Flanders broke the quiet of the sunny afternoon, reminded the little funeral party that they were indeed burying one whose life had been sacrificed in the Great War.

The Grave in Chart Sutton

Surely those who pass through the old churchyard will pause by the grave, with its beautiful gray cross, and the children growing up in the parish will come there sometimes, and will read and remember the simple inscription on it.

"In the Great War, by word and deed, at home and abroad, she served her country even unto death."

And if any ghosts hover around the little place, they will be the ghosts of a purity, a kindness, and of a love for humanity not often met with in this workaday world.

Chapter 17
Conclusion

"A roadside cemetery near Neuve Eglise, in the French region of Alsace," by Capt. George Edmund Butler, a New Zealand war artist who carried a sketchbook to create drawings, often under enemy fire, as a basis for his paintings. (1917). Courtesy Wikimedia Commons.

Reminisces in 1918 by the Author's Niece Betty

I stayed with my aunt for one night: Aug. 7, 1914, the day the first British troops landed in France. During the previous three days after Britain declared war on Germany, most people had scarcely begun to realize there was a war. I was recalled by telegram from Northamptonshire to the headquarters of my Voluntary Aid Detachment in Kent, and spent a night in town en route, to get a uniform, etc. At my aunt's house my eyes were opened a little about what lay before us. She was on fire with patriotism and a burning wish to help her country, and I immediately caught some of her enthusiasm.

The Strange Side of War: A Woman's WWI Diary 313

"A war crowd gathers on Downing Street in London," by *Bain News Service* (1914). Courtesy the Library of Congress.

Every hour we rushed out to buy papers, every minute seemed consecrated to preparation for what we could do. There were uniforms to buy, notes of Red Cross lectures to "rub up," and, in my aunt's case, she was busy offering her services in every direction in which they could be of use.

My aunt must surely have been one of the first people to begin voluntary rationing. We had the simplest possible meals during my visit. Although she was proud of her housekeeping and usually provided perfect food, on this occasion she said how impossible it was for her to indulge in anything but necessities when our soldiers would so soon have to endure hardships of every kind. She said we ought to be particularly careful to eat very little meat, because there would certainly be a shortage of it later on.

I recall there was some hitch about my departure from Norfolk Street on August 8. It did not seem clear whether my Voluntary Aid Detachment was going to provide billets for all recalled members, and I remember my aunt's absolute scorn of difficulties at such a time.

"British recruitment poster," Parliamentary Recruiting Committee (1914). Courtesy the Library of Congress.

"Of course, go straight to Kent and obey orders," she cried. "If you can't get a bed, come back here; but at least go and see what you can do."

That was typical of my aunt. Difficulties did not exist for her. As a young girl she made up her mind that no lack of money, time, or strength should ever prevent her doing anything she wanted to do. It certainly never prevented her doing anything she felt she ought to do.

The war provided her with a supreme opportunity for service, and she did not fail to take advantage of it. Of her work in Belgium, especially at the soup kitchen, I believe it is impossible to say too much. According to *The Times*, "The lady with the soup was everything to thousands of stricken men, who would otherwise have gone on their way fasting."

Among individual cases, too, there were many men who benefited by some special care bestowed on them by her. There was one wounded Belgian to whom my aunt gave my address before she left for Russia so he could have someone he might correspond with. I used to hear from him regularly. In every letter breathed gratitude to *"la dame écossaise"* [the Scottish lady]. He said she had saved his life.

"English women making airplane shafts during World War I," *Bain News Service* (circa 1914 to 1918). Courtesy the Library of Congress.

My aunt's lectures to munitions workers were, perhaps, the best work she did during the war. She was a charming speaker. I never heard anyone who got more quickly into touch with an audience. As I saw it expressed in one of the newspapers: "Stiffness and depression vanished from any company when she took the platform." Her enunciation was extraordinarily distinct, and she had an arresting delivery of speech that compelled attention from her first word to the last.

She never minced words about the truth about the war, but showed people at home how far removed it was from being a "merry picnic."

"British women ambulance drivers in World War I," by B*ain News Service* (circa 1914 to 1918). Courtesy the Library of Congress.

"They say recruiting will stop if people know what is going on at the Front," she used to tell them. "I am a woman, but I know what I would do if I were a man when I heard of these things. I would do my durndest."

All through her life the idea of personal service appealed to her. She never sent a message of sympathy or a gift of help unless it was quite impossible to go herself to the sufferer.

She was only a girl when she heard about what proved to be the fatal accident of her eldest brother in the Argentina. She went to him by the next ship, alone, except for the escort of his old yacht's skipper. A journey to the Argentina in those days was a big undertaking for a delicate young girl.

On another occasion, she was in Switzerland when she heard of the death of a little niece in Northamptonshire. She left for England the same day to go and offer her sympathy, and try to comfort the child's mother.

"When I hear of trouble I always go at once," she used to say.

The Strange Side of War: A Woman's WWI Diary 317

"British women ambulance drivers near the Front during World War I," by *Bain News Service* (circa 1914 to 1918). Courtesy the Library of Congress.

I have known her drive in her brougham [carriage] to the most horrible slum in the East End to see what she could do for a woman who had begged from her in the street—yes, and go there again and again until she had done all that was possible to help the sad case.

It was this burning zeal to help that sent her to Belgium and carried her through the long dark winter there. It was, perhaps, the same feeling which obscured her judgment when her expedition to Russia was contemplated. She was a delicate woman, and there did not seem to be much scope for her services in Russia. She was not a qualified nurse. The distance from home and handicap of her ignorance of the Russian language would probably have prevented her organizing anything like comforts for the soldiers there as she had done in Belgium. To those of us who loved her, the very uselessness of her efforts in Russia adds to the poignancy of the tragedy of the death which resulted from them.

The old question arises: "To what purpose is this waste?"

And the old answer comes still to teach us the underlying meaning and beauty of what seems to be unnecessary sacrifice: "She hath done what she could."

Indeed, that epitaph might describe my aunt's war work. She begrudged nothing, she gave her strength, her money, her very life. The precious ointment was poured out in the service of her King and country and for the Master she served so faithfully.

I have been looking through some articles that appeared in the press after Sarah's death. Some of them elude to her wit, her energy and vivacity, the humor that was "without a touch of cynicism." Others discuss her inexhaustible spirit, her geniality, and the "powers of sarcasm, which she used with strong reserve." Others, again, see through to the faith and philosophy behind her humor, "Scottish in its penetrating tenderness."

In my opinion my aunt's strongest characteristic was a dazzling purity of soul, mind, and body. She was a person whose very presence lifted the tone of the conversation. It was impossible to think of telling her a nasty story, a "double entendre" fell flat when she was there. She was the least prudish person in the world, but no one who knew her could doubt for an instant her transparent goodness. I have read every word of her diary. There is not in it the record of an ugly thought, or of one action that would not bear the full light of day. About her books she used to say she had tried never to publish one word that her father would not like her to have written.

She had a tremendous capacity for affection, and when she once loved, she loved most faithfully. Her devotion to her father and to her eldest brother influenced her whole life. It would have been impossible for those she loved to make too heavy claims on her kindness.

My aunt had great social charm. She was friendly and easy to know. She had a wonderful power of finding out the interesting side of people and of seeing their good points. Her popularity was extraordinary, although hers was too strong a personality to command universal affection. Among her friends were people of the most varied types and circumstances. Distinction of birth, position, or intellect appealed to her. She was always glad to meet a celebrity, but distinction was no passport to her favor unless it was accompanied by character. To her poorer and humbler friends, she was kindness itself, and she was extraordinarily staunch in her friendships. Nothing would make her "drop" a person with whom she had once been intimate.

In attempting to provide a character sketch of a person whose nature was as complex as Sarah's, you admit defeat from the start. She had so many interests, so many sides to her character, that it seems impossible to present them all fairly. Her love of music, literature, and art was coupled with an enthusiasm for sport, big-game shooting, riding, travel, and adventure of every kind. She was an ambitious woman and a brilliantly clever one. Her clearness of perception and wonderful intuition gave her a quick grasp of a subject or idea. She had a thirst for knowledge that made learning easy, but hers was the brain of the poet and philosopher, not of the mathematician. Accuracy of thought or information was often lacking. Her imagination led the way and left her with a picture of a situation or a subject, but she was very vague about facts and statistics.

As a woman of business she was shrewd, with all a Scotchwoman's power of looking at both sides of a bawbee [Scottish halfpenny] before she spent it. But she was also extraordinarily generous in a very simple and unostentatious way, and her hospitality was boundless.

My aunt was almost hypersensitive to criticism. Her intense desire to do right and serve her fellow-beings animated her whole life, and it seemed to her rather hard to be found fault with. Indeed, she had not many faults, and the defects of her character were mostly temperamental. As a girl she was unpunctual and subject to fits of indecision when it seemed impossible for her to make up her mind one way or the other. The inconvenience caused by her frequent changes of times and plans were probably not realized by her.

> **BAD FORM IN DRESS.**
>
> The National Organizing Committee for War Savings appeals against extravagance in women's dress.
>
> Many women have already recognized that elaboration and variety in dress are bad form in the present crisis, but there is still a large section of the community, both amongst the rich and amongst the less well-to-do, who appear to make little or no difference in their habits.
>
> New clothes should only be bought when absolutely necessary, and these should be durable and suitable for all occasions. Luxurious forms, for example, of hats, boots, shoes, stockings, gloves, and veils should be avoided.
>
> It is essential, not only that money should be saved, but that labour employed in the clothing trades should be set free.

"British poster for women during World War I," by the National Organizing Committee for War Savings in London, (1915). Courtesy the Library of Congress.

Later in life, when she lived so much alone, she did not always see that difficulties which appeared nothing to her might be almost insuperable to other people, and that in houses where there are several members of a family to be considered, no individual can be quite as free to carry out his own plans as a person who is independent of family ties. But when you remembered how splendidly she always responded to any claim on her own kindness you forgave her for being a little exacting.

Perhaps her greatest handicap in life was her immense capacity for suffering—suffering poignantly, unbearably, not only for her own sorrows but for the sorrows of others.

Only those who appealed to her in trouble knew the depth of her sympathy and how absolutely she shared the burden of the grief.

But perhaps they did not always know how she agonized over their misfortunes and at what price her sympathy was given.

My aunt was a passionately religious woman. Her faith was the inspiration of her whole life. It is safe to say that from the smallest to the greatest things there was never a struggle between conscience and inclination in which conscience was not victorious.

As she grew older, I believe she became a less orthodox member of the Church of England, to which she belonged, but her love for Christ and for his people never wavered.

As each Sunday came around during her last illness, when she could not go to church, she used to say to a very dear sister, "Now, J., we must have our little service."

Then the bedroom door was left ajar, and her sister would go down to the drawing room and play the simple hymns they had sung together in childhood.

And on the last Sunday, the day before her death, when the invalid lay in a stupor and seemed scarcely conscious, that same dear sister played the old hymns once more, and as the sound floated up to the room above those who watched there saw a gleam of pleasure on the dying woman's face.

My aunt had no fear of death.

There had been a time, some weeks before the end, when her feet had wandered very close to the waters dividing us from the unknown shore.

She told her sisters afterwards that she had almost seemed to see over to the "other side" and so many of those she loved were waiting for her, and saying, "Come over to us, Sally. We are all here to welcome you."

Perhaps just at the last, when her body had grown weak, the journey seemed rather far, and she clung to earth more closely, but such weakness was purely physical.

The brave spirit was ready to go, and as the music of her favorite hymn pierced her consciousness when she lay dying, so surely the words summed up all that she felt or wished to say, and formed her last prayer in death, as they had been her constant prayer in life:

> "In death's dark vale I fear no ill
> With Thee, dear Lord, beside me;
> Thy rod and staff my comfort still,
> Thy Cross before to guide me.
>
> "And so through all the length of days
> Thy goodness faileth never;
> Good Shepherd, may I sing Thy praise
> Within Thy house for ever."

Chapter 18
Afterword

BY NOËL FLETCHER

for Women as Well as Men: A New Order.

"Insignia of the Order of the British Empire: The 1st Class Badge and Star. The King has instituted two new Orders, both open to women as well as men... the Order of the British Empire and the Order of the Companions of Honor. The 1st two classes of the former will carry, for men, the honor of Knighthood, and for women, the title of Dame. There are five classes each for men and women," *The Illustrated War News,* (July 27, 1916).

King Albert I of Belgium

- Ruled Belgium until 1934 when he died in a rock climbing accident in the mountains in southwest Belgium. He was 58.

Queen Elisabeth of Belgium

- Used her influence as a Dowager Queen to promote humanitarian causes.
- Israel bestowed upon her the title Righteous Among Nations after World War II for her efforts rescuing hundreds of Jewish children during Germany's occupation of Belgium.
- Died in November 1985 a few months after her 89th birthday.

Prince Alexander of Teck

- Was highly decorated for his work during the war.
- In 1917, he and his family relinquished their German titles from the Kingdom of Württemberg due to anti-German sentiment in Britain. He changed his name to Cambridge after his grandfather, the Duke of Cambridge.
- After the war, he embarked on a notable career as a statesman, serving first in South Africa and then in Canada during World War II.
- Died in 1957 at age 82. At the time of his death, he was known as the Earl of Athlone.

Mabel St. Clair Stobart

- Became an active lecturer in Ireland and Canada.
- Outlived her second husband as well as her two sons, who died from Spanish influenza.
- Her active life took her to South Africa and British Colombia.
- Lived in Dorset in England and died there in December 1954 at 92 years of age.

"Medal of Queen Elisabeth of the Belgians," presented after World War I.

Lady Susan Elizabeth Clementine Waring

+ For her work at Lennel House, Lady Clementine was made a Commander of the British Empire and awarded the Medal of Queen Elisabeth of the Belgians in recognition of her war efforts.
+ Died in 1962.
+ Lennel House was sold by the family sold in the 1990s. It is now a nursing home.

The Illustrated War News, (Sept. 13, 1916).

Lady Dorothie Fielding

- Received many commendations for her war efforts. She became the first woman to be awarded the British Military Medal for bravery in the field. In addition, she received the Order of Leopold II from Belgium and the French Croix de Guerre from France.
- In 1917, left Flanders to marry Capt. Charles Moore, who received a Military Cross. They lived in Ireland after World War I.
- She died at age 46 in 1935.
-

Mrs. Hilda Wynne

- Moved from the Russian front to Italy, assisting both soldiers and civilians while treating the wounded and helping with soup kitchens. Remained with the Italian fighting forces until the Armistice was signed.
- For her efforts in Russia, she was awarded the Order of St. George, the highest military decoration. After using some of her inherited money for humanitarian efforts in wartime Europe, she continued to support relief efforts. After the war, she raised funds for the benefit of disabled veterans of the war.
- She died in January 1923 at the Hotel Meurice in Paris.

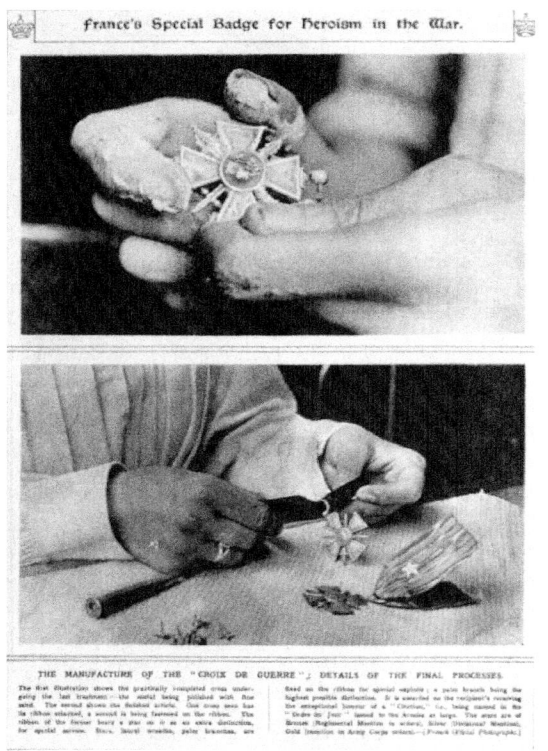

"Making the Croix de Guerre in France," *The Illustrated War News*, (Jan. 10, 1917).

Millicent, Duchess of Sutherland

✦ Left England to oversee medical relief at field hospitals in northern France.

✦ In June 1918, moved with her unit to Roubaix, France near the Belgian border.

✦ Was awarded the Royal Red Cross from Belgium, the Croix de Guerre from France, and the British Red Cross medal for her activities during World War I.

✦ A society hostess, she married three times and was an accomplished author. She died in August 1955 at age 87.

Chapter 19
About the Author/Editor
Noël Marie Fletcher

Noël Marie Fletcher is a career print and broadcast journalist who has lived and worked in Asia and Europe. As a financial journalist, she covered international trade in many Asian countries including Hong Kong, South Korea, Singapore and Thailand. As a Beijing Correspondent, she was one of the few female journalists living in China who experienced the events surrounding the Tiananmen Square uprising. She has also worked as a journalist in Palm Springs and in broadcast television in the San Francisco Bay area. She is the author of numerous nonfiction books. She served as Acting Bureau Chief for The Times of London in Berlin in 2017. She is a reciprocal member of the National Press Club in Washington, D.C. and a member of the Geneva Press Club. Her books often involve investigative research. She seeks to incorporate art into her work, including her own photography and historical images.

Fletcher & Co. Publishers

Fletcher & Co. Publishers is an independent, art-house publishing company. We use new media and graphic design techniques to transport you into the world of the novel. Our books aren't just written words. They're experiences: international cultures, art, suspense, history & adventure. Here are some other titles you may be interested in reading.

Edge of Suspicion
by Zita Steele

Take a journey into danger and suspense. South Korean detective Moon chases an elusive cybercriminal and matches wits with a deadly blonde in Singapore.

Forts of the Old West: A Journey across New Mexico
by Noël Marie Fletcher

Take a journey into the lives of people who vanished in the Wild West. Explore true stories and eyewitness accounts of the kidnappings and experiences of Anglos, Hispanics, and Native Americans taken captive in New Mexico and the Southwest.

Erwin Rommel: Photographer, Vol. 1: A Survey
by Erwin Rommel & Zita Steele

Take a journey behind the camera of a world-famous military commander. Experience WWII firsthand from Field Marshal Rommel's private photo collection, seized by U.S. forces in 1945. View 340+ images, including photos Rommel took during campaigns in France and North Africa and others which he collected. Join Rommel in the air and in his command vehicle as he captures majestic desert landscapes, Panzer maneuvers, battlefield action, soldiers on the frontlines, and graves of the fallen. Also included are Rommel's personal photos of family and friends. The photos are digitally restored and enhanced for detail. Some are accompanied by Rommel's own handwritten photo captions. Author/artist Zita Steele uses her knowledge of German language and culture, with in-depth research about Rommel and his campaigns, to provide context for the photos. Zita also analyzes patterns in Rommel's photography to shed a unique light on the artistic personality of this notable military leader.

Vol. 2: Rommel & His Men

Experience life on the frontlines with Field Marshal Erwin Rommel. View 200+ images from Rommel's private photo collection, seized by U.S. forces in 1945. Join Rommel as he interacts with his German and Italian troops. See him and his men at work, at rest, and on the move. View Rommel's mementos of his men and military leaders. This book provides a candid view of Rommel as an ordinary soldier rather than a general.

My Time in Another World: Experiences as a Foreign Correspondent in China

by Noël Marie Fletcher

A richly detailed and gripping firsthand account of the infancy of modern China as experienced by American journalist Noël-Marie Fletcher, a young professional woman tasked with reporting news on developing trade and industry from teeming Chinese cities and isolated hinterlands in the 1980s. In this series of personal anecdotes, Noël-Marie recounts her adventures with realism, humor, and key insights, guiding the reader on an informative and engaging journey from her first awkward encounters with back-country Chinese manufacturers to the dramatic hardships she experienced during the Tiananmen Square uprising and its aftermath. An engrossing eyewitness account, "My Time in Another World," provides a rare personal perspective of China before its climactic transformation into a global superpower.

Pathways in Time: Photo Journeys

by Noël Marie Fletcher

Travel along many roads and witness simple and abstract forms of beauty. Featuring over 160 photos, "Pathways in Time: Photo Journeys" shows the wonder of nature such as in rainbows, birds, trees, leaves, raindrops, and the earth. It also reveals abstract views of architecture, urban settings, and found objects. Author/photographer Noël-Marie Fletcher shows how to find beauty in ordinary life and the world that surrounds us all.

Two Years in the Forbidden City *by* Princess Der Ling

This true story, first eyewitness account of the Imperial Court written by a Chinese aristocrat for Western readers. It provides an up-close personal view of the notorious Dowager Empress Tzu-hsi in her final years. Enhanced with rich imagery and historical notes, this story takes you on a vivid trip into the grandeur and intrigue of China's last dynasty. Includes 100+ interesting historical details along with photos, illustrations, and paintings from the late 1800s to early 1900s showing the Dowager Empress, the Boxer Rebellion, the Imperial Court, and other people featured in the narrative.

Lantern of the Wicked *by* Charles Clement

Shanghai, 1929. Ace is an all-American pilot, enjoying a carefree life in a Chinese paradise. Everything changes drastically when Ace is accused of a murder he didn't commit, and an international police squad launches a manhunt for him. Now, alone in a foreign city, Ace may be forced to rely on a mysterious Taoist gangster, Pockmarked Fang, for help.

The Spy *by* James Fenimore Cooper

During the dark days of the Revolutionary War, America struggles for nationhood. Meanwhile, in the shadows, a spy is trading secrets of vital importance to the cause – but for whose side? Colonials and loyalists play a game of cloak and daggers in America's first spy novel. Our edition features 30+ color photographs designed to give you a front-seat experience.

Envoy: Rule of Silence *by* Zita Steele

Take a journey into a thrilling world of secrets and lies in modern-day Europe. Polish ex-secret policeman Michal Krynski is tired of working as a double agent for France's security bureau. His last mission - to track down a runaway DJ. As he travels to the strange island of Malta, Krynski plots revenge against the system that ruined his life. Will he catch the DJ or kill him? Zita Steele is a novelist and artist. She writes with an expertise in criminology, cybercrime, and international relations. She creates her own illustrations.

Mystery of the Yellow Room *by* Gaston Leroux

News of a strange crime spreads like wildfire in Paris. Someone has attempted to murder the daughter of a brilliant scientist. But nobody can explain how the murderer got in and out of the locked room of her isolated country home. Only Joseph Rouletabille, an impatient young journalist, has the genius to solve this crime. But can he match wits with a seemingly supernatural killer?

Two if by Sea *by* Zita Steele

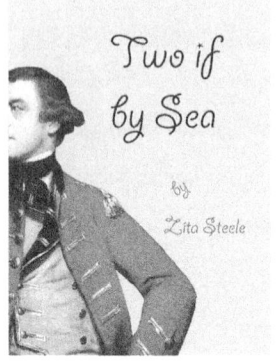

A theatre production about a Revolutionary War hero goes awry when the wrong actor takes the stage, sparking a series of epic consequences.

Ruthless Shadow *by* Zita Steele

It's 1948. The postwar world is in chaos and Mitch Day is looking for trouble. He's fast, dangerous, and Irish-American—he's always been lucky. But a failed robbery attempt lands him in a small Arizona town with a dark secret. Life gets complicated when he crosses paths with two very different women—Kika, a beautiful young woman who falls passionately in love with him, and Winnie, the icy and manipulative heiress of Baylor & Cromwell Real Estate Co. In over his head, Mitch must fight his way out of a sinister situation to survive.

River of My Ancestors: The Rio Grande in Pictures
by Noël-Marie Fletcher

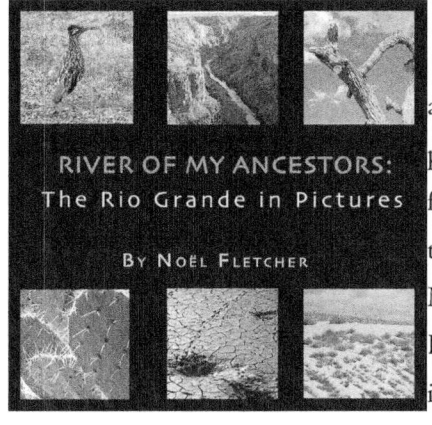

Take a journey along the wild and rugged Rio Grande. Beautiful pictures capture the essence of the famous river and its importance in the arid Southwest. Native New Mexican author/photographer Noël Fletcher provides family stories and insights about frontier life. Follow the Rio Grande through deserts, wetlands, and rocky cliffs. Experience natural wonders, including volcanic lands and river rapids, and encounter wildlife such as snakes, wolves, cranes, and bighorn sheep. With 180+ striking color photos, the book combines vivid photos and the written word to tell a living history of the famous Rio Grande and the beautiful desert land of New Mexico.

Windows into the Beauty of Flowers & Nature
by Noël-Marie Fletcher

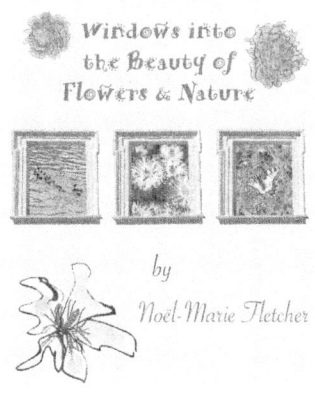

Take a journey into the beauty of life. Featuring over 450 photos, "Windows into the Beauty of Flowers & Nature" shows flowers in their many forms and types in an array of resplendent colors. Stunning high-quality images capture the essences of various insects and animals who live among us, including butterflies, lizards, birds, bees, and rabbits.

Author/photographer Noel-Marie Fletcher also compliments her photos by including some of her freehand pastel and ink artwork.

Printed in Great Britain
by Amazon